W9-DDL-145

FUNDAMENTALS
OF
SPORT
MANAGEMENT

*Human Kinetics' Fundamentals of
Sport and Exercise Science Series*

Robert E. Baker, EdD
Craig Esherick, JD

George Mason University, Fairfax, VA

HUMAN KINETICS

Library of Congress Cataloging-in-Publication Data

Baker, Robert E., 1957-
  Fundamentals of sport management / Robert E. Baker, Craig Esherick.
     p. ; cm. -- (Human Kinetics' fundamentals of sport and exercise science series)
  Includes bibliographical references and index.
  1. Sports--Management. 2. Sports administration. I. Esherick, Craig. II. Title.
  GV713.B32 2013
  796.06'9--dc23

2012030722

ISBN-10: 0-7360-9108-4 (print)
ISBN-13: 978-0-7360-9108-4 (print)

The web addresses cited in this text were current as of August 13, 2012, unless otherwise noted.

Acquisitions Editor: Myles Schrag
Developmental Editor: Christine M. Drews
Assistant Editors: Brendan Shea, PhD, Susan Huls, Amy Akin, and Amanda S. Ewing
Copyeditor: Tom Tiller
Indexer: Gerry Lynn Shipe
Permissions Manager: Dalene Reeder
Graphic Designers: Bob Reuther and Fred Starbird
Cover Designer: Keith Blomberg
Photo Asset Manager: Laura Fitch
Photo Production Manager: Jason Allen
Art Manager: Kelly Hendren
Associate Art Manager: Alan L. Wilborn
Illustrations: © Human Kinetics, unless otherwise noted
Printer: Versa Press

Printed in the United States of America   10 9 8 7 6 5 4 3 2 1

The paper in this book is certified under a sustainable forestry program.

Human Kinetics
Website: www.HumanKinetics.com

United States: Human Kinetics
P.O. Box 5076
Champaign, IL 61825-5076
800-747-4457
e-mail: humank@hkusa.com

Canada: Human Kinetics
475 Devonshire Road Unit 100
Windsor, ON N8Y 2L5
800-465-7301 (in Canada only)
e-mail: info@hkcanada.com

Europe: Human Kinetics
107 Bradford Road
Stanningley
Leeds LS28 6AT, United Kingdom
+44 (0) 113 255 5665
e-mail: hk@hkeurope.com

Australia: Human Kinetics
57A Price Avenue
Lower Mitcham, South Australia 5062
08 8372 0999
e-mail: info@hkaustralia.com

New Zealand: Human Kinetics
P.O. Box 80
Torrens Park, South Australia 5062
0800 222 062
e-mail: info@hknewzealand.com

E5088

I cannot adequately express my appreciation for the enduring support of my wife, Pam Hudson Baker, throughout this journey.

This book is dedicated to all sport management students, graduates, and faculty who advance the discipline and the conduct of sport.

—**Bob Baker**

I would like to thank my wife, Theo, and my sons, Nicko and Zachary, for their unstinting support during the many months I spent on my laptop writing this book.

I dedicate this book to the many hard-working students in sport management at George Mason University who inspire me every day.

—**Craig Esherick**

We would also like to acknowledge Myles Schrag, Chris Drews, Brendan Shea, and Susi Huls at Human Kinetics for their dedicated work in moving this project to completion.

Contents

Series Preface

The sport sciences have matured impressively over the past 40 years. Subdisciplines in kinesiology have established their own rigorous paths of research, and physical education in its many forms is now an accepted discipline in higher education. Our need now is not only for comprehensive resources that contain all the knowledge that the field has acquired, but also for resources that summarize the foundations of each of the sport sciences for the variety of people who make use of that information today. Understanding the basic topics, goals, and applications of the subdisciplines in kinesiology is critical for students and professionals in many walks of life. Human Kinetics has developed the Fundamentals of Sport and Exercise Science series with these needs in mind.

This and the other books in the series will not provide you with all the in-depth knowledge required for earning an advanced degree or for opening a practice in this subject area. This book will not make you an expert on the subject. What this book will do is give you an excellent grounding in the key themes, terms, history, and status of the subject in both the academic and professional worlds. You can use this grounding as a jumping-off point for studying more in-depth resources and for generating questions for more experienced people in the field. We've even included a list of additional resources for you to consult as you continue your journey.

Key to Icons

 Look for the giant quotation marks, which set off noteworthy quotes from researchers and professionals in the field.

 Management Insights go behind the scenes to explain the background of relevant sport management issues.

 Quick Facts include quirky or surprising "Did you know?" types of information.

 International Application sections profile a person or organization to illustrate a global perspective of the topic discussed.

 Success Stories highlight influential individuals in the field. Through these sidebars, you will learn how researchers and professionals apply their knowledge of the subject to their work, and you'll be able to explore possible career paths in the field.

You might be using this book to help you improve your professional skills or to assess the potential job market. You might want to learn about a new subject, supplement a textbook, or introduce a colleague or client to this exciting subject area. In any of these cases, this book will be your guide to the basics of this subject. It is succinct, informative, and entertaining. You will begin the book with many questions, and you will surely finish it with many more questions. But they will be more thoughtful, complex, substantive questions. We hope that you will use this book to help the sport sciences, and this subject in particular, continue to prosper for another generation.

Preface

Fundamentals of Sport Management is an introduction to the interdisciplinary field of sport management. This book is for those curious about the field of study as well as those who wish to refresh their knowledge of the options available in sport management. High school students who want to learn what sport management is and what sport managers do will find this text useful. University undergraduates who have heard of sport management and want an overview of the essential content in the field can benefit from this book as well. Undergraduates majoring in another field who might be interested in pursuing graduate study in sport management may also gain perspective through this book. Additionally, sport practitioners who want to reinforce or challenge their perceptions of the core concepts in sport management may enhance their professional capacity. Serving as a handy reference on basic concepts in various areas of sport management, this book will be a valuable addition to many practitioners' libraries. Those trained in other fields may gain insights into sport management and options for a career change.

Sport management has evolved as both a popular and respected discipline in higher education. Academic programs in sport management take an interdisciplinary approach in preparing students for work in the field. This book addresses each of the academic areas (business, management, economics, marketing, communications, physical education, law, ethics, government, and psychology) and the contribution of each area to the field of sport management.

These basic questions are addressed in *Fundamentals of Sport Management*: What is sport management, and what can I do with the principles I learn from sport management? The text contains fundamental academic *and* practical information on sport management.

Part I presents an introduction to the field of sport management. Beginning with the origins of the discipline, chapter 1 focuses on the development of the field, its professional associations, and professional preparation through academic programs.

Concluding part I, chapter 2 focuses on career opportunities in sport management. The various paths to employment and professional development in sport management are central to this chapter. The value of field experiences and internships is discussed as well.

Each of the chapters in part II focuses on a specific academic building block in the field. Chapter 3 presents management principles in sport, examining such functions as planning, organizing, and controlling. Chapter 4 deals with leadership in sport organizations, including a discussion of organizational studies, the social psychological foundations of leadership, communication techniques, and strategies of leaders. Chapter 5 examines the development of sport policy and the governance of scholastic, intercollegiate, professional, and private and public sport enterprises.

Chapter 6 presents sport operations, the functioning of sport events, and the management of venues in which events take place. Chapter 7 addresses the legal aspects

eBook
available at
HumanKinetics.com

of sport, including tort law and negligence, Title IX, and the Americans With Disabilities Act. Chapter 8 addresses the basics of sport marketing, including public relations, promotions, sponsorships, and advertising.

Chapter 9 addresses sport and the media, including print, broadcast, and electronic media. Chapter 10 presents the economics of the sport industry. Chapter 11 presents fundamental aspects of the financing of sport, including balance sheets and income statements, nonprofit and for-profit finances, and the influence of television rights. Chapter 12 examines ethical foundations in sport, including a discussion of sportsmanship. The epilogue discusses the future of sport management. It suggests possible trends and examines developments in such areas as entrepreneurship, technology, globalization, and sport as an agent for social change.

Each chapter contains sections and sidebars expanding on the main topics. The section titled International Application offers a global perspective of the topic discussed. A Success Story offers a summary of an achievement in sport management. Management Insights explain the background of relevant sport management issues. Quick Facts highlight surprising facts about sport management. Quotes provide meaningful insights from experts. The Short of It offers a summary of the key points in the chapter.

Appendix A contains resources (including books, journals, and websites) to help you keep up with and learn more about sport management. Appendix B offers tips for prospective sport management students and professionals on applying the principles of sport management in various positions. The book concludes with a list of references and an index.

This book offers insights into the exciting world of sport management, the impact of the sport industry, and the possibilities for employment in sport. If you are curious about the field or seek a refresher on the content and current status of sport management, then this book is for you. Enjoy this journey into *Fundamentals of Sport Management*.

DESCRIPTION OF SELECT CHAPTER OPENER PHOTOS

Many of the chapter opener photos feature people, places, and events that are worthy of further description:

- Chapter 1: Roman Abramovich, owner of Chelsea Football Club
- Chapter 2: Chris Antonetti, general manager and executive vice president of the Cleveland Indians
- Chapter 4: Paul Hewitt, head basketball coach at George Mason University and former head basketball coach at Georgia Institute of Technology
- Chapter 5: NCAA headquarters in Indianapolis, Indiana
- Chapter 6: The Colosseum in Rome, Italy
- Chapter 10: Coors Field in Denver, Colorado, home of the Colorado Rockies
- Chapter 12: Wolverhampton Wanderers goalkeeper Wayne Hennessey and Notts County's Kevin Smith

Welcome to Sport Management

Part I of *Fundamentals of Sport Management* presents an overview of sport management and of the many professional opportunities it encompasses. This section of the book provides information about sport management as an academic discipline and as a profession. Chapter 1 addresses a seemingly simple question: What is sport management? It answers this question by exploring characteristics of the sport industry, as well as the origins and development of professional preparation programs in sport management. It also addresses the complex relationship between sport management academic programs and the sport industry.

Chapter 2 explores the varied career opportunities made possible by the considerable size and scope of the sport industry. This chapter discusses the advantages of professional education in sport management and covers what to look for in a sport management education—from faculty to experiential and networking opportunities. Viewing life as a contact sport, the chapter addresses the importance of internships in developing a solid skill set and discusses how field experiences can help students develop their resumes and establish contacts in the industry. It is also critical for students to understand the many stakeholders in sport management, and this chapter describes many careers available in the various sport segments, from recreational to professional sport. It also highlights the knowledge, attitudes, and skills that students need in order to distinguish themselves in their pursuit of a career in the sport industry.

CHAPTER 1

What Is Sport Management?

PA Photos

In this chapter, you will learn the following:

✓ How sport management is defined as an academic discipline
✓ How the academic discipline of sport management developed in response to sport industry needs
✓ The importance of professional preparation for students of sport management

> In the past 20 years, college sports-management programs have grown nearly as exponentially as the sports business itself has.
>
> **John Helyar
> (2000)**

Belmont Abbey College was established by Catholic monks in 1876 as a small liberal arts school in the middle of predominantly Protestant North Carolina. By the turn of the 21st century, the university's leaders had decided that the institution needed a change, and in 2004 they brought in William Thierfelder as president to boost enrollment and plot a new course for the school. Thierfelder and a member of the board of directors, H.A. "Humpy" Wheeler, came up with a novel idea to garner national attention and put the school on firmer financial footing (Thompson, 2007).

It is no coincidence that both of these men have a background in sport. Thierfelder holds a doctorate in sport psychology and worked previously as president of the York Barbell Company and as director of an agency serving NFL players. Wheeler, whose father was athletic director at Belmont Abbey for more than 30 years, served as president of Charlotte Motor Speedway. Their idea was to start the first motorsport management program at a university in the United States. The resulting program takes advantage of its proximity to the Charlotte Motor Speedway, NASCAR headquarters, the Carolina Speedway, and the Dirt Track Racing School. Thus Thierfelder and Wheeler have helped Belmont Abbey carve out a niche that has not only increased enrollment but also grabbed the attention of an industry that employs thousands of North Carolinians (Thompson, 2007).

sport management—Both a professional career path and an academic content area that includes all activities, individuals, and organizations involved in the conduct of sport in all its dimensions—youth and adult, play and work, amateur and professional, for-profit and nonprofit, community and international, recreation and performance oriented, and public and private.

Sport management is both a professional career path and an academic content area. In the broadest sense, sport management includes all activities, individuals, and organizations involved in the conduct of sport in all of its dimensions—youth and adult, play and work, amateur and professional, for-profit and nonprofit, community and international, recreational and performance oriented, and public and private. The field also includes the management of sport as entertainment.

Sport is a pervasive social institution that has grown into an estimated $425 billion per year industry (Plunkett, 2011; Coakley, 2009), and the emergence and evolution of academic sport management programs parallels the growth of the industry. Indeed, the impetus for professional preparation in sport management came from the industry itself and ultimately prompted the development of the academic discipline (Gillentine & Crow, 2005). As an academic content area, sport management includes professional preparation programs intended to help students learn foundational knowledge and best practices. It also includes the study of the conduct of the sport industry from a variety of disciplinary perspectives. For example, economists might examine the economic impact of sport globally or in a specific region. Sociologists might investigate the role of sport as a social institution. Business scholars might study the financial, strategic, or organizational aspects of sport. Psychologists might research group dynamics, leadership, or other interpersonal factors that affect sport. In addition to such scholarly study, sport management also involves applying these theoretical underpinnings in the specialized professional preparation of sport practitioners—that is, exploring how research findings should inform the day-to-day practice of, for example, a sport marketer, broadcaster, or facility manager.

Sport management is a relatively young academic discipline (Masteralexis, Barr, & Hums, 2012). In fact, it still goes by several names, including sport management, sports management, athletic administration, and sports administration. So, what's in a name? The terms *sport* and *sports* appear to be interchangeable, but when used in describing this field of study they carry different connotations. For example, the term *sport* implies a broader concept, similar to the function of the terms *government* and *religion*. The study of *government*, for instance, involves broad knowledge of how people organize and rule themselves, whereas the study of *governments* focuses on specific applications, such as those in the United States, Brazil, India, and China. Similarly, the study of *religion* involves broad knowledge of spiritual beliefs and foundations, whereas the study of *religions* would focus on, say, Buddhism, Catholicism, Islam, or Judaism. In much the same way, the study of *sport management* takes a broad perspective on the concepts and foundations of the conduct of sport, and the study of *sports management* implies an examination of, for example, basketball, hockey, football, tennis, or golf.

The terms **administration** and **management** also involve distinctions. The difference in terminology may appear inconsequential, yet each term carries its own implications. *Administration* refers to the performance of tasks related to the process of management, whereas *management* refers to the process of organizing, directing, and overseeing the achievement of objectives. Each of these terms is applicable to the study of the organization and conduct of the sport industry.

administration—Performance of tasks related to the process of management.

management—Act of organizing, directing, and overseeing the achievement of objectives.

Ultimately, though *sport management* has come to be the most widely used term to identify this field, all of these terms retain relevance in professional preparation for sport managers. In the end, the quality of the program is far more important than its name.

Origins in Physical Education, Athletics, and Business

The professional preparation of sport management practitioners originated in response to identified needs of the sport industry. Often, in their early stages of development, collegiate athletic programs were incorporated in physical education academic units. As a result, sport management programs first emerged in the physical education curriculum, and classes focused on the administration of physical activity have since developed into the specialized sport management courses we know today. Comprehensive sport management education can draw from such specialized curricular areas as accounting, communication, economics, ethics, event planning and execution, facilities, finance, governance, law, leadership, management, marketing, public relations, operations, and sales, among others. Thus, in the university structure, the ongoing evolution of sport management continues to be defined not only by its origins in physical education but also by curricular influences from diverse disciplines, including business, communication, education, recreation, and the social sciences. Increasing scholarly interest in sport management as a unique field of study has aided its progression from merely practitioner training to a serious academic undertaking bolstered by its own body of knowledge and research agendas.

In the last 40 years, the number of university-based sport management programs has increased dramatically (Stier, 2001), and more than 300 professional preparation programs are now offered in sport management in countries around the globe (North American Society for Sport Management, 2012). Universities have seen burgeoning interest in sport management curricula as more students have pursued employment in the sport industry (Parkhouse & Pitts, 1996). The following chronological summary of the evolution of sport management reveals that, despite a sluggish start, sport management has become a common academic program that attracts considerable student interest.

Sport Management: 1900 to 1965

Despite two world wars and a worldwide economic depression, sport thrived through the first half of the 20th century, and by 1950 the sport industry was well entrenched in U.S. society. Football was king of the vibrant intercollegiate sport scene, which had emerged from student-led clubs to be subsumed under faculty, and later professional, coaches and managers. The National Collegiate Athletic Association (NCAA) was formed in 1906 as a self-regulatory body at the behest of President Theodore Roosevelt. Baseball led the field in professional sport, which also included football, boxing, golf, tennis, and many others. And the Olympics had reemerged to popularize global sport competition. Despite all of this, no formal preparation existed for sport managers.

Nonetheless, the incentive to win, combined with the growing power of sport, led some to apply scientific research to sport. Specifically, during this era, psychology, physiology, and other scholarly disciplines turned some of their attention to the phenomenon of sport. As a result, academic programs were established to advance knowledge and apply specific theoretical foundations to sport. In similar fashion, sport management emerged from both academic curiosity and industry needs. Sport management was unique, however, in that, from its inception, it was intended to provide professional preparation for sport management practitioners. Thus the application of scientific management concepts to sport lagged behind the evolution of some other research-grounded, sport-related disciplines.

The first attempt to provide professional preparation in sport management began in 1949 at Florida Southern College (Isaacs, 1964). It was a curricular program, approved by the Florida Department of Education, in baseball business administration. The curriculum included numerous specialized courses similar in content to those typically covered in modern sport management programs. This isolated attempt was short-lived, operating between 1949 and 1959, and did not promote a theoretically grounded research program typical of established academic disciplines. Nor did it directly produce a body of knowledge or the timely emergence of similar programs. As a result, it is not widely heralded as the first sport management program; that program would not begin until years later.

In 1957, Walter O'Malley, president of the Brooklyn Dodgers, approached James Mason, professor at the University of Miami, and proposed the concept of specialized education for aspiring managers in the thriving sport industry. Though the curriculum was not implemented at Miami, the concept would serve as the basis for the first graduate program in sport administration.

Sport Management: 1966 to 1979

The proposed sport management curriculum conceived by O'Malley and Mason became a reality in 1966 at Ohio University, which established the first master's degree in sport administration. Shortly afterward, Biscayne College (now Saint Thomas University) and Saint John's University offered the first undergraduate sport management degree programs. In 1971, the University of Massachusetts established the second master's degree program. At this point, academic preparation in sport management had been established. By 1980, 20 graduate programs in sport management had been developed in the United States; even so, true proliferation would take another decade.

1825
The first sports page, Sporting Olio, is published in the *American Farmer* in Baltimore, Maryland.

1844
The Young Men's Christian Association (YMCA) is founded.

1852
Yale and Harvard compete against each other in the sport of rowing; this event took place in Lake Winnipesaukee, New Hampshire, and is recognized as the first intercollegiate sport competition.

1891
Dr. James Naismith invents the game of basketball at a YMCA in Springfield, Massachusetts.

1893
The first sports section in a newspaper is published by the *New York World*, owned by Joseph Pulitzer.

1896
Athens hosts the first modern Olympics.

1897
The first Boston Marathon is held.

1900–1965

1904
The International Federation of Association Football (FIFA, after its French name, Fédération Internationale de Football Association) is established as the international sport federation for soccer.

1906
The Intercollegiate Athletic Association of the United States is formed at the behest of President Theodore Roosevelt; it becomes the National Collegiate Athletic Association (NCAA) in 1910.

1917
The National Hockey League is established with four teams in Canada.

1920
In response to the Black Sox scandal, Kenesaw Mountain Landis is appointed the first commissioner of Major League Baseball.

1921
Radio is used for the first time to broadcast a boxing match between Jack Dempsey and Georges Carpentier.

(continued)

Sport Management: 1980 to 1999

By 1985, a sport management boom had resulted in the establishment of 83 academic sport management programs in the United States (Lambrecht & Kraft, 2009), and there were well over 100 programs by the late 1980s and nearly 200 by the mid-1990s. That number rose above 200, including more than 20 doctoral programs, before the start of the new millennium. By that point, undergraduate, master's, and doctoral programs had developed to meet the needs of various stakeholders. At one extreme, undergraduate programs sought to meet the sport industry's need for effective practitioners; doctoral programs, meanwhile, sought to expand the knowledge base of the new discipline and prepare a discipline-specific professoriate.

From their inception, sport management programs have fulfilled multiple purposes and existed in every size and variety of institution. Despite a lack of coordination, the development of academic programs in sport management has attracted considerable attention from students. In fact, the field has seen continuous growth not only in the number of sport management programs but also in the number of students attracted to those programs.

The explosive growth of sport management underscored the need for wide-ranging organization in the academic discipline. The Sport Management Arts and Science Society (SMARTS), formed at the University of Massachusetts, discussed common curriculum standards. In 1985, the North American Society for Sport Management (NASSM), the first academic association for sport management, was formed for the purpose of encouraging theoretical and applied scholarly pursuits and professional development in sport management. In 1986, NASSM cooperated with the National Association for Sport and Physical Education (NASPE) to form a joint sport management task force charged with developing standardized curricular areas. In 1993, NASSM and NASPE jointly formed the Sport Management Program Review Council (SMPRC) to oversee a process by which sport management programs could be approved as meeting the established program and curriculum standards. This effort marked the first attempt at self-regulation in the academic discipline of sport management.

Sport Management: 2000 and Beyond—Current Status

In the new millennium, sport management programs have continued to proliferate with varying purposes, curricula, and institutional characteristics. However, despite the availability of SMPRC program approval and content standards, only 25 percent of programs had obtained approval (Commission on Sport Management Accreditation, 2012). In response, in 2005, NASSM and NASPE formed two additional joint task forces—the Accreditation Task Force and the Standards Task Force—to explore the option of accrediting sport management programs. As a result, the Commission on Sport Management Accreditation (COSMA) was formally established in 2008. COSMA is "a specialized accrediting body whose purpose is to promote and recognize excellence in sport management education in colleges and universities at the baccalaureate and graduate levels" (Commission on Sport Management Accreditation, 2012). COSMA accreditation focuses on the following factors: outcomes assessment, strategic planning, curriculum, faculty, scholarly and professional activities, resources, internal and external relationships, and educational innovation.

NASSM has identified more than 300 academic programs in sport management. For decades, the promulgation of sport management programs has paralleled the elevation of sport's cultural status and socioeconomic power; in short, as the sport industry goes, so goes professional preparation in sport management. Chapter 2 more closely investigates the sport industry and its relationship to professional preparation in sport management; however, one issue that concerns both of these sides of the sport management coin should be addressed here. As is the case with other segments of the economy, the economic downturn has reduced employment opportunities in the sport industry. At the same time, limitations on employment opportunities can encourage individuals to further their education in preparation for a career. As a result, most sport management programs continue to enjoy healthy enrollment numbers.

Because university sport management programs continue to fill seats, they may sometimes be viewed as "cash cows." However, though the importance of enrollment to institutional health is undeniable (as illustrated in the case, discussed earlier, of Belmont Abbey), sport management cannot base its identity solely on generating tuition revenue; rather, it must be recognized as a legitimate academic discipline. Toward that end, each level of academic preparation serves distinctive purposes. For example, doctoral sport management programs advance disciplinary knowledge through a research agenda that can also inform the sport industry. They also prepare future faculty members to continue expanding the knowledge base in sport management. Master's programs provide a scholarly foundation upon which advanced doctoral studies are built; they also prepare future sport

Quick Facts

The North American Society for Sport Management (NASSM) website lists 333 sport management programs, including 282 in the United States and 13 in Canada. The site also lists 19 programs in Europe, 8 in Australia, 4 in New Zealand, 3 in Africa, 3 in Asia, and 1 in India, but there is no comprehensive global listing of sport management programs.

1900-1965
(continued)

1930
Uruguay, the host country, wins FIFA's inaugural World Cup.

1936
Jesse Owens wins four gold medals in the Olympic Games hosted by Nazi Germany in Berlin.

1939
NBC airs the first broadcast of a Major League Baseball game (featuring the Cincinnati Reds and the Brooklyn Dodgers) and the first broadcast of a pro football game (featuring the Philadelphia Eagles and the Brooklyn Dodgers).

1947
Jackie Robinson becomes the first African American to play Major League Baseball.

1950
Before 200,000 stunned fans in the Maracanã stadium in Rio de Janeiro, Uruguay beats Brazil to capture the FIFA World Cup.

1951
Walter Byers is named the first president of the NCAA.

1954
The magazine *Sports Illustrated* publishes its first issue.

1957
Althea Gibson wins the Wimbledon singles tennis title and becomes the first African American woman to appear on the cover of *Sports Illustrated*.

1961
Congress passes the Sports Broadcasting Act, thus permitting National Football League commissioner Pete Rozelle to negotiate with television networks on behalf of all teams in the league.

1964
Cassius Clay (Muhammad Ali) defeats Sonny Liston to become heavyweight boxing champion.

1966-1979

1966
Ohio University starts a master's degree program in sport administration.

1967
The first Super Bowl is played; it features the Green Bay Packers and the Kansas City Chiefs.

(continued)

Packianathan Chelladurai and Janet Parks, Sport Management Scholars

Photo courtesy of Packianathan Chelladurai.

Photo courtesy of Janet Parks.

Sport management faculty members are the keystone of academic preparation in sport management; without them, the discipline would not exist. Packianathan Chelladurai and Janet Parks are two highly respected scholars who epitomize the successful faculty member in sport management.

Packianathan Chelladurai received a MASc and a PhD in management science from the University of Waterloo. He is a universally respected sport management scholar and educator, having taught for 40 years in both Canada and the United States. Chelladurai currently serves as professor of sport management at Troy University. He was a founding member of the North American Society for Sport Management (NASSM) and the European Association of Sport Management (EASM). He has also served as editor of the *Journal of Sport Management* and authored several books, more than 80 journal articles, and 21 book chapters. Chelladurai developed the multidimensional model of sport leadership and the Leadership Scale for Sports. In 1991, he was the first recipient of NASSM's most prestigious honor, the Earle F. Zeigler Award. In 2005, he became the first to receive EASM's Merit Award for Distinguished Service to Sport Management Education. He was recently named one of the 50 most influential contributors in sport psychology for his work in leadership.

Janet B. Parks received her doctor of arts degree in physical education from Middle Tennessee State University and completed postdoctoral study at the University of Wisconsin–Madison. Prior to her retirement, she served as distinguished sport management professor and chair of the School of Human Movement, Sport, and Leisure Studies at Bowling Green State University in Ohio. She was a founding member of NASSM and served as founding coeditor of the *Journal of Sport Management*. In addition to her teaching and professional service activities, Parks has published textbooks, book chapters, journal articles, and research reports on sport management topics related to career development, gender issues in sport, and other aspects of the field. Having gained widespread respect in sport management, Parks has made countless presentations to professional societies. She received NASSM's Earle F. Zeigler Award for professional achievement in 1992 and its Garth Paton Distinguished Service Award in 2001, as well as the Outstanding Achievement Award from the NASPE Sport Management Council. She is a NASSM research fellow and a research consortium fellow of the American Alliance for Health, Physical Education, Recreation and Dance (AAHPERD).

industry professionals on the basis of theoretically grounded applications. Bachelor's programs tend to focus on scientifically based professional preparation of aspiring sport industry practitioners. Each individual program is unique, however, in pursuing its specific aims. Thus a given program might focus on social responsibility and social justice, on international development, or on a specific segment of the industry, such as intercollegiate athletics, motorsport, or professional sport enterprises.

Because sport management serves as both a scholarly discipline and a professional preparation program, the field faces the ongoing challenge of balancing theoretical research and practical application, as participants pursue both scholarly and professional preparation agendas. As a result, sport management programs must maintain both academic rigor and professional relevance, which means that they must offer benefits to multiple stakeholders, including students preparing for careers in the sport industry and the organizations who employ them. These considerations also raise a broader question: What is sport management's relationship to the sport industry?

The sport industry has generally embraced the benefits provided by academic sport management programs, but a gap remains between the industry and the academy. As is typical with professional preparation programs, practical applications put forth by people in the sport management discipline are often valued or adopted by the industry. However, theoretical research can be ignored—or worse, it may never reach industry practitioners. Thus, while it is incumbent on the industry to implement changes in best practices based upon foundational discovery research, it is evident that the direct relevance of contributions by academic sport management programs is the key to building bridges with the industry. In addition, the growing number of sport industry practitioners who have undergone professional preparation in sport management has generated growing acceptance of the academic degree.

Sport industry acceptance of sport management is one consideration in the move toward program accreditation. If the industry values accreditation, it increases an incentive for programs to pursue accreditation. However, if academic sport management programs themselves value the accreditation process, sport management programs will be optimally conceived and implemented, and the accreditation of academic programs will ensure the quality and subsequent acceptance of professional preparation in sport management. At the same time, issues are plentiful in sport management education. The continuously evolving sport management discipline must situate itself amid changing universities, changing work environments, changing industry opportunities, and changing workforces.

1966-1979
(continued)

1970
Brazil wins the FIFA World Cup, which is held in Mexico and broadcast for the first time in color.

1971
Nine American table tennis players participate in a historic series of matches between the United States and communist China.

1972
Nike is founded by Bill Bowerman and Phil Knight.

1972
President Richard M. Nixon signs into law Title IX, which bars discrimination based on a person's sex.

1972
Terrorists kill 10 members of the Israeli team during an attack at the Summer Olympics in Munich.

1973
Secretariat wins the Triple Crown of horse racing.

1979
The Entertainment and Sports Programming Network, now known as ESPN, is launched.

1980-1999

1985
The North American Society for Sport Management is established.

1987
The *Journal of Sport Management* is launched.

1987
WFAN in New York City changes its format to sports talk radio.

1989
Wayne Gretzky wins the Hart Memorial Trophy as MVP of the NHL for the ninth time.

1990
Martina Navratilova wins the women's tennis singles title at Wimbledon for the ninth time.

1992
Michael Jordan, Larry Bird, and Magic Johnson lead the Dream Team to gold at the Summer Olympics in Barcelona.

1992
The English Premier League is formed with 20 teams from the Football League.

1992
ESPN invests in its first ESPN-branded radio station.

(continued)

Sport management programs are currently affiliated with a variety of units, including kinesiology, education, business, and separate professional schools (Fink & Barr, 2012). Is one location better than the others? Where are the best programs housed? And which are the best ones? There is no current systematic ranking of sport management programs; we can, however, consider benchmarks for comparing programs. Regardless of where a sport management program is housed, the faculty must be qualified, the essential curriculum content must be covered, industry connections must be established, and experiential opportunities must be made available.

Professional Preparation in Sport Management

Many positive outcomes await not only the sport industry and its current and future employees but also those sport management academic programs that effectively manage these four benchmarks. To put it more specifically, a sport management program must include (a) a faculty that balances industry experience and scholarly productivity, (b) a theoretically grounded curriculum that provides depth and breadth of coverage in relevant content areas as identified by the Commission on Sport Management Accreditation (COSMA) (see table 1.1), (c) a network of affiliated

TABLE 1.1 COSMA Common Professional Core

A. Social, psychological, and international foundations of sport management

    1. Sport management principles

    2. Sport leadership

    3. Operations management/event and venue management

    4. Sport governance

B. Ethics

C. Sport marketing and communication

D. Finance/accounting/economics

    1. Sport finance

    2. Accounting

    3. Economics of sport

E. Legal aspects of sport

F. Integrative experience

    1. Strategic management/policy

    2. Internship

    3. Capstone experience

Reprinted from Commission on Sport Management Accreditation 2010.

Quick Facts

Thirty-one institutions are charter members of the Commission on Sport Management Accreditation (COSMA).

sport management industry professionals and organizations, and (d) multiple field-based experiential learning opportunities that complement the curriculum. Managing these benchmarks successfully can enhance the effectiveness of professional preparation at the diverse institutions that offer sport management.

Just as each college or university has a distinctive purpose, each academic program for professional preparation in sport management is unique. However, these benchmarks might be considered as the universal elements of professional preparation in sport management. While COSMA accreditation is mission driven and outcome based, thus taking into account institutional individuality, these common elements inform us about what to look for when considering sport management programs and provide one basis for evaluating programs.

No singular sport management curriculum exists, but COSMA has identified common professional components (CPCs) that serve as foundational content areas essential to all sport management programs. These are the components listed in table 1.1. How a given CPC is addressed in an individual sport management program is unique to that program, but the CPCs listed in the table are foundational components of any sport management education.

As in any academic discipline, the qualifications of a sport management program's faculty serve as a cornerstone of that program's quality. Though faculty qualifications vary by individual programmatic goals, faculty members in professional preparation programs for sport management must generally display evidence of both practical experience in the sport industry and substantive scholarly production. Balancing these two focuses within the faculty is one key to a program's relevance in both preparing students professionally and contributing to the discipline's scholarly knowledge base.

While some may say that "who you know is more important than what you know," this is not really the case. Actually, both are important. Who you know (your network) can open doors, but what you know (your ability to perform) is essential for success in the sport industry. Others suggest that beyond the effect of "who you know" lies the essential factor of "who knows you." Regardless of the turn of phrase, however, it is essential to develop a professional network. Sport management programs that foster networking opportunities

1980-1999
(continued)

1993
The European Association for Sport Management is established.

1995
The Sport Management Association of Australia and New Zealand is founded.

2000s

2001
Alex Rodriguez signs a 10-year contract with MLB's Texas Rangers worth $250 million.

2002
A group of sport management researchers founds the Asian Association for Sport Management.

2003
The Special Olympics are held in Dublin, Ireland, with the help of 30,000 volunteers.

2004
Michael Schumacher of Germany becomes the world champion of Formula One racing for the seventh time.

2006
ESPN Radio grows to 700 affiliated radio stations.

2008
Beijing hosts the Summer Olympic Games. The Olympic Broadcasting Services use 1,000 cameras to cover the Games. Some 6 million people in the United States watch at least one event via mobile phone, and 842 million Chinese people watch at least part of the opening ceremonies. The official Beijing Games website draws 105.7 million unique users during the month of August.

2008
The last game is played in the original Yankee Stadium on September 21, by which time more than 150,000,000 fans have attended events there since the stadium opened.

2008
The Indian Premier League (IPL) crowns its first cricket champion, the Rajasthan Royals.

2009
The Latin American Association for Sport Management (Asociación Latinoamericana de Gerencia Deportiva) is formed in March.

(continued)

> *Administrators, professors, and students know that "breaking into" sports is tough, so sports management programs work hard to place students in internships with sports firms. Any experience in sports is better than none, but sports management programs must make sure that both students and employers understand the purpose and value of an internship.*
>
> **Scott Wysong (2006)**

enhance their students' chances of success. If, as another maxim puts it, life is a contact sport, then a program must develop and maintain a professional network into which its students can be integrated.

In the sport industry, experience is paramount in obtaining employment. Often, even entry-level positions require experience in the field; therefore, it is critical that sport management students have the opportunity to gain hands-on work experience through their professional preparation program. A professionally supervised, credit-bearing field experience allows students not only to apply what they have learned in the classroom but also to demonstrate their skills to prospective employers.

Professional Associations in Sport Management

Sport management is home to several categories of related professional associations (see table 1.2). Academic associations are organized on the basis of related academic content areas. For example, the North American Society for Sport History revolves around the historical analysis of sport, and the Sport and Recreation Law Association advances the study of the legal aspects of sport. Such associations serve the sport management discipline, as well as institutional and individual members, through the advancement of scholarship, teaching, and service. Some are global, such as the World Association for Sport Management (WASM). Others are regional, such as NASSM, which is a prominent association of sport management faculty scholars in Canada and the United States that is intended to represent the interests of the sport management academy, as noted in its statement of purpose: "The purpose of the North American Society for Sport Management is to promote, stimulate, and encourage study, research, scholarly writing, and professional development in the area of sport management—both theoretical and applied aspects" (North American Society for Sport Management, 2012).

Sport associations are organized on the basis of the governance and conduct of specific sports or segments of the sport industry. Sport-specific governing bodies include, among many others, the International Federation of Association Football (FIFA), the United States Tennis Association (USTA), and USA Swimming. These organizations may be national governing bodies, such as USA Basketball, or global ones, such as the International Basketball Federation (FIBA). Some sport governance organizations address multiple sports—for example, the International Olympic Committee (IOC), the National Federation of State High School Associations (NFHS),

TABLE 1.2 Associations and Journals in Sport Management

Type	Examples
Academic association	American Alliance for Health, Physical Education, Recreation and Dance (AAHPERD)
	Asian Association for Sport Management (AASM)
	North American Society for Sport Management (NASSM)
	North American Society for the Sociology of Sport (NASSS)
	Sport Marketing Association (SMA)
Sport association	International Basketball Federation (FIBA)
	International Federation of Association Football (FIFA)
	International Wheelchair Basketball Federation
	National Association for Stock Car Auto Racing (NASCAR)
	National Collegiate Athletic Association (NCAA)
	Professional Golfers' Association (PGA)
	United States Olympic Committee (USOC)
	USA Swimming
Practitioner organization	National Association of Basketball Coaches (NABC)
	National Association of Collegiate Directors of Athletics (NACDA)
	National Interscholastic Athletic Administrators Association (NIAAA)
Hall of fame	International Boxing Hall of Fame
	International Gymnastics Hall of Fame
	Naismith Memorial Basketball Hall of Fame
Professional journal	*Athletic Business*
	Coach and Athletic Director
	SportsBusiness Journal
Academic journal	*Case Studies in Sport Management*
	Journal of Sport Management
	Sport Management Review

2000s
(continued)

2010
IPL games are broadcast live via YouTube.

2010
South Africa hosts the men's FIFA World Cup, which is won by Spain.

2010
The NCAA signs a contract worth US$11 billion with CBS and Turner Sports to televise the Men's Division I Basketball Championship.

2010
The African Sport Management Association is founded in June during the 17th Biennial Conference of the International Society for Comparative Physical Education and Sport held at Kenyatta University in Nairobi, Kenya.

2011
New Zealand's squad, known as the "All Blacks," one of the most recognized licensed products in sports, wins the Rugby World Cup, which takes place in its home country.

2012
The World Association of Sport Management is founded.

2012
London Summer Olympics held. Michael Phelps retires from swimming after becoming the Olympian with the most medals in the history of the modern Games. Oscar Pistorius, a South African sprinter known as "the blade runner," ran in the Olympics and later took part in the Summer Paralympics setting a Paralympic record time and obtaining a gold medal in the 400-metre race.

the National Collegiate Athletic Association (NCAA), and the Special Olympics. More information on the governance of sport is provided in chapter 5.

Practitioner organizations represent the interests of industry segments. Examples include the Sports and Fitness Industry Association (SFIA) and the International Association of Venue Managers (IAVM). Such organizations also directly represent practitioners in specific careers—for example, the International Sports Press Association (AIPS), the National Association of Collegiate Directors of Athletics (NACDA), the National Soccer Coaches Association of America (NSCAA), and the Sports Lawyers Association (SLA).

The public nature of the sport industry has also led to the creation of another type of association—the hall of fame. Halls of fame recognize outstanding long-term achievement in specific areas of sport.

 INTERNATIONAL APPLICATION

Global Academic Associations and Exchanges

Globalization in the field of sport management has yielded opportunities that have been seized by sport enterprises as well as academic coalitions. For example, the recently formed World Association for Sport Management (WASM) has received international support from leaders in the sport management discipline. Like its predecessor, the International Sport Management Alliance (a consortium of sport management academic associations), WASM facilitates cross-cultural understanding and global cooperation in the sport management discipline. The regional sport management associations have aligned with one another to form an international cooperative to further the interests of the sport management discipline. Specifically, the association was developed by representatives of the European Association for Sport Management, the Sport Management Association of Australia and New Zealand, the Asian Association for Sport Management, the Latin American Organization for Sport Management, the African Sport Management Association, and the North American Society for Sport Management. Individually, each association represents regional academic interests in sport management, yet the recognition of the global nature of sport prompted a united approach to the academic discipline of sport management on a worldwide scale.

On a smaller scale, individual institutions engage in similar cooperative arrangements to further their global presence. As a result, joint degree programs and international student exchanges have become increasingly commonplace. For example, SUNY Cortland and London Metropolitan University offer a dual degree program in international sport management. The University of the West Indies, FIFA, and the International Centre for Sports Studies have collaborated on an executive sport management program. Many colleges and universities offer student exchange opportunities through formal articulation agreements. For example, U.S. students can study abroad through Florida State University, George Mason University, Slippery Rock University, Wingate University, the University of South Carolina, and other institutions. Many institutions, both in the United States and in other nations, offer students the opportunity to go abroad for a course, a semester, or an even longer unit as a component of their sport management degree.

In addition to organizations and halls of fame, of interest to both the industry and the sport management academy are the relevant professional and academic journals (see table 1.2).

The Short of It

- Like the sport industry, the academic discipline that we call sport management has become a global affair.
- Trailblazers such as Packianathan Chelladurai and Janet Parks have helped expand this discipline into one of the fastest-growing academic concentrations at colleges and universities around the world.
- Sport management practitioners and faculty have formed many professional associations (e.g., NASSM, SLA) to foster new research ideas and develop best practices.
- Cooperation between the sport industry and the academic community can enhance the academic discipline of sport management and improve the functioning of the sport industry.

CHAPTER

What Can I Do With Sport Management?

Photo courtesy of Cleveland Indians.

✓ What job opportunities are available for sport management students in the sport industry

✓ How internships can help sport management students develop a solid skill base and industry contacts

✓ How to define the sport industry

✓ How different paths to employment exist in the sport industry

> Even if you're on the right track, you'll get run over if you just sit there.
>
> **Will Rogers,** vaudeville performer and social commentator

Chris Antonetti was about to graduate from Georgetown University with a degree in business administration. While serving as a manager for the men's basketball team, he had enjoyed not only being involved in college athletics but also learning about the *business* of college basketball. The more he thought about his career path, the more he came to the conclusion that he wanted to work in the sport industry.

Antonetti decided that the key to acquiring a job would be further study at the master's degree level in sport management. He researched sport management programs around the country and decided to enroll at the University of Massachusetts Amherst. As part of his degree requirements, he interned with Major League Baseball's Montreal Expos in the club's player development department in Florida. He was then hired full-time as assistant director of player development. A year later, he was hired by the Cleveland Indians as general manager Mark Shapiro's top assistant and got involved in player acquisitions, the farm system, contract negotiations, scouting, and statistical analysis. When Shapiro moved into upper management as the club's president, the selection of Chris Antonetti as general manager came as no surprise.

Antonetti's story is, of course, just one of many in the business of sport, which is a global phenomenon. Indeed, sport wields considerable economic influence around the world. It contributes $425 billion annually to the U.S. economy alone (Plunkett, 2011). Sport is big business, and the sport industry consistently ranks as one of the top sectors of the United States' economy. Yet it is difficult to examine sport as a singular entity; in fact, the multifaceted **sport industry** includes such diverse segments as sport-related media; legal and financial services; sponsorships, advertising, and endorsements; ticketing, events, and facility operations; wholesale and retail sporting goods; education, nonprofit work, and community development; and entertainment, gaming, recreation, and sport tourism (golf resorts and ski resorts hire many managers, and sport tourists travel to participate in events and visit nostalgic sites).

sport industry—Industry including such diverse segments as sport-related media; legal and financial services; sponsorships, advertising, and endorsements; ticketing, events, and facility operations; wholesale and retail sporting goods; education, nonprofit work, and community development; and entertainment, gaming, recreation, and sport tourism.

This variety reflects the interests of myriad stakeholders and yields equally diverse opportunities for employment. For example, sport participants, spectators, and business managers each hold unique interests in the sport industry. Stakeholders also include educators, tourists, gamblers, and gamers. Educators, for instance, are involved in the delivery of sport through collegiate and scholastic settings. Sport participants are provided with a means to pursue self-fulfillment, recreation, or competition. Gamers find a setting in which to experience entertainment, and gamblers approach sport as the backdrop for a potentially lucrative trade. In addition, hundreds of millions of fans and spectators follow sporting events that are provided through various media outlets on a daily basis. Overall, the sport industry serves as the setting for millions of employees across its many segments.

This rich interest in sport provides many distinctive sport-related employment opportunities throughout the world. In fact, in many developed nations, a significant portion of the workforce is employed in sport. In the United States, direct participants include nearly 14,000 professional athletes, more than 175,000 coaches and scouts, and almost 13,000 officials earning their livelihood in sports. Beyond that, nearly a million Americans work in fitness centers, snow skiing facilities, bowling centers, country clubs, and golf courses. Approximately 1.5 million Americans work directly in the amusement, sport gambling, and recreation sectors, and another 250,000 are employed in wholesale and retail sporting goods (U.S. Bureau of Labor Statistics, 2011).

Even beyond its direct economic importance, sport functions as a powerful component of many societies. One way of thinking about this power has been provided by Wolf (1990), who delineated four modes of power: (1) Power can be viewed as a personal attribute similar to individual capability. (2) As a transactional or transformational agent, power can be influential in framing interpersonal interactions. (3) Tactical power can be employed at the organizational level to establish control of the environment. (4) Structural power can shape the settings of power on a large scale. Sport is associated with each of these modes of power.

The power of sport can be used to address myriad social objectives. As a powerful and emotive socioeconomic institution, sport offers a way for individuals, groups, and cultures to build relationships and engage with one another. On a local level, sport provides an arena for individual engagement and exchange; at the same time, its structural power and function as a social institution mean that it can also be used to influence societies on a large scale (Coakley, 2009). Because sport is enormously popular and, indeed, pervades the social fabric of many countries, "its ability to reach across social, political, and economic divides . . . makes sport one of the few institutions that can serve as a catalyst for change" (Pederson, 2011, p. 385). The power of the social institution of sport generates huge economic investment, which creates opportunity for extensive social impact. Whether or not that opportunity is realized depends on the conduct of sport, and that conduct is ultimately determined by current practitioners and by aspiring sport managers embarking on careers in the industry.

Quick Facts

- Approximately 3.3 million people are employed directly in the sport industry in the United States.
- Football (soccer) is the most attended and watched sport in the world.
- Fishing is the largest individual participant sport in the world.
- It takes 3,000 cows to supply the National Football League with enough leather for a year's supply of footballs.
- Major League Baseball teams use about 850,000 balls per season.
- Each year, about 42,000 tennis balls are used in approximately 650 matches during the Wimbledon Championships.

Careers in Sport Management

Careers in the sport industry are extremely varied. Some require specialized education and expertise, whereas others are a bit more generic. For example, sport agents often possess law degrees in order to enhance their effectiveness in negotiating contracts, and accountants in sport organizations must possess appropriate skills and certifications to ply their trade regardless of the economic segment within which they work. In contrast, no specific training is required for sport-related sales careers, but preparation in these skills often opens the door to entry-level positions in the sport industry.

Positions in sport are available in all facets of the industry, ranging from high-profile professional and international sport organizations to local enterprises and events. Indeed, the multibillion dollar global sport industry offers abundant employment opportunities for aspiring sport management professionals at all levels. A wide variety of jobs can be had, for example, in the following settings:

- Academic institutions (e.g., scholastic and collegiate athletic programs)
- Major and minor league professional leagues and franchises
- Independent sport federations, including governing bodies, representative bodies, and not-for-profit and profit-based organizations
- Sporting goods companies
- Independent sport management and marketing firms
- Media groups
- Corporate entities with sport marketing departments
- Sport agencies, which provide athlete representation
- Health and fitness facilities
- Golf courses and ski resorts
- Halls of fame

- Community parks and recreation organizations
- Extreme and adventure sport providers
- Sponsors
- Special event management providers
- Venues and facility management providers
- Enterprises related to sport entertainment or sport tourism

Specific positions available in the sport industry range widely and include those in marketing, sales, promotions, sponsorship, ticketing, development, public and media relations, venues and events, finance and accounting, and human resources management. For example, specific positions available in intercollegiate athletics include sports information director, development director, ticket manager, marketing director, event coordinator, financial manager, and athletic director, to name just a few. A professional franchise can employ dozens, even hundreds, including coaches and players, event staff, external (public, corporate, and community) relations associates, marketers, fiscal managers (e.g., salary cap analysts), a general manager, and a president. A private enterprise such as a sport management firm might employ legal counsel, human resources managers, financial managers, marketing and promotions managers, and public relations specialists.

Whatever the specific sport industry setting, if you plan to pursue a sport management career you should prepare for daily challenges, occasional instability, intense competition, long hours, and wide-ranging rewards. Entry-level positions offer varied starting salaries, and some provide opportunities for rapid advancement. Whether seeking an entry-level or an advanced position in sport, you can use many websites to identify available positions, such as firstjobinsports.com, precisionhire.com, teamworkonline.com, and workinsports.com. Some are free and readily available for use, others require registration, and some require paid membership; the most useful sites often provide detailed position descriptions, educational and experiential requirements, and other information related to specific career opportunities in sport management.

Professional Sport

Professional leagues govern the competition of their member teams; they devise and enforce the rules. League structure varies; some leagues use a board of governors and a commissioner, whereas others function as single-entity structures in which the league owns the franchises. Examples of professional sport leagues include Major League Baseball (MLB), Major League Lacrosse (MLL), the English Premier League (soccer), the Australian Football League, Serie A (Italian football), the J. League (Japanese football), the Bundesliga (German football), the Hellenic

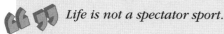

Life is not a spectator sport.

Jackie Robinson

Basketball Clubs Association, Major League Soccer (MLS), the National Basketball Association (NBA), the Canadian Football League (CFL), the National Football League (NFL), the National Hockey League (NHL), the Indian Premier League (IPL), the Women's National Basketball Association (WNBA), and National Pro Fastpitch (U.S. women's softball league).

Professional minor leagues are similar to professional major leagues. In some cases, they are affiliated with a major league, or their teams are affiliated with major league teams; in other cases, they operate as independent structures. In Triple-A baseball (the International and Pacific Coast Leagues), Double-A baseball (the Eastern, Southern, and Texas Leagues), and Class A baseball (the California, Carolina, and Florida State leagues), teams such as the Potomac Nationals and Toledo Mud Hens are affiliated with MLB franchises such as the Washington Nationals and Detroit Tigers. Other types of minor league sport organizations in the United States include the National Basketball Development League, the American Basketball Association, and the East Coast Hockey League. Competitive second-tier leagues, such as Serie B in Italy and the English Premier League's Football Championship League, can be found throughout the world.

Individual professional sport franchises compete within professional leagues. For example, the Pittsburgh Steelers compete in the NFL, the Los Angeles Lakers compete in the NBA, the Montreal Canadiens compete in the NHL, Real Madrid competes in La Liga (Spain's top-level soccer league), the Denver Outlaws compete in MLL, the Melbourne Demons compete in the Australian Football League, the Washington Mystics compete in the WNBA, the San Francisco Giants compete in MLB, the Delhi Daredevils compete in the IPL, and Manchester United competes in the Premier League.

Intercollegiate and Interscholastic Athletics

Collegiate athletics provides another setting for employment in the sport industry. The National Collegiate Athletic Association (NCAA) is the governing body for most college sport in the United States. Other U.S. governing bodies include the National Association of Intercollegiate Athletics and the National Junior College Athletic Association. Employment positions are available not only with these governing bodies but also with individual conferences, such as the Big Ten, the Pac-12, the Southeastern Conference, the Atlantic Coast Conference, and the Big East Conference. Within NCAA conferences, intercollegiate programs compete on three levels. Division I, the highest level of competition, includes institutions such as University of Illinois, Stanford University, the University of Florida, and the University of Texas. Division II, with the fewest institutions, includes schools such as Barry University; California State University, East Bay; Bemidji State University; West Texas A&M University; and Slippery Rock University. Division III is home to the largest number of schools, including, for example, Occidental College, Johns Hopkins University, Massachusetts Institute of Technology, the Emory and Henry College, Juniata College, the College at Brockport (SUNY), Kenyon College, Christopher Newport University, Greensboro College, and the University of Mount Union.

Interscholastic athletics, governed by the National Federation of State High School Associations, also involves many state associations, such as the Arizona Interscholastic Association, the Pennsylvania Interscholastic Athletic Association, and the Virginia High School League. Sport personnel are also employed by public school systems, such as the Fairfax County Public Schools, the Los Angeles Unified School District, and the Seattle Public Schools; these systems, of course, include individual high schools, middle schools, and other schools that offer athletic programming. Sport programs are also offered at private schools, such as DeMatha Catholic High School and Hampton Roads Academy. Other sport-oriented scholastic associations include the National High School Coaches Association and the National Interscholastic Athletic Administrators Association.

Organizations, Foundations, and Associations

National and international sport organizations are abundant, and they may focus on specific sports or on sport in general. Examples include the International Olympic Committee, the United States Olympic Committee, and dozens of national and international sport governing bodies. Sport leagues and organizations can be found in many countries for most sports, including, for example, basketball, cricket, football (soccer), golf, martial arts, rugby, and volleyball. Employment opportunities can also be found at the Young Men's Christian Association, the Young Women's Christian Association, the Special Olympics, the International Paralympic Committee, the Boys & Girls Clubs of America, the Amateur Athletic Union, Peace and Sport, and the United Nations Office on Sport for Development and Peace. Governmental sport-related organizations include state and city sport commissions and government sport agencies; community sport clubs; community parks and recreation departments; and municipal golf, tennis, and fitness venues. Various federal agencies also offer sport-related opportunities; see chapter 5 for information about governmental involvement in sport and the related employment opportunities.

Employment opportunities are also available at nonprofit sport-related foundations and associations. There are a variety of not-for-profit organizations, including trade associations, representative associations, educational organizations, and charitable foundations. Examples include the Sports and Fitness Industry Association; the National Association for Sport and Physical Education; various professional players unions and associations (e.g., the National Football League Players Association); the National Association of Governor's Councils on Physical Fitness and Sports; the National Congress of State Games; the President's Council on Physical Fitness, Sports, and Nutrition; and the Women's Sports Foundation.

Manufacturing, Sales, Marketing, and Media

The manufacture and sale of sporting goods constitute a major economic segment that offers many employment opportunities. For example, sports equipment, shoes, and apparel are manufactured and distributed by Adidas, Head, MacGregor, New Balance, Nike, Spalding, Wilson, and many others. Sporting goods retail outlets include, among many others, Dick's Sporting Goods and Sports Authority. Sport-related job opportunities can also be found with a wide variety of facilities and service providers who hire professionals for positions that include sales and marketing, business development, facility management, and sport instruction in settings such as extreme and adventure sports, sport leagues, training facilities for the martial arts or other specific sports, bowling alleys, water parks, ski resorts, tennis and racquet clubs, golf courses, health spas, and fitness clubs.

Professional positions are also available at sport management and marketing firms, such as Octagon, IMG, Gaylord Sports Management, Creative Artists Agency, Lagardère Unlimited, Wasserman Media Group, and Sport Management Group Worldwide. Though sport agents who negotiate contracts often need a law degree, sport agencies also employ a wide range of other personnel. For example, major corporations (e.g., Coca-Cola, McDonald's, Anheuser-Busch, Gatorade) often operate in-house marketing, promotions, and sponsorship departments that offer opportunities for sport managers. Jobs are also available in many forms in special event management, as well as venue and facility management—for example, through specialized firms and at sport stadiums and arenas. Sport-related consultants and architects often opt for entrepreneurial opportunities, but some work is also available at private architectural and construction firms that specialize in designing and building sport facilities.

Many jobs are available in sport-related media, which now include newspaper, radio, television, online publishing, special-interest sport publications, and sport-related publishers. Sport managers are employed by individual sport-specific associations, such as the Professional Golfers' Association Tour and the Ladies Professional Golf Association, as well as motorsport organizations such as Formula One racing, the National Association for Stock Car Auto Racing, Championship Auto Racing Teams, IndyCar, and the National Hot Rod Association. Sport management graduates may also find work with individual race teams or companies (e.g., Joe Gibbs Racing, Hendrick Motorsports) or racetracks (e.g., Daytona International Speedway, Talladega Superspeedway, Indianapolis Motor Speedway).

Paths to Employment

There is no official, prescribed career path in the sport industry. Where you start does not dictate where you ultimately want to go in your career. Thanks to the sport industry's international scope, sport management careers are available both locally and globally. Some sport managers remain with a single sport organization for their entire career, whereas others move frequently between organizations. This chapter presents diverse examples of careers available in the industry, but not all career opportunities can even be foreseen. As new careers emerge, they are quickly adapted to the sport industry. For example, as blogging became a viable career option, sport bloggers emerged as a component of the industry. Some sport managers continue their education with a graduate degree such as an MBA or a master's in sport management; others obtain a doctorate in order to pursue an academic career, and still others pursue a law degree in order to become sport agents.

⭐ SUCCESS STORY

Charley Casserly, NFL Manager, Executive, Broadcaster, and Professor

Charley Casserly was a 16-year National Football League (NFL) general manager for the Washington Redskins and Houston Texans. He currently works for the NFL Network as an analyst.

Over the course of his 29-year NFL career, Casserly became one of the most respected general managers in the league. In his 23 years with the Washington Redskins, he was known for his tireless work ethic and keen eye for football talent. During Casserly's tenure, Washington went to four Super Bowls and won three. Casserly then served as senior vice president and general manager of football operations for the expansion franchise Houston Texans, where for four years in a row his draft selection earned Rookie of the Year honors or was selected for the Pro Bowl (no other team in that four-year period could say the same). In 2003, NFL commissioner Paul Tagliabue appointed him to the prestigious NFL Competition Committee for the second time (he served on the committee from 1996 to 1999 and from 2003 to 2006).

Casserly's earlier experience included serving as an assistant coach at Cathedral High School and at Springfield College, as an athletic director at Cathedral, and as a head football coach at Minnechaug High School. He began his work with the Redskins in 1977 as an unpaid intern under Hall of Fame coach George Allen. Washington hired him as a scout for the next season, then elevated him to assistant general manager in 1982. The Redskins went on to capture their first Super Bowl in 1983. Elevated to general manager in 1989, Casserly sustained the organization's history of uncovering high-quality players in the later rounds of the draft. In 1999, *Sports Illustrated, Pro Football Weekly, SportingNews,* and *USA Today* named Casserly as NFL Executive of the Year at midseason. During Casserly's years with Washington and Houston, he instituted internship programs that have produced more than 30 league executives, staff members, and other professionals in the sport world.

Casserly has enjoyed extensive experience in radio and television. While he was a general manager, he had both a radio and television show in Houston and Washington, DC. Since becoming a full-time member of the media in 2006, he has worked for the NFL Network, Comcast Sports, *The NFL Today* (CBS Sports), CBS Sports Line, NFL.com, and the Westwood One pregame show, along with a number of other media outlets.

Casserly and his wife, Beverley, have been married more than 30 years and have one daughter, Shannon. He holds a bachelor's degree in education, a master's degree in guidance, and an honorary doctorate from Springfield College, where he also played football. He is also a member of the Springfield College Sports Hall of Fame and the Bergen Catholic High School Hall of Fame. In addition to his television work, he is an adjunct professor in the MBA program at Georgetown University. Professor Casserly also assists students as an executive in residence and instructor of sport management in George Mason University's sport management program.

Professional Preparation
for a Sport Management Career

Aspiring sport managers can choose from multiple paths to employment in the sport industry, but they must prepare in some way for their future career. Professional preparation incorporates both educational and experiential opportunities. The fundamental content areas that every prospective sport manager should master were developed by the Commission on Sport Management Accreditation (COSMA); they are listed in table 1.1.

On-the-job training occurs in every profession and provides specific education for specific positions. Specialized academic preparation in sport management provides many aspiring sport managers with professional preparation that they need in order to succeed. One major component of any professional preparation program is an internship, which enables the student to obtain valuable work experience in the industry and serves as a recognized pathway to employment. Thus internships function as a link between the industry and academic sport management programs.

The "carefully orchestrated beginning" of professional preparation in sport management emerged from the sport industry itself (Gillentine & Crow, 2005, p. 5; Pederson, 2011). Clearly, academic programs in sport management can serve the industry by preparing future sport managers to maximize appropriate skills and to avoid the mistakes of their predecessors. Sport management programs must remain useful to the industry while also maintaining their academic integrity (Wysong, 2006). Achieving this balance requires a commitment to both professional relevance and academic rigor.

In order to maximize students' employment prospects, sport management programs should include these four key elements:

1. Comprehensive curriculum that meets or exceeds COSMA curricular content guidelines
2. Diverse faculty that balances academic credentials and scholarly contributions with industry experience and application
3. Variety of real-world opportunities through field-based experiential learning (e.g., volunteer opportunities, practicums, internships)
4. Opportunities for networking with professionals in the sport industry

Appropriate academic content (Commission on Sport Management Accreditation, 2010) can be combined with industry applications to enhance experiential opportunities for students. This combination can be accomplished through a curricular approach that requires credit-bearing, field-based experiences such as practicums and internships. It can also be enhanced through individual classes that use links to industry for class projects that provide additional experiential learning opportunities. Strategic linkages with the industry can also be fostered through individuals. For example, former NFL executive Charley Casserly noted, upon teaching an undergraduate professional development seminar in sport management, that students would "use the fundamentals of this [class content] for the rest of your life" (Bishop, 2008). Industry and academic expectations are not always in sync, and sport management programs must bridge the gap and connect with the sport industry. Doing so is in the best interests of students, universities, and the industry.

Through their professional preparation, students should develop knowledge, skills, abilities, and dispositions that enhance their opportunity for employment in the sport industry. The requisite knowledge is grounded in the COSMA curricular content. Students must gain a factual, theoretical, and applied knowledge base before they enter the professional ranks. Essential skills and abilities begin with effective communication—both verbal and written. For example, common tasks for sport industry personnel include writing media releases, developing marketing plans, and negotiating with service providers. Aspiring professionals also need skills in organization, time management, planning, and multitasking. Since most employers will let you know what they want, it is also essential to be able to learn from constructive feedback. At the same time, you will sometimes be put into situations where little guidance is provided, which means you must develop the ability to figure things out on your own as needed. The sport industry does little hand-holding for its employees; therefore, working independently is often required. On the other hand, 80 percent of American employees work in groups, and you must also be able to collaborate effectively (Caroselli, 1998). In addition, long hours are common in the sport industry, whether for on-site game management or for sales calls, and disposition is often what separates those who succeed in sport from those who don't. Students who hone their attitudes to enhance their goal orientation, work ethic, determination, focus, and adaptability also enhance their chances for success. More generally, students who develop and apply these key elements—knowledge, skills, abilities, and helpful dispositions—can find a wide variety of internships and jobs in the sport industry (see table 2.1 for examples of jobs that can result from particular internships).

It is also crucial that students build relationships with sport industry professionals. As the saying goes, life is a contact sport, and expanding a sport management program's network opens opportunities for students, alumni, faculty, and all stakeholders. It allows students to get behind the scenes to meet the professionals who create the world of sport (Robinson, Hums, Crow, & Philips, 2000), thus giving them enhanced learning opportunities and improved prospects for job placement. Getting an internship or job is a difficult task—and one, of course, that is of great concern to students. One key to success is for sport management programs and their students to connect with people in the sport industry (Masteralexis, Barr, & Hums, 2012).

 Do what you can, with what you have, where you are.

Theodore Roosevelt

TABLE 2.1   Jobs That Can Result From Successful Internships

An internship as a . . .	Might lead to a job as a . . .
Media assistant	Journalist, broadcaster, or media relations coordinator
Facility or events assistant	Facility manager or event coordinator for a university or professional team
Ticket sales representative	Ticket sales associate, groups sales associate, sales manager, marketer, public relations associate, customer service representative, or human resources associate
Public relations or community relations assistant	Public relations associate, community relations associate or coordinator, or development officer for a college athletic department, a league, or a professional team
Game operations assistant	Operations manager or event coordinator for a stadium or arena
Marketing or promotions assistant	Marketing associate or coordinator, sponsorship coordinator, or public relations associate for an agency, a league, or a professional team
Player personnel assistant	Player personnel associate or human resources coordinator for a professional sport organization or a sporting goods manufacturer

Professional Development in Sport Management

One major way to link the sport industry with academic preparation in sport management is through the professional field experience or internship. When an internship is developed and implemented properly, it serves as a worthy academic component (Young & Baker, 2004). Through industry-based internships, students gain the experience necessary to obtain employment in sport. At the same time, many sport industry segments have come to depend on this source of free labor; in fact, as the availability of able and willing sport management students has steadily increased, former entry-level jobs have at times evolved into credit-bearing internships. This approach can benefit both the student, who gains experience and networking opportunities, and the organization, which reduces expenses; however, in difficult economic times, it can also contribute to a decline in employment opportunities for graduates.

Given the intense competition for positions in the sport industry, it is essential that aspiring sport managers prepare themselves not only in the necessary content and with the necessary experiential applications but also as prospective professionals. Professional development opportunities can enhance students' success in identifying, obtaining, and performing well in a position in the competitive sport industry. Beyond work experience, professional development should also involve researching prospective employers, developing skills in resume writing and interviewing, and enhancing your understanding of typical work requirements and conduct. The student is ultimately preparing to become a professional sport manager.

🌐 INTERNATIONAL APPLICATION

John David Walsh, Founder of jdBASKETBALL

John David "JD" Walsh is a former college basketball player who graduated from the University of Maryland in 1996. He went on to coach basketball at Roslyn High School in 1998 and then at St. John the Baptist Diocesan High School from 1999 to 2004. Aiming to create "a dialogue for mankind," Walsh founded jdBASKETBALL with a two-fold mission: (a) to use basketball as a way to educate youth and enable social change and (b) to promote and grow the game of basketball worldwide and particularly in India. Since its inception in 1998, jdBASKETBALL has grown from a program with the simple intention of teaching basketball to kids in the New

Photo courtesy of JD Walsh.

York metro area into a global enterprise that has operated in eight countries on three continents and has touched more than 20,000 lives and counting. Walsh has toured and held camps in countries including China, the Dominican Republic, India, Italy, Kashmir, Qatar, and Taiwan.

The program has operated throughout India for several years to promote both the game of basketball and positive social change. Walsh engages multinational corporations, governments, and regional social educators to develop sustainable programs that deliver results. In partnership with George Mason University, jdBASKETBALL received funding from the U.S. State Department as a sport diplomat to implement an international sport programming initiative to promote cross-cultural goodwill and ambassadorship between the United States and India. The group has also worked with various nongovernmental organizations, such as Big Brothers Big Sisters and Sulha (a peacemaking group in Israel), and has won numerous awards, including the 2008 Ashoka Nike Changemaker award for its work with CHINAR and orphan youths in Kashmir.

Walsh's work has been recognized by the deputy secretary of state in a Senate hearing (April 24, 2008): "You know the most effective public diplomacy I've seen? It's been basketball. . . . There's a JD Walsh right now in basketball; he's a Maryland graduate, he's in India doing this same thing, but he's expanded on the idea. He's using it to also, as they teach basketball, to have HIV/AIDS testing, to teach courses in nonviolent conflict resolution. He's not talking about Arab–Israeli peace issues, or al-Qaeda, for that matter, but he's having more effect in diplomacy than you can imagine."

Walsh not only teaches basketball skills on the world stage; he also teaches participants around the world to use the game to communicate, grow community, and promote peace and cross-cultural understanding. Employing sport as a vehicle for development, peace, and positive social change across the gamut of humanity, jdBASKETBALL has indeed helped lay a foundation for a worldwide "dialogue for mankind."

The Short of It

- The sport industry accounts for a considerable part of the world economy and offers a wide range of job opportunities.
- Students must develop a solid foundation in the academic study of sport management.
- Students who take advantage of opportunities to work in the sport industry while in school will learn valuable skills and make industry contacts that can be valuable in their careers.
- Students can distinguish themselves by developing key knowledge, skills, abilities, and dispositions as they pursue employment in the sport industry.

Building Blocks of Sport Management

Part II of *Fundamentals of Sport Management* presents the multidisciplinary areas of study within the field of sport management. These chapters collectively focus on the fundamental content knowledge of the sport management discipline. Chapter 3 addresses the principles and functions of management, the roles of sport managers, and the skills required to fulfill those roles. It also covers the types of sport organization within which these functions take place. Chapter 4 explores leadership in sport organizations, including the antecedents, best practices, and consequences of leadership. It also describes the application of leader theory within organizational systems. Chapter 5 addresses governance of sport organizations and how it connects to policy. The chapter also describes governance structures found at the scholastic, collegiate, and professional levels of sport.

Chapter 6 examines sport venues and the interrelated operations and management of the sporting events that take place in them. The chapter also covers venue design and staffing, as well as risk management. Chapter 7 presents the legal aspects of sport, including contract, intellectual property, and tort law, as well as how sport managers are affected by specific legislation, such as Title IX and the Americans With Disabilities Act. Chapter 8 focuses on marketing the vast array of sport products. It explains the marketing mix, segmentation, and consumer behavior. Chapter 9 explores the relationship between sport and the media in its various forms—from print to broadcast to web-based outlets. The chapter also addresses the skills needed to succeed in contemporary sport journalism.

Chapter 10 examines the economics of sport; specifically, it explains micro- and macroeconomics, supply and demand, and the importance of economic impact studies in sport. It also describes the unique economic circumstances of both professional and collegiate sport. Chapter 11 addresses finance within the sport enterprise, including major revenue sources, expenses, balance sheets, and income statements. It also provides insight into the importance of television revenue in the distinctly different college and professional sport systems. Part II concludes with chapter 12, which describes how to develop a professional philosophy to support your application of ethics and morals in making sport management decisions.

CHAPTER 3

Sport Management Principles and Functions

Photo courtesy of Evan Cantwell/Creative Services/George Mason University.

In this chapter, you will learn the following:

✓ Multiple functions of management in sport
✓ Common characteristics of sport organizations
✓ The 10 roles of sport managers
✓ Skill sets required of sport managers

> Management is, above all, a practice where art, science, and craft meet.
>
> **Henry Mintzberg**, author on business and management

In order to win games, every team in the National Basketball Association (NBA) needs to identify, sign, and retain talented players, but how they manage those tasks varies from team to team. Most teams maintain a division that deals with what is called basketball operations. Within that division, responsibilities are distributed among the general manager (GM) and assistant GMs, the player personnel director and staff, the scouting staff, and the coaching staff; for example, scouts evaluate talent, the GM obtains talented players, and the coaches use strategy to guide players in ways that produce winning teams. Within this general approach, however, each team—and each individual in any of these positions—organizes and manages these responsibilities in a unique fashion. One team might use a lean, efficient division with clearly defined roles for a small number of hard-working staff, whereas another team might use a very large staff assigned to fill overlapping roles. To evaluate a team's success, we might examine the results of the annual NBA draft to determine whether drafted players were evaluated appropriately and produced effectively over time. We might also examine the team's payroll, statistics, and winning percentage to determine whether it efficiently produced desired results. Ultimately, the effectiveness of a team's full management structure and practices is reflected in the team's success or lack thereof. Coaches are often fired for losing too many games, but a thorough examination might reveal that many other managerial decisions affected a team's lack of success.

Management has been defined as "the process of working with and through individuals and groups to accomplish organizational goals" (Hersey, Blanchard, & Johnson, 2001). In its myriad applications, management, at its core, involves using resources to achieve objectives and goals. The general principles and functions of management apply to sport settings, and the general roles and responsibilities associated with those functions apply to sport managers, who affect the overall success of the sport organization in which they work. They are responsible for executing general management functions within the specific context of the sport organization.

 The aim proposed here for any organization is for everybody to gain—stockholders, employees, suppliers, customers, community, the environment—over the long term.

W. Edwards Deming, management consultant

Organizations in Sport

Like all organizations, **sport organizations** possess four defining elements: multiple members, specialization of member contributions, coordination of specialized functions, and a common goal (Chelladurai, 2009). The common features present within organizations are as follows: an identity, instrumentality, a program of activity, membership, boundaries, permanency, a division of labor, a hierarchy of authority, rules, and procedures (Chelladurai).

An organization is greater than the sum of its parts. Every organization has its own identity, apart from the identities of its individual members. For example, you probably have a view about the National Football League (NFL), the National Collegiate Athletic Association (NCAA), and the National Hockey League (NHL), even though you may not personally know the people within those organizations. One fundamental purpose of an organization, then, is to be instrumental in its collective capacity to pursue its goals. In doing so, an organization engages in a specified program of activities (e.g., marketing, selling). It attracts members and establishes either formal or informal eligibility criteria for membership. It establishes clear boundaries for what it does, why it does it, and who is involved. Organizations also have permanence beyond their individual members. They become efficient through a rational division of labor, which is reflected in specialization of both members and tasks. Organizations use a hierarchy of authority to manage their members and tasks; indeed, every organization establishes rules and procedures to direct and control its members' activities.

Take, for example, Nike, which has established a definite identity, both as a brand and as an organization. Nike maintains distinct boundaries to avoid being confused with its competitors (e.g., Adidas) or with the retail outlets that sell Nike products (e.g., Sports Authority). It pursues established corporate goals by engaging in specific activities that include, among others, product development, manufacturing, distribution, and sales. It has a permanence that goes beyond its current workforce, but those employees are its membership and are bound by corporate rules and procedures. Beginning with co-founder and chairman Phil Knight, Nike has a clearly defined hierarchy that is evident in its corporate structure. This division of labor—from executives to factory workers to regional sales associates—allows Nike to efficiently pursue its corporate goals.

Sport organizations can be categorized in various ways. For example, they can be classified on the basis of profit orientation. **Profit-based organizations** are intended to make a profit, unlike **nonprofit organizations**, whose purpose does not include profit making. Of course, both profit-based and nonprofit organizations seek to maximize revenue in order to attain organizational goals; however, highly successful nonprofit organizations reinvest surplus in the organization rather than generating pure profit.

sport organization—Unit that has identity, instrumentality, a program of activity, membership, boundaries, permanency, division of labor, hierarchy of authority, and rules and procedures.

profit-based organization—Organization whose goal includes generating more revenue than expenses.

nonprofit organization—Organization whose purpose does not include making a profit yet still seeks to generate revenue.

Sport organizations can also be classified on the basis of their beneficiary (Blau & Scott, 1960). Mutual benefit organizations, such as a players union (e.g., the NFL Players Association), focus their benefits and concerns on their members. Organizations with business concerns, such as professional sport franchises and many other private sport enterprises, focus their benefits on owners and managers. Service-oriented organizations, such as the YMCA, focus their benefits on clients or participants. And commonwealth organizations, such as public education institutions, focus their benefits on the general public, serving the greater society.

Sport organizations can also be perceived as machines, in that they can be rigid, repetitive, and impersonal and they operate by means of interrelated parts. Or they can be viewed as organisms, insofar as they exhibit lifelike systems influenced by their environment. More specifically, organizations are sometimes compared with brains that wield huge information-processing capacity. Often, organizations have something in common with cultures, in that minisocieties influence the design, operation, and life of an organization and its membership. They can also be perceived as political systems, wherein multiple agendas and power plays make up the politics of the organization and its members.

Regardless of how a sport organization is conceptualized, its function influences its organizational structure, which in turn influences, and reflects, its operation. Structures vary based on several factors. The organization's complexity or simplicity influences its level of need for multiple departments, numerous job titles, and a deep hierarchical chain of command. The organization's ratio of formalized control to tolerance for flexibility influences how people do their jobs, as well as what policies and procedures are needed. The degree to which the organization is centralized or decentralized determines where authority rests, how activities are controlled,

Quick Facts

- Rinus Michels, a Dutch native who died in 2005, was named coach of the century by the International Federation of Association Football (FIFA) in 1999.

- Numerous variations of sport management software allow for virtual management of franchises in a variety of sports, including Formula One, NASCAR, rugby, U.S. football, and many others.

- The All India Football Federation, the governing body for soccer in India, signed IMG-Reliance (a joint venture between IMG Worldwide and Reliance Industries) to a 15-year agreement for the commercial rights to soccer in India.

- Octagon manages more than 13,000 events worldwide each year (about 36 events each day) and offers the world's largest sponsorship consulting with more than 800 people worldwide.

whether delegation is used, and how participatory the decision making is. All of these variables affect the organization's configuration. For example, a small agency might use a single administrative office staffer to support the agent, whereas a large full-service agency might employ hundreds or even thousands of people on a global scale. Naturally, these two organizations will be structured very differently. Although they perform some similar services, one is simple, whereas the other is complex. The simple organization uses centralized control but may be more flexible. The complex, global organization may be much more decentralized yet maintain formalized control (though it could, if desired, maintain either flexibility or centralization). In any case, the two organizations will definitely function differently.

For further discussion of organizational systems in sport management, see chapter 4. For the purposes of this chapter, however, this basic discussion is sufficient to give you some idea of sport organizations as a setting where management functions are used.

Management Functions

The **functions of management** have been divided into categories that are widely discussed but not always agreed upon (Chelladurai, 2009; Hersey et al., 2008; Jordan & Kent, 2005). Regardless of the terms used, the process of management involves nine common functions presented here within four functional processes: (a) planning; (b) organizing; (c) staffing, directing, motivating, and leading; and (d) controlling, monitoring, and evaluating. Theoretically, the managerial process starts with planning and ends with controlling or evaluating. In practice, however, managers rarely employ these functions in a standardized sequence; rather, they must generally engage in several functions simultaneously in order to meet their job responsibilities. For example, if a ticket sales manager departs from a Major League Baseball franchise with the season rapidly approaching, the staffing function will take precedence in order to maintain ticket sales.

Planning

Planning involves developing organizational goals and objectives, then establishing the necessary methods, processes, and activities to attain those goals. Plans are not dissimilar to road maps or GPS guidance systems. They indicate where the organization intends to go and how it intends to get there. Effective planning, then, requires both strategy and tactics. Strategy involves establishing broad organizational goals and specific measureable objectives to pursue. Tactics involve identifying the methods, processes, and activities to use in pursuing desired outcomes.

The process of planning includes several common steps, the first of which is establishing goals, or broad targets that

functions of management— Functional processes that include planning, organizing, staffing, directing, motivating, leading, controlling, monitoring, and evaluating.

planning—Process of developing organizational goals and objectives and then establishing the methods, processes, and activities necessary for attaining those goals.

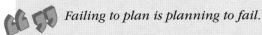
Failing to plan is planning to fail.

Anonymous

set the course for the organization. Objectives are more specific and measureable and can be used to facilitate evaluation. Both goals and objectives should be guided by the organizational mission, which encompasses the fundamental rationale and principles upon which the organization is grounded. For example, the Special Olympics would establish its goals and objectives based upon its stated mission, which reads as follows:

> The mission of Special Olympics is to provide year-round sports training and athletic competition in a variety of Olympic-type sports for children and adults with intellectual disabilities, giving them continuing opportunities to develop physical fitness, demonstrate courage, experience joy and participate in a sharing of gifts, skills and friendship with their families, other Special Olympics athletes and the community. (Special Olympics, 2012)

Another step in the planning process involves assessing options and influences—both positive and negative, as well as internal and external. One way of doing so is to conduct a **SWOT analysis**, which, as the acronym reflects, examines the organization's strengths, weaknesses, opportunities, and threats. Strengths are generally positive internal features and dynamics, whereas weaknesses, of course, are negative internal factors. Opportunities are favorable external conditions, whereas threats are external conditions that might constrain the organization. For example, a nonprofit sport foundation seeking to establish itself in a certain region must examine both the internal and external environments. It must accurately assess both its own strengths (e.g., dedicated staff) and its weaknesses (e.g., lack of financial resources). It must also understand its opportunities (e.g., a prevailing interest in the region in using sport for community building) and any threats (e.g., other organizations offering similar programs in the region).

SWOT analysis—Analysis of strengths, weaknesses, opportunities, and threats, wherein strengths are conceived as generally positive internal features and dynamics, weaknesses as negative internal factors, opportunities as favorable external conditions, and threats as constraining external conditions.

Performing a SWOT analysis allows an organization to move on to another step in the planning process: identifying possible courses of action. Action plans indicate how the strategic plan will be implemented; essentially, they are the plan for executing the plan. The performance criteria included in the action plan should be informed by the desired outcome. For example, if that same nonprofit sport foundation needs to raise a specific amount of money in order to fund an important project or build a facility, it can develop an action plan for generating the needed income. Its measure of success in this case would simply be the quantity of money raised in relation to the targeted amount.

Plans come in several varieties, one of which is the long-term plan. For example, a professional franchise might decide to build its roster by developing young talent

Strategy without tactics is the slowest route to victory. Tactics without strategy is the noise before defeat.

Sun Tzu, ancient author of *The Art of War*

rather than by acquiring established players; by its very nature, this approach must be executed over a long period of time. Strategic planning is usually long-term. It establishes guiding goals and key objectives that the organization can use to drive into its future. For instance, an academic unit that offers a bachelor's degree in sport management might use strategic planning to determine the feasibility, or enhance the chance of success, of offering graduate degrees. If the unit's plans align with its program mission, it would undertake a SWOT analysis in the strategic planning process.

It is critical for an organization to purposefully determine who is involved in the planning process. This involvement can take many forms. Grand, long-term, strategic plans can be undertaken from the top down; in this approach, only top executives are engaged in the process, which will affect the future of the entire organization. Alternately, the organization might engage many members in the planning process. One common example of this bottom-up approach is brainstorming.

As with long-term plans, short-term plans can also engage many or just a few employees. One type of short-term plan is the operational or tactical plan, which focuses on tactics used in pursuit of organizational goals and objectives. These plans are generally guided by measurable, outcome-based objectives. For example, if a sport management academic unit sets a strategic goal of establishing a graduate program, its operational plan might include specific marketing tactics to attract the targeted number of enrollees—for example, advertising in trade journals and establishing articulation agreements with undergraduate programs from which it could recruit students. It could measure the success of its plan by monitoring responses to the ads and, ultimately, by tracking the number of enrollees.

Plans can be made for a single situation, thus enacted only once, or for a standing purpose. Cities planning for a special sport event such as a Super Bowl or World Cup match often develop a one-time plan that is customized to the parameters of that event and thus not generally applicable to other events. The city might plan for transportation, vendors, event registration, housing for participants and spectators, and so on. In contrast, sport and fitness facilities often develop a risk management plan to minimize identifiable risks for their patrons, and this type of plan addresses not a one-time event, or a single day of activity, but a set of ongoing actions.

Planning is not intended to forecast the future but to move an organization and its members toward the future in a desired way. It means taking a purposeful approach toward harnessing an organization's resources in a coordinated effort to achieve its goals. Once plans have been established, they are executed by means of the organizing and controlling functions, which therefore can greatly affect the organization's future.

Organizing

Organizing means deciding how the plan will come to fruition. It addresses questions such as these: What tasks must be done? Who is going to complete them? How will they be systematized? Where will decisions be made? Organizing involves effectively integrating various resources—human, financial, and material—to accomplish the plan (Hersey et al., 2008). Simply put, once plans are in place, organizing consists of five elements: (1) identifying the tasks necessary to execute the plan, (2) determining who will complete those tasks, (3) establishing how resources will be allocated toward the tasks, (4) developing an organizational structure to enhance effectiveness, and (5) dividing the tasks and delegating them to the responsible parties.

> **organizing**—Effectively integrating various human, financial, and material resources to accomplish a plan.

Organizing often involves specialization or departmentalization, which requires a hierarchical structure and the division of labor to accomplish the tasks at hand. For example, in a professional sport franchise, the marketing department fulfills a very different purpose by means of different procedures from those that characterize the player personnel department, and the work of a sport marketer is quite distinct from that of a scout. When tasks are distributed to specific work groups, this division of labor allows for specialization of performance. Most professional franchises institute separate departments to assume responsibility for tasks such as marketing the sport product, conducting game-day event operations, scouting players, coaching the team, and selling tickets. The configuration of these tasks and work groups constitutes the organizational structure. This type of hierarchical structure, as displayed in figure 3.1, establishes lines of communication, as well as a chain of command or authority for decision making.

One common organizational structure used in the sport industry is called a bureaucracy, a term coined by Max Weber (1947). Bureaucratic organization distributes complex tasks into simple, clarified duties, thereby dividing labor's specialized efforts. These efforts are governed by a top-down hierarchy of authority. Bureaucracies also establish rules and regulations that are impersonal and categorical. These bureaucratic principles allow us to proactively organize and control the organization. Though bureaucracies are common, they are often maligned for the "red tape" that employees must navigate in order to complete their assigned tasks. Regardless of the structure used by an organization, it must place qualified individuals in well-defined positions that direct their work toward established goals and objectives.

Surround yourself with the best people you can find, delegate authority, and don't interfere as long as the policy you've decided upon is being carried out.

Ronald Reagan

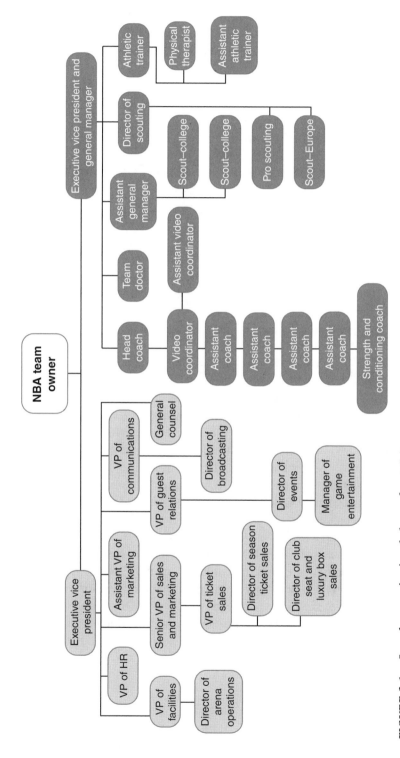

FIGURE 3.1 Sample organizational chart of an NBA team.

Staffing, Directing, Motivating, and Leading

All organizations, including those in sport, accomplish their goals through people. The coach does not play the game, and the manager does not accomplish company goals in a vacuum. Both must surround themselves with qualified personnel. Staffing involves an organization's selection, development, and retention of able employees. For example, a football team uses a hierarchical organizational structure in which specific, talented players are recruited to play specialized positions. They are further developed and trained through effective coaching. In the same way, every department in every organization must attract and develop employees whose talent is used appropriately in pursuit of the goals and objectives established within the organization's structured system. This perspective illuminates how sport management graduates who have been properly prepared can serve as a valuable resource to a sport organization. Staffing is inextricably part of the directing function, which involves motivating and guiding employees toward achieving organizational goals.

Even in a well-planned, well-organized system, staff motivation greatly affects success in attaining organizational goals. Evolving from previous definitions (Hoy & Miskel, 2006; BusinessDictionary.com, 2011), **motivation**, from the Latin *movere* ("to move"), can be viewed as involving the complex internal and external forces and mechanisms that stimulate a person's interest, desire, and energy to initiate and sustain committed effort that is directed toward attaining a goal. Motivating employees is difficult. Each employee may respond differently to direction and motivational efforts. Think about something you have done when you were highly motivated to do it well. What motivated you? Did your supervisor do something that motivated you well or poorly? As with coaches and players, sport managers might challenge, support, instruct, or direct different employees toward the same outcomes. Effective managers help employees achieve. They provide the resources necessary for employees to complete tasks. They also identify and meet employees' needs.

motivation—Complex internal and external forces and mechanisms that stimulate one's interest, desire, and energy to initiate and sustain committed effort that is manifested in activity directed toward attaining a goal.

In merging the works of Maslow (1943), Adams (1977), McClelland (1975), and Davis (1991), Berryman-Fink and Fink (1996) identified seven needs that motivate employees: achievement, affiliation, autonomy, equity, esteem, power, and safety and security. Within this broad view, different people have different needs and are therefore motivated by different things. Consider, for example, a sport team. Some members just want to be a part of the team; they need affiliation. Others seek power within the team, and still others base their identity and self-worth

Management by objectives works—if you know the objectives.

Peter Drucker, management consultant

on playing the sport. Some derive satisfaction from being treated fairly, whereas others are motivated by the opportunity to achieve. To illustrate the importance of managers' recognition of differing needs, consider another scenario—that of an emergency medical technician (EMT) responding to an emergency in which it is clear who needs cardiopulmonary resuscitation (CPR) and who does not. Responding to an emergency call, the EMT arrives to find an unconscious fan who exhibits symptoms calling for resuscitation. It would be appropriate and requisite for the EMT to provide CPR to the fan in need. It would be inappropriate, however, to assume that all fans have the same need and require each fan in the venue to undergo CPR. It is clear that various fans' needs are different. Granted, it can be more difficult to see difference in needs among employees, but effective managers must do so in order to effectively motivate employees. In meeting employees' needs, "effective motivation requires an appropriate balance of tangible, intangible, intrinsic, extrinsic, monetary, and non-monetary rewards" (Jordan & Kent, 2005). Going back to the instance of the sport team, motivated players will be more satisfied and will perform better in pursuit of team goals than those who are not appropriately motivated. The same can be said more generally for employees in sport organizations.

Sport managers often engage in the leading function by motivating and guiding individuals and teams to accomplish organizational goals. Top-level managers, or executives, form a relatively small group, but they wield abundant power, authority, and responsibility. To illustrate, the president of a professional sport franchise is a top-level executive, whereas the director of marketing is a middle manager. Middle or mid-level managers must be both leaders and followers. Supervisory-level or frontline managers serve as points of contact between labor or technical staff and management. For example, the events coordinator serves as a supervisory-level manager who is responsible for the event staff and the conduct of events.

The most effective managers in sport organizations are those who integrate managerial and leadership skills into a coherent approach. Managerial leaders attain results by working with and through other people—namely, their employees (Quarterman, Li, & Parks, 2011). They demonstrate leadership by influencing their employees' behavior and coordinating efforts to achieve identified goals.

An expanded discussion of leadership is provided in chapter 4. For now, suffice it to say that the interrelated management functions of staffing, directing, motivating, and leading are essential to executing the organizational plan through the established organizational structure. Achievement is made possible only through the diligent, motivated efforts of employees who are guided by effective managerial leaders.

Efficient management without effective leadership is like rearranging the chairs on the deck of the Titanic.

Stephen Covey, author of *7 Habits of Highly Effective People*

Controlling, Monitoring, and Evaluating

The interrelated management functions of controlling, monitoring, and evaluating address questions such as the following: How are achievements measured? Are organizational goals being achieved? How will the outcomes affect planning, organizing, and leading? In sport organizations, is winning the only bottom line? Is profit the real bottom line? Or, for a collegiate athletic program, is educational attainment the bottom line? For any organization, the assessment of goal-related performance outcomes is an essential component of management. Thus sport managers must determine whether specified organizational goals and objectives have been achieved. Toward this end, managers who perform the function of controlling use "results and follow-up to compare accomplishments with plans and to make appropriate adjustments where outcomes have deviated from expectations" (Hersey et al., 2008, p. 8). In other words, if winning is the objective, the measurement could simply be the win-loss record. If the team won enough games, then the organization achieved satisfactory success. If not, then what can be done to improve? If, however, the analyst uses more detailed measures, such as the effect of turnovers or scoring efficiency or opponents' percentages, the analysis might provide more insight into *how* to improve. The same can be said for any objective in a sport organization: winning, profit, education, physical fitness, and so on. In any aspect of the organization, managerial control involves setting standards directed toward achieving goals, effectively measuring related performance outcomes, and initiating any necessary corrective action.

Sport managers use five steps in the control process: (a) establishing performance standards, (b) accurately measuring performance, (c) comparing performance with the established standards, (d) analyzing and correcting deviations from the standards, and (e) reinforcing performance at or above expectations. The monitoring function is integral to managerial control. In monitoring, managers apply standard criteria and assess performance outcomes by first determining accurate measures of outcomes. For example, the performance of a direct ticket salesperson might be viewed as including both the number of phone calls made and the number of sales closed. Monitoring can involve both quantitative and qualitative measures. Quantitative assessments are measured numerically and thus provide relatively clear, easily comparable data (e.g., wins, tickets sold, profits generated). Qualitative measures are more difficult in that they can be somewhat subjective, and they are often combined with quantitative measures. Qualitative measures can be obtained through interviews, focus groups, and surveys. For example, in the case of the direct salesperson, the manager might evaluate his or her attitude or overall contributions to the organization beyond the sales figures. This approach, though difficult, could produce an insightful qualitative assessment. The manager might perform this assessment by seeking feedback from people who were called by the salesperson or by directly observing the employee's interactions. In sport, it is commonplace to seek feedback from fans, which helps sport managers evaluate everything from fan satisfaction to the feasibility of introducing a new product.

Evaluation can be performed at various levels, and it typically includes individual performance appraisals, departmental program evaluations, and organizational effectiveness measures (Chelladurai, 2009). For example, evaluating the ticket salesperson's performance is just a beginning. The ticket manager must also determine whether the entire ticket sales department is effectively meeting collective goals. Upper-level executives will also want to know whether ticket operations can be improved—and if so, how.

In the evaluating function, the manager judges performance based on established objectives. Evaluation can be either summative or formative. In a summative appraisal, performance is measured against common, standardized criteria in order to help the manager decide how to distribute rewards. For example, if a sales target of 100 calls per day is achieved by most salespersons but one staffer makes only 40 calls per day, that staffer will likely be terminated after a summative evaluation. Formative evaluation, on the other hand, is used to inform managers and employees of strengths and weaknesses in order to help the employee enhance his or her performance related to expectations. For example, in the same ticket sales scenario, the manager could use formative evaluation to provide feedback and help to the underperforming staffer (e.g., training in time management or sales techniques) in order to give him or her the best opportunity to improve. Ultimately, both the staffer and the organization could benefit from this improvement, which could allow the staffer to retain his or her job and improve the department's sales figures.

Evaluations extend to programs, which are resources and activities used in pursuit of a common objective on a continuous (rather than a one-time) basis (Chelladurai, 2009). A comprehensive program evaluation process begins by assessing program objectives, such as the number of sales calls, the amount of revenue generated, or the win-loss record. Managers should evaluate if the objectives are appropriate to the mission. The evaluation goes on to measure programmatic outcomes and determine whether objectives were met. For example, did the program meet the goal for ticket sales, revenue projections, or expected wins? On an even broader level, **organizational effectiveness** refers to the extent to which the sport organization as a whole achieves its goals. This determination is made by assessing the organization's performance in relation to agreed-upon standards. Managers determine **organizational efficiency**, on the other hand, by using a cost-benefit approach to examine resource use in relation to goal achievement. For example, if two NBA franchises each set a goal of increasing attendance to a minimum of 19,000 for each home game and both franchises do so, then they have both been *effective* in attaining the goal. However, if franchise A achieves the goal by spending half the money that franchise B spends in order to obtain the same results, then franchise A has demonstrated not only effectiveness but also greater organizational *efficiency*.

organizational effectiveness—Extent to which a sport organization achieves its goals by assessing its performance in relation to desired standards.

organizational efficiency—Amount of resources used as considered in relation to the organization's level of goal attainment.

In any evaluation process, if the established goals and standards are not met, the assessment should determine why. Were the goals appropriate and attainable? Were tasks clearly defined? Were sufficient resources available? Were the necessary skills effectively used? Was the planning and organizing adequate? Sport managers must ensure that the resources needed to accomplish the goals are available. They must also determine the reason for failure in order to facilitate future success. For example, ticket sales staff need functioning telephones and proper ticket software in order to succeed. If sales techniques are lacking, the ticket manager should provide the staff with appropriate training. The manager might also offer incentives to sales staff to encourage their emotional investment in increasing ticket sales.

Through controlling, monitoring, and evaluating, sport managers can limit repeated errors, enact corrective measures, and enhance performance in order to meet established standards and achieve organizational goals in a desired manner. Controlling, monitoring, and evaluating are continuous management processes that should be entrenched at various levels in a sport organization. They are closely connected to the planning function, as they assist sport managers in looking forward by using outcomes to inform plans. Together, these sport management functions serve as a tool that managers can use not only to measure performance but also to help the organization attain its goals.

Universality of Management

Socrates asserted that management is a universal concept. The principles, functions, processes, and practices of management apply to all types and sizes of organizations; this includes sport organizations. Whether large or small, nonprofit or profit-based, all sport organizations need management at all levels. For example, the manager of a ticket office must plan for all local aspects of ticket distribution, including staffing and other resources needed to accomplish the task at hand. In doing so, the ticket manager often works with other units to accomplish the goal of ticket distribution. For example, the ticket manager might join the sport marketing staff in planning, organizing, directing, and controlling the marketing and promotions activities used to support ticket sales. The manager might also work with event and facility managers to plan, organize, and direct the distribution of tickets—electronically or in person—for single-game or package ticket holders. The manager monitors the entire process, both during the season and in an end-of-season summative evaluation that begins the planning process for the next round of ticket sales and distribution.

On a more global scale, top-level sport executives plan comprehensively, develop a systematic organizational structure, direct the organization's activities toward a vision, ensure adequate staffing, and control operations broadly by monitoring and evaluating activities and outcomes related to the organization's goals. This broad level of management informs, and is accomplished through, mid-level managers, who apply these managerial functions more locally. Think of the sport executive as the prime minister or president of a country. Though this person is ultimately responsible for all functions of the government, he or she does not individually perform these functions at the local level. Similarly, the sport CEO plans broadly for the organization. The team president, for example, develops a strategy for the franchise, and the team's general manager then informs the director of player personnel, who in turn plans implementation at the local level. Planning, direction, and staffing are often handled at the top of a sport organization, but mid-level and frontline sport managers organize, staff, and direct their divisions in order to meet upper management's expectations. In addition, sport executives use middle and frontline sport managers to obtain the performance measures needed in the process of controlling, monitoring, and evaluating. These evaluations provide necessary feedback and are best used as the first step in planning. Thus all of these management functions are continually in progress in a sport organization.

Sport organizations may differ from one another in their organizational structure, governance procedures, objectives, personnel, and many other aspects, but the functions and principles of management are universally applicable to them all. Similarly, the fundamental roles and responsibilities of sport managers are generally constant despite the varied organizations and levels in which they are found.

Skills, Roles, and Responsibilities of Managers

In order to fulfill the common managerial roles and meet their many responsibilities, successful sport managers often employ a common set of skills. Not to be confused with motivation, desire, or willingness, skills involve the *ability* to perform tasks at hand. Whether innate or learned through experience and professional training, sport management skills are needed by all managers in all sport organizations.

Technical skills are based on specialized knowledge of the techniques, operations, activities, methods, resources, and processes used to attain organizational goals. Sport managers must use technical skills and help others use them. For example, a marketing director must be aware of and demonstrate the communication skills desired in the marketing staff that he or she supervises. Sport managers must also possess and apply interpersonal or human skills. A collegiate sport development officer, for instance, must use effective interpersonal skills with both internal and external stakeholders in order to coordinate with staff, satisfy clients, and raise funds for the athletic program. Indeed, interacting effectively with people (whether one to one or in a group) is an essential sport management skill if one is to achieve organizational goals and objectives. A sport manager must be effective in motivating, supervising, and communicating with a multitude of diverse individuals and stakeholders. For example, a sport manager might use interpersonal skills with his or her supervisor by "managing up" to obtain the resources necessary to achieve departmental goals. With external clients, the sport manager might use interpersonal skills in providing expert customer service. Interpersonal skills are also essential in simply helping subordinates (e.g., sport management interns) succeed in performing their assigned tasks. Through such varied uses of interpersonal skills, a sport manager coordinates individual and group efforts toward achieving organizational goals.

SUCCESS STORY

Laurel J. Richie, President of the WNBA

As the third president of the Women's National Basketball Association (WNBA), Laurel J. Richie is responsible for the league's daily operations. According to the WNBA (2011), Richie is a graduate of Dartmouth College who amassed a wealth of experience in managerial positions prior to taking the reins of the league. In fact, she possesses more than three decades of management and marketing experience. She served formerly as senior vice president and chief marketing officer of Girl Scouts of the USA, where she directed branding, communications, marketing, and online projects. Earlier, after a stint at a Chicago-based advertising agency, Richie spent 20 years at Ogilvy & Mather, climbing to senior partner and executive group director while serving premier clients such as American Express, Unilever, and others. She managed her team to become the most productive and profitable and became a founding member of the organization's diversity advisory board. Upon assuming the WNBA's top spot, Richie said, "I am fortunate to have worked with an organization as inspiring as Girl Scouts, and I'm thrilled to have the opportunity to build upon the successes of the WNBA and help grow this league into a world-class business" (Smith, 2011).

The WNBA is the premier professional league in women's sport, and it attracts the best female basketball players in the world. President Richie is well aware of her league's vital signs. She points to recent increases in fan attendance (6 percent), gate receipts (3 percent), renewals (35 percent), web page visits (3 million), and sponsorships (25 percent) as indicators of the league's health (Coward, 2011). Richie plans to continue to expand the league's fan base by focusing on marketing (Lombardo, 2011; Horrow, 2011), which she views in light of her experience with grassroots marketing with the Big Brothers Big Sisters program. Richie also acknowledges the importance of media exposure at the national level:

> I'm excited by the fact that we are moving beyond the novelty of a national professional woman's sports league and what we're really talking about is the level of play. And our friends at ESPN even this week, two times we have been featured in the top 10 plays and again shifting the dialogue from "isn't it interesting they're here" to "oh my gosh, look what they're doing." I think that really bodes well for just the level of play today in the WNBA. (Freelantz Sports Media, 2011)

Richie has been resolute in promoting the viability of the WNBA in a tough economic market. Despite the labor issues experienced by other professional sport leagues, Richie has planned for the needs of her league, which is affiliated with the NBA but characterized by very different labor dynamics. For example, many WNBA basketball players regularly supplement their income by playing overseas. Richie plans for the WNBA to thrive by focusing on providing premier competition. As part of her mission, Richie plans for the WNBA to lead the way in enhancing the visibility of and respect for elite women's sport:

> I think we have taken a stand [for women's equality]. I think every time the 132 players of the WNBA take the court, in my opinion they're taking a stand because they are showing their athleticism, their skill, and their talent. I hope that we all

look back on the summer of 2011 and say what happened with soccer [the successful staging of the sixth FIFA Women's World Cup] and the 15th anniversary of the WNBA, that was a milestone and a turning point. Because I think at the end of the day, what changes perceptions or expands perceptions is when people can actually experience the game. I'm thrilled with all of the attention on soccer because I think the general public saw women competing at a level that might have surprised them and I think we just have to keep going at it. I think that's the best sort of ambassador for women's sports. (Freelantz Sports Media, 2011)

As the spokesperson for the WNBA, Richie has displayed pride in the league and its players. She has emphasized facilitating the pursuit of goals both on and off the court, and her accomplishments provide a role model for all. Richie has received recognition as one of *Ebony* magazine's Outstanding Women in Marketing and Communication and as a recipient of the YMCA Black Achievers Award. She was also named one of *Network Journal's* 25 Influential Black Women in Business (2011).

Another set of complex skills—conceptual skills—are required for the sport manager to understand the organization's big picture. These skills enable sport managers to recognize the relationships between different parts of the organization and how they fit together. For example, a sport manager in collegiate athletics must understand the role of athletics in the university and how other units in the athletic department bear related responsibilities (e.g., a fundraising officer who understands his or her connection to marketing, events, and facilities managers). Sport managers must understand both internal and external interdependence (or independence), as well as the social, economic, political, legal, ethical, and cultural environments that shape relationships. For instance, sport managers in a national governing body such as USA Basketball must understand their relationship with the United States Olympic Committee, the NCAA, the NBA, and numerous other sport governing bodies. They must also understand the organization's relationship to international governing bodies, such as the International Basketball Federation, the International Olympic Committee (IOC), and the World Anti-Doping Agency. And they must understand the legal parameters, both within the United States and in other regions, as well as the role of basketball in various cultures around the world.

Sport managers apply conceptual skills through the process of decision making. No decision is small, but decisions must often be made quickly. Whether it is a general manager deciding whether to spend millions of dollars on a point guard, or a frontline event manager deciding how to provide security for an upcoming game, sport managers make daily decisions that affect many stakeholders. Indeed, effective decision making, and the ability to be decisive, are requisite skills in themselves. Using all of these skills, sport managers must gather and evaluate relevant information in a timely manner in order to make informed and effective decisions.

All sport managers should employ technical, human, conceptual, and decision-making skills in a variety of roles as managerial leaders. The typical sport manager plays roles in the following three categories: interpersonal, informational, and decisional. The interpersonal roles of a managerial position include figurehead, leader, and liaison (Mintzberg, 1975), and sport managers fulfill all of these inter-personal roles. As a figurehead, the manager must fulfill symbolic and ceremonial responsibilities in the public eye. As a leader, the manager must motivate and direct members to complete assigned tasks in pursuit of organizational goals. As a liai-son, the manager must develop and sustain relationships with internal and external stakeholders. A university athletics director, for example, represents the athletic department in public appearances as a figurehead, leads all department staff (from administrators to coaches), and develops appropriate relationships with both external boosters and academic stakeholders on campus.

As a result of their access to a large amount of relevant information, sport man-agers also fill the informational roles of monitor, disseminator, and spokesperson (Mintzberg, 1975). As an information monitor, the sport manager purposefully searches both internally and externally (e.g., in the sport industry) for information relevant to the organization. As an information disseminator, the manager screens and subsequently distributes relevant information to subordinates. For example, if a GM for a minor league baseball team learns that the team will be joined by a major league pitching star for a rehabilitation appearance in an upcoming game, that GM would disseminate this information to department managers (e.g., ticket office, concessions, and promotions managers) in order to allow them to prepare their offices and staff for an expected increase in attendance. As a spokesperson, the sport manager communicates selected information with external audiences, which usually involves explaining or justifying activities, handling general public relations, and otherwise promoting the organization's interests. For example, several sport organizations, including the NCAA, employ people specifically to lobby the U.S. Congress in order to promote the organization's interests and to minimize the likelihood of legislation being enacted counter to those interests. Most professional franchises employ a specific spokesperson, who is often the public relations (PR) manager. When a major story needs to be told—or, if generated elsewhere, responded to—it is often the PR manager's responsibility to do so. This work might range from the positive (e.g., the breaking of a record) to the negative (e.g., a player's arrest) and even to the tragic (e.g., the death of a beloved coach). In any circumstance, the franchise usually responds through its spokesperson.

As a result of the sport manager's position of authority, he or she also assumes four distinct decisional roles: entrepreneur, disturbance handler, resource allocator, and negotiator (Mintzberg, 1975). As an entrepreneur, the sport manager strives to augment the organization's capabilities and efficacy. The entrepreneurial manager initiates improved processes, anticipates and adapts to changes in the organization, and discovers new growth opportunities. Sport entrepreneurship can occur in many contexts, ranging from a private venture such as a fitness center to a nonprofit orga-nization aimed at using sport for conflict resolution. For example, the production manager for a sports apparel manufacturer might investigate the manufacturing process and find that some simple changes could increase the production of apparel while lowering costs. This entrepreneurial manager might go on to find that engaging a new supplier of raw materials will not only save money and increase environmental responsibility but also form the basis of an entirely new product line.

If, due to a natural disaster, for example, this same apparel manufacturer found itself facing a shortage of its newly anticipated raw material, thus jeopardizing its ongoing profitability, its management would need to respond in the role of disturbance handler. What are the alternatives? Is the new raw material available elsewhere? How much will prices rise? How will the profit margin be affected? Responding to this kind of unanticipated change, which goes beyond the scope of organizational control, the sport manager becomes a disturbance handler.

As a resource allocator, the manager distributes resources to units or sub-units in pursuit of organizational goals. For example, if the apparel manufacturer experiences rapid growth in demand for its product but still has only limited resources for hiring additional people, it may find multiple departments understaffed, and the sport manager, as the resource allocator, will have to determine where to invest. Will staffing be geared toward increasing production, advancing marketing and sales efforts, or improving delivery of the product to retailers? How does each prospective investment fit within the organization's mission and goals? Where is investment needed the most? Which allocation will maximize benefits? The manager's decision will be guided by determining the best return on investment or "bang for the buck."

As a negotiator, the sport manager identifies, mitigates, and resolves issues between organizational stakeholders—both internal and external. For example, during the 2011 labor–management discontent over the NFL's expiring collective bargaining agreement (CBA), the owners and the NFL Players Association disagreed sharply enough that owners decided to lock out the players. The lockout was eventually resolved, as sport managers on both sides fulfilled the role of negotiator and agreed upon a new CBA that allowed the NFL to resume its regular season play.

In a comprehensive example of these management roles, consider an advertising manager for a startup skateboard company who is approached by an online gaming site with the opportunity to reach a large new market through a never-before-used product placement campaign. Suddenly, in a bidding war with a competitor, the advertising manager must be an entrepreneur, disturbance handler, resource allocator, and negotiator all at once in order to outmaneuver the competitor and secure the lucrative new opportunity.

In practice, these ten managerial roles—the interpersonal (figurehead, leader, liaison), the informational (monitor, disseminator, spokesperson), and the decisional (entrepreneur, disturbance handler, resource allocator, negotiator)—are interdependent and inseparable (Mintzberg, 1975). A successful sport manager must possess the skills and motivation to readily assume each role as required by circumstances in pursuit of established organizational goals. Every sport manager must fulfill each of these roles as needed in order to carry out the nine managerial functions of planning, organizing, staffing, directing, motivating, leading, controlling, monitoring, and evaluating.

FIFA

Founded in Paris in 1904, the International Federation of Association Football (FIFA) is the international governing body of soccer (or football, as it is known in most of the world). It also governs futsal (an indoor version of soccer and beach soccer). Its membership consists of more than 200 national governing bodies (NGBs) of soccer throughout the world, including some that represent nonsovereign entities, such as Palestine (FIFA, 2012). FIFA enjoys a larger membership than either the International Olympic Committee (IOC) or the United Nations.

National associations account for FIFA's members, and membership in a continental confederation is a prerequisite for a NGB's membership in FIFA. There are six continental confederations: the Asian Football Confederation; the Confederation of African Football; the Confederation of North, Central American and Caribbean Association Football; the Confederación Sudamericana de Fútbol (CONMEBOL); the Oceania Football Confederation; and the Union of European Football Associations.

The statutes governing FIFA operations, eligibility, and legislation emerge from the FIFA Congress, which serves as FIFA's primary legislative body and meets annually. The Congress addresses global issues and elects the president of FIFA. President Joseph "Sepp" Blatter, eight vice presidents, and 15 appointed members form the executive committee, which appoints the secretary general, a position currently filled by Jerome Valcke (FIFA, 2012). Along with 25 standing committees, they are responsible for the overall administration of FIFA affairs. The FIFA Executive Committee, chaired by the FIFA president, is responsible for making decisions within the parameters of FIFA's congressional statutes. The standing committees (e.g., finance, disciplinary, referee) act on behalf of and under the direction of the FIFA Executive Committee or the congress itself. The general secretariat employs more than 350 people and is headquartered in Zurich, where it manages FIFA's daily operations (FIFA).

The World Cup, which is FIFA's premier event and one of the most prominent mega-events in the world, is both governed and organized by FIFA. Every four years since 1930, people from all over the world travel to the host nation of the World Cup to attend 64 matches. Hundreds of millions more watch media coverage of the event. FIFA controls event coverage and broadcast rights. In 2010, more than 700 million viewers watched the World Cup, which took place in South Africa, where more than 18,000 volunteers were selected from 70,000 applicants worldwide to help conduct the event (Clothier, 2010; Wyatt, 2010).

FIFA also operates other international events, produces world team rankings, and recognizes the FIFA World Player of the Year. Its other tournaments include the Women's World Cup, the Confederations Cup, the U-20 and U-17 World Cups, the U-20 and U-17 Women's World Cups, the Club World Cup, the Blue Stars/FIFA Youth Cup, the Futsal World Cup, and the Beach Soccer World Cup (FIFA, 2012). FIFA is responsible for rule compliance and enforcement and can sanction its members for violations. FIFA rankings, based on team performance in friendly matches, as well as international competitions and qualifiers, are released monthly for men and quarterly for women. FIFA has also adopted a musical anthem, which is played at the onset of most FIFA-sanctioned events.

The Short of It

- The nine functions of sport management are planning, organizing, staffing, directing, motivating, leading, controlling, monitoring, and evaluating.

- Sport managers must use conceptual, human, technical, and decision-making skills in a variety of roles.

- The 10 roles of sport managers are figurehead, leader, liaison, monitor, disseminator, spokesperson, entrepreneur, disturbance handler, resource allocator, and negotiator.

- The common elements of sport organizations include multiple members, specialization, coordination of specialized functions, and pursuit of an established goal.

- All sport organizations possess an identity, instrumentality, a program of activity, a membership, boundaries, permanency, a division of labor, a hierarchy of authority, rules, and procedures.

Leadership in Sport Organizations

Photo courtesy of George Mason Athletics.

In this chapter, you will learn the following:

✓ What makes an effective leader
✓ How the culture of an organization can be important to the success of the leader
✓ The important role that feedback plays in leadership and organizational improvement
✓ The roles of goal setting and motivation in leadership

> Leadership and learning are indispensable to each other.
>
> **John F. Kennedy**

The Special Olympics has been providing opportunities for intellectually challenged athletes for almost 50 years. The organization was the brainchild of Eunice Kennedy Shriver. Through her leadership, a camp she founded in her backyard in Potomac, Maryland, grew into an organization that now has more than 200 locations around the world and holds 50,000 athletic competitions each year.

Shriver's academic background focused on sociology, and she developed a passion for working with intellectually challenged young people when she took over the administration of her family's foundation. The Joseph P. Kennedy, Jr. Foundation's mission was to improve the lives of intellectually challenged persons by developing understanding of disability and educating others about the lives of persons living with disability. In 1968, Camp Shriver turned into the first International Special Olympics Summer Games in Chicago.

Shriver and her organization developed partnerships with the U.S. Olympic Committee, the International Federation of Association Football (FIFA), the Union of European Football Associations (UEFA), and the International Olympic Committee (IOC). Shriver's fundraising skill and vision have produced partnerships with sponsors such as Mattel and Coca-Cola. Her enthusiasm and her skill at hiring good people to run the organization have been instrumental in recruiting Special Olympics Ambassadors such as Vanessa Williams (actress and singer), Yao Ming (basketball star), Larry Lucchino (president of the Boston Red Sox), and Nelson Mandela. These highly accomplished individuals have helped spread the word about the positive ways in which sport can affect the lives of the young people who participate in Special Olympics competitions all over the globe. One of the great testaments to Shriver's leadership is the Special Olympics motto: "Let me win, but if I cannot win, let me be brave in the attempt."

Leadership Versus Management

Management is the process of using available resources to attain organizational goals. The resources used by managers to accomplish their goals include people, capital, equipment, and technology. When dealing with human resources and interactions, how do we distinguish between management and leadership? Effective managers may also be effective leaders, but that cannot be assumed. Likewise,

Management is doing things right. Leadership is doing the right things.

Peter Drucker, management consultant

The manager asks how and when; the leader asks what and why.

Warren Bennis, pioneer of the contemporary field of leadership

effective leaders may or may not be effective managers. Without a doubt, however, leadership is a crucial managerial function in engaging people to pursue common organizational goals. Leadership cannot exist in a vacuum; it requires more than a single individual. As with managers, leaders' success is achieved through others, yet leadership is broader in scope than management. How, then, does management differ from leadership?

Hersey, Blanchard, and Johnson (2008) define **leadership** as "the process of influencing the activities of an individual or a group toward reaching goal achievement in a given situation" (p. 62). Whereas managers are asked to efficiently accomplish organizational goals (e.g., planning, budgeting, organizing, staffing, and controlling) while coping with the entailed complexities, leaders are called on to establish a vision, communicate a common purpose, motivate, and inspire people to move toward the chosen goals while coping with the constant of change (Kottner, 1990). The sport industry needs individuals who are both managers and leaders (Quarterman, Li, & Parks, 2007). This chapter focuses on the ABCs of leadership in order to summarize and integrate a variety of theories and enhance your understanding of leadership in sport organizations.

> **leadership**—Process of influencing the actions of an individual or a group toward achieving intended goals.

The ABCs of Sport Leadership: Antecedents, Best Practices, and Consequences

Leadership is a complex concept. Its study is supported by an array of foundational theories, and it deserves in-depth analysis. Nonetheless, given the purpose and scope of this text, the fundamentals of sport leadership are presented here in a basic ABC format: (a) antecedents, (b) best practices, and (c) consequences (see figure 4.1). The antecedents of leadership involve everything that comes before leadership actually occurs. These precursors set the stage for leadership, and they include everything from the mind-sets of leaders and members to environmental circumstances and

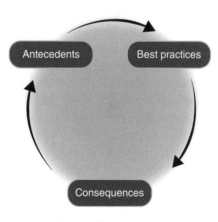

FIGURE 4.1 Basic ABC model.
Adapted from Baker 2003.

specific situational characteristics. Anteced-ents clearly influence best practices for lead-ers, which focus on leadership behaviors and interventions, interaction between leaders and members, and other moderating factors in the process of leadership. The consequences or results of leadership conclude the initial leadership process. Leaders address con-sequences by assessing outcomes, and the resulting feedback becomes an antecedent in the continuing leadership process.

This ABC format synthesizes prominent leadership theory and applications and pro-vides a framework for examining leadership. In fact, all leadership concepts—whether pertaining to leaders, members, organizations, or environments—can be viewed within the ABC framework. See figure 4.2 for a visual representation of the interdependence of these key constituents in the leadership process.

FIGURE 4.2   Interdependence of leadership constituents.

Adapted from R.E. Baker and P.H. Baker, 1999, *Professional dominance or personal autonomy: Achieving the win-zone in the decision-making process for athletic inclusion,* Sociology of Sport Conference (Cleveland, OH: North American Society); Adapted from R.E. Baker and P.H. Baker, 1999, *Athletic inclusion: Accommodating athletes with special needs* (Marquette, MI: International Conference on Sport and Society).

Antecedents of Leadership

Complex antecedents form the starting point for the leadership process, and there is a seemingly infinite array of these precursors. Antecedents are discussed here both separately and in conjunction with best practices. The discussion begins by addressing the characteristics and dynamics associated with members and leaders, then examines organizations; it also addresses environmental and situational ante-cedents in conjunction with the theories presented.

You are probably familiar with situations in which an average-skilled basketball team, led by a new head coach, rose above its skill level to achieve great things. The new coach likely had excellent leadership skills. One of the key roles of a leader is to motivate, and in the case of sport management a leader must motivate the sport organization's staff or members. Motivation, or willingness, to put forth effort is often discussed in terms of reinforcement and punishment; however, this simple carrot-and-stick approach does not always maximize motivation for either leaders or members. Many scholars have researched what motivates people. Pink (2011) proposes that individuals are maximally motivated by autonomy, mastery, and purpose. Herzberg (1968) noted a difference between simple maintenance factors and motivation factors. A car, for example, must receive basic maintenance simply to be ready to drive. Maslow's (1943) hierarchy of needs identified the following areas of human need: physiology, safety and security, social aspects, self-esteem, and autonomy. Davis (1991) expanded on Maslow's work to suggest that both humans' and organizations' needs are not hierarchical but fluid. In align-ment with Herzberg's view, these human needs may involve maintenance factors (e.g., physiological needs) that do not motivate, as well as motivation factors (e.g., autonomy) that do engage human drive. In this view, basic needs (e.g., resolving hunger) must be met before a person can be motivated. For a comparison of the needs theories, see figure 4.3. McClelland and colleagues (McClelland, Atkinson, Clark, & Lowell, 1953; McClelland, 1961, 1975; McClelland & Burnham, 1976) identified three human needs that serve to motivate: achievement, affiliation, and power. Motivation derived through meeting a person's needs can be further understood in light of Adams' (1977) theory of inequity, which posits that one compares his or her efforts and results with those of others. For example, if a ticket salesperson works longer hours and sells more tickets but is rewarded at the same level as a lower performer, the higher performer's satisfaction is likely to be affected by the apparent inequity of the treatment.

Does the fulfillment of a need automatically result in satisfaction and performance? In his preference-expectancy theory, Vroom (1964) suggested that individuals choose courses of action that they expect to result in their preferred outcomes based on such factors as how strong their desire is, what type of outcome they expect, and how directly the results are connected to their actions. Thus goal setting can be used as a vehicle for motivation at the individual level (see chapter 3 for a discussion of goals from an organizational perspective). The key to using goals effectively in human

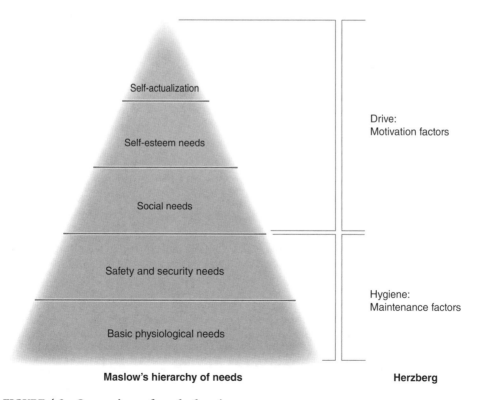

FIGURE 4.3 Comparison of needs theories.
Based on Maslow 1943 and Herzberg 1968.

Specific

Measurable

Achievable, attainable, action oriented, agreed upon

Realistic, relevant, results oriented

Time based, tangible, trackable

FIGURE 4.4   SMART goals.

motivation is to set appropriate goals. More specifically, setting what are referred to as SMART goals motivates individuals to stretch their abilities in order to attain their goals; see figure 4.4 for a description of the characteristics denoted by the SMART acronym. For example, if a direct salesperson sets a goal of initiating 150 sales calls per day, that is a more measurable and motivational goal than simply saying that he or she should call a lot of people.

Another antecedent in the leadership process is **power**, which is the ability to influence others. Power stems from many sources. Burbules (1986), for example, viewed power as interactive, relationship based, and reciprocal. He described authority as legitimized power supported by rituals, symbols, expertise, and organizational configurations. Etzioni (1961) differentiated between personal power (generated from below, from the members) and positional power (generated from above, from the organization or position).

power—Ability to influence others.

Organizationally generated power is commonly classified as one of three types: positional, reward, or coercive. Legitimate positional power is based on the managerial position held by a person within the organizational structure. For example, the general manager (GM) of a professional sport franchise wields positional power simply by serving in that role. The GM can also use reward power, based on his or her ability to distribute rewards that are valued by others, in order to compensate employees for excellent performance. Conversely, coercive power hinges on the ability to reprimand and can be used to punish low performers. In sport, for example, referees, officials, and umpires wield coercive power, as do coaches and managers.

Individually generated power, on the other hand, is classified as referent, expert, or informational (Quarterman, Li, & Parks, 2011). In contrast to organizationally based forms of power, referent power is based on individual personality and charismatic appeal. People who gain the admiration of others often possess referent power but don't have to do anything specific in order to obtain it. Nor is it inherent in their organizational position. An individual's expert power, in contrast, depends on specific knowledge and skills. People generally place high value on perceived expertise. For example, a GM who has proven to be an excellent talent evaluator holds expert power in that area. People also value information, and informational power derives from possessing desired information. For example, if a sport organization is short on technological knowledge and capabilities, then a sport management graduate who possesses this particular knowledge may find an opportunity to gain power in the organization. Each of these types of personal power depends entirely on the individual, whereas organizationally based power held by an individual can be withdrawn by the organization.

Wolf (1990) presented a broader view of power as occurring in four modes. As a personal attribute, power is something to be possessed in the form of personal capacity or capability. In the form of interpersonal relations, power shapes and directs interactions and transactions in human relationships. In its tactical and organizational mode, power controls the settings of power play and is political in nature. Finally, structural power shapes the underpinnings of all power play; in fact, sport carries structural power in many societies, though it varies from one culture to another.

Another leadership antecedent is efficacy, or individuals' perceptions of their own capacity to perform (Bandura, 1986). Individuals who are provided with adequate resources and given a specific task form a perception of their ability to complete that task, and this belief about what they can do lies at the heart of efficacy. For example, if a coach believes strongly in her or his ability to maximize the performance of a prospect who is known as an underachiever, the coach is more likely to support a trade for that talent. One caveat: Efficacy can vary from task to task. For example, that same coach, who enjoys high efficacy regarding the ability to maximize talent, may believe himself or herself to be ineffective in conducting media relations, and this low efficacy may lead the coach to shy away from interviews, media conferences, or any other contact with reporters.

One more antecedent of leadership involves group dynamics and cohesion. **Cohesion** is "a dynamic process, which is often reflected in the tendency for a group to stick together and remain united in the pursuit of goals and objectives" (Carron, 1982, p. 124). Because cohesion affects performance, it is important in any small group setting (Carron, Colman, Wheeler, & Stevens, 2002). Cohesion can involve both social and task aspects. **Social cohesion** involves social interaction and individual members' attraction to one another. For example, the leader of a marketing and management agency might foster cohesion by providing many social opportunities for employees (e.g., family picnics, lunch meetings, out-of-office conferences, happy hour meetings).

cohesion—Process wherein a group sticks together and remains unified in the pursuit of goals.

social cohesion—Process involving social interaction and individual members' attraction to other group members.

task cohesion—Process involving individual commitment to formal group goals and identification with achieving those goals.

Task cohesion, on the other hand, revolves around individuals' commitment to the formal group's goals and their identification with achieving those goals. For instance, a season ticket sales manager for a sport franchise might design her staff's office in such a way that everyone sits in one "bullpen" where sales slogans are displayed on the wall and charts depicting past successes and current goals are posted within view of each team member. The task in this case is to sell, and reminders of that focus can be seen everywhere. These two types of cohesion—social and task—can operate jointly or independently.

Group tasks can also vary in terms of dependence and independence. Independent group tasks do not require interaction with other group members, whereas dependent ones do. In coactive dependence, tasks have a common external connection; in reactively-proactive dependence, one member completes a task initiated by another; and in interactive dependence, interactions between members are required in order to complete the task (Carron & Chelladurai, 1981). For example, soccer is an interactive team task, whereas wrestling involves coactive team members performing relatively independently. Just as group tasks vary in terms of dependence and group cohesion, so too leadership styles must vary.

Sport Organizations as Systems

To establish the context of leadership in the sport industry, we must look at the organizations in which that leadership is exercised. Organizations serve as the playing field where leaders and members perform. Sometimes viewed as living organisms, organizations can evolve and even learn. The academic concept of learning organizations first emerged in the 1970s (Argyris & Schön, 1978, 1995). A complex, dynamic organization excels only if it and all of its members are committed to maximizing their capacity to (a) generate and share new ideas, (b) understand operations, and (c) establish and pursue a collective vision. Argyris and Schön (1995) suggested that reliance on single-loop learning—in which organizations correct faults by using only existing mind-sets, goals, and policies—hinders employees' initiative and creativity. Instead, they suggested using double-loop learning, in which organizations and leaders adapt new mind-sets and goals where needed in order to correct organizational errors. For example, sport facility managers who seek feedback from spectators, vendors, and employees are engaging in double-loop learning; indeed, constructive criticism from stakeholders can be a great source of new ideas for an organization that is not afraid to change.

Senge (1990), noting that both individuals and organizations learn, framed learning organizations as systems that require leaders to think differently. Deming's (1993) system of profound knowledge, based on the interrelatedness of people and processes in organizational systems, requires that leaders think in terms of systems in order to positively affect quality. A learning organization is built on trust and engagement, which results not simply in compliance but in genuine commitment among leaders and members alike.

Sport organizations are open systems influenced by both internal and external environments. These environments include both task environments (which consist of customer, competition, labor, and supplier subcomponents) and general environments (which consist of economic, social, political, legal, and technological subcomponents) (Certo, 1992). For example, a sports apparel company must take into account not only its customers but also its competitors. Has a competitor captured a large share of loyal customers? The company must also be aware of the capacity of both its labor pool and its suppliers. Can it get the raw materials it needs in a timely manner? Do the questionable cheap labor practices in some countries influence where the company chooses to produce its products? Prevailing environmental factors can also be influential. Would any pending legislation affect the apparel industry? Are new product technologies possible? Does the state of the economy facilitate increased production?

Chelladurai (2009) has conceptualized **organizational systems** as inputs, throughputs, and outcomes occurring in relationship to its environment. In this model, inputs include human and material resources, values, and purpose. Throughputs include the transformational structures, processes, and interactions that convert inputs into outputs; they include management and operations. Outputs are composed of the products, goods, and services produced, as well as the maintenance of members' satisfaction.

organizational systems—Inputs, throughputs, and outcomes occurring within an organization's environment.

In a college athletic department, for example, inputs include the students, coaches, and administrators who make up the teams and managers. They also include physical structures, such as the offices of the coaches and athletic director, stadiums and arenas, and other campus locations where competition, practice, conditioning, and instruction take place. The last major input in this type of sport organization is the annual budget under which the department operates—that is, the financial resources at its disposal. The department's throughputs include the leadership and management skill provided by the athletic director and other managers, as well as the coaching, conditioning, weight training instruction, and medical attention provided by the teams' coaches and staff members. Outputs include the revenue generated by each team's activities, the satisfaction of each team member in pursuing athletic excellence, and the enjoyment experienced by students, alumni, and other fans who follow the teams.

Senge (1990) noted that each system is perfectly created to yield the results that occur. In other words, the results achieved by a winning franchise are a result of the system in place. As a system, the organization can learn to continually refine and improve its performance. Viewing organizations as systems allows for a big picture perspective that focuses on the interrelationship of subsystems, stakeholders, and environments. Systems thinking allows leaders, members, and teams alike to be crucial learners and contributors who go beyond the limits of the nonlearning organization.

Another key factor is organizational culture, which can be seen as a pattern of assumptions that evolves as an organization learns to adapt to external circumstances and integrate its internal thinking (Schein, 2004). Organizational culture is driven by an organization's values, beliefs, and customs. In reframing organizational culture, Bolman and Deal (2008) identify a symbolic frame in which culture is shaped through purposeful work and esprit de corps is built through myths, heroes, rituals, ceremonies, physical settings, humor, and jargon, as well as symbolic anecdotes, legends, and chronicles. For example, Knute Rockne is a legendary figure at the University of Notre Dame, Wrigley Field symbolizes the Chicago Cubs, the ceremonial touching of Howard's Rock unites the football team at Clemson University, and John Wooden's Pyramid of Success created a specialized jargon for his UCLA teams. Each of these practices generates pride and spirit among organizational stakeholders.

It is inevitable that any organizational culture will change. But how does this happen? Schein (2004) has suggested that consensus must develop around the organization's mission, goals, means, assessments, and strategies. Kanter (1983) held that successful change involves innovation, integrative leadership, and empowerment of

Quick Facts

- Most modern U.S. presidents have had a background in sport—whether baseball, basketball, bowling, boxing, cheerleading, football, or golf. They have also routinely hosted star athletes and teams to honor championships won on both the professional and collegiate levels. In short, they have embraced sport as part of their leadership role.

- President Theodore Roosevelt, in responding to deaths in college football, was instrumental in the formation of what would become the National Collegiate Athletic Association (NCAA).

- In 2011, Joseph "Sepp" Blatter, a Swiss citizen, was re-elected as president of the world's soccer governing body, FIFA, at the age of 75.

- Nelson Mandela, the inspirational leader of post-apartheid South Africa, used the sport of rugby and the springbok symbol from the top national team's jersey to help unite and heal the citizens of South Africa.

members. Collins and Porras (2004) posit that an organization is enabled to adapt to change by core values that influence a shared vision. Davis and Meyer (1998) have contended that change is not a monster to be feared; rather, it is commonplace. Certainly, in the world of sport, the only constant is change. Fullan (2008) identified what organizations need in order to facilitate successful change: (a) foster love for one's fellow members in the organization; (b) connect peers with organizational purpose; (c) build individual and organizational capacity for achieving organizational goals; (d) remember that organizations learn and that learning is central to change; and (e) understand that transparency is essential. Fullan also offers these related strategies for leading an organization through change: (a) develop collegiality, (b) be open-minded in planning, (c) value all members, (d) provide abundant learning opportunities, (e) develop leaders at all levels, and (f) apply unavoidable positive pressure (Fullan, 2008). If members are committed to the organization and the process of change both individually and (more important) collectively, the organization will change successfully (Fullan, 2001). Fullan (2008) further advises energetic, enthusiastic, and hopeful leaders to (a) have a moral purpose, (b) understand how change occurs, (c) build relationships, (d) share knowledge, and (e) create coherence within the complex process of organizational change.

Best Practices: The Art and Science of Leadership

Having discussed antecedents, or factors that affect leadership, we turn now to the second part of the ABC model of sport leadership: best practices of leadership, and of sport leadership in particular. Do clearly defined best practices exist for sport leaders? How does effective leadership work? Here, both the art and the science of leadership are relevant. We can learn how leadership works by examining the science of leadership, including the foundations of leadership theory. The art of leadership focuses on applying complicated leadership interventions and techniques.

The Science of Sport Leadership: Theoretical Foundations

Are leaders born or made? Researchers have sought to answer this question by providing insights into how leadership works. Along the way, the study of leadership itself has evolved, and established leadership theories include the following distinctive approaches: (a) trait theories, (b) behavioral theories, (c) cognitive theories, (d) situational and contingency theories, and (e) contemporary integrative theories.

Trait theories investigate characteristics of successful leaders to explore whether certain traits are inherent in leaders. The so-called great man theories suggested that the keys to leadership were innate, even instinctual, qualities. Trait theorists address central questions such as the following: What common characteristics are displayed by leaders? Do natural-born leaders exist? Can leadership be learned?

Within this approach, Weese (1996) identified five components of sport leaders: (a) credible character, including trustworthiness and reliability; (b) compelling vision, which creates focus; (c) charismatic communication ability; (d) contagious enthusiasm; and (e) the capacity to build a culture in which shared values align with vision. Bennis and Nanus (2003) identified four common skills in leaders—specifically, being able to manage attention, meaning, trust, and self. These abilities to communicate direction, to facilitate meaning and understanding, to be reliable and consistent, and to know one's own skills and limits led to seven characteristics of effective leaders: (a) business knowledge, (b) people skills, (c) conceptual thinking skills, (d) track record, (e) choice of people to meet organizational needs, (f) sound judgment and quick decision making, and (g) strong character (Bennis & Nanus, 2003).

Like any corporate executive, the GM of a professional sport franchise must know the business and know people. The GM must have a vision and select high-quality personnel to carry out that vision. Decision making is also important. Which players and staff will be chosen? Who will coach? How will the team invest its money? What experience will be provided to spectators? If a GM doesn't purposefully answer the seemingly endless questions, they will be answered for her or him. In this environment, perhaps it is not surprising that one common attribute of successful leaders is strength of character. Enthusiasm and ability are critical leadership qualities, but character is the most important. A leader with ability and enthusiasm, but without character, can hinder both long- and short-term goal attainment.

McGregor's (1960, 1966, 2005) Theory X and Theory Y reveal basic assumptions underlying a leader's beliefs about members. Theory X describes leaders who believe that people are basically lazy and unreliable and therefore require structured, task-oriented, authoritarian leadership that includes direct supervision and control. One good example of Theory X leadership would be the owner of a professional sport team who wants to be involved in every coaching decision, every marketing plan, and every player personnel change. Theory Y, on the other hand, describes leaders who believe that motivated members are creative and self-directed and therefore require

Nearly all men can stand adversity, but if you want to test a man's character, give him power.

Abraham Lincoln

confidence, trust, support, and facilitative, team-oriented leadership. In contrast to Theory X, then, a Theory Y owner hires the best possible managers and trusts them to achieve. These basic assumptions correspond with Likert's (1967) formulation of management systems, wherein System I behaviors are aligned with Theory X but System IV behaviors are aligned with Theory Y. The view put forth by McGregor and Likert is supported by Argyris' (1964) immaturity–maturity continuum, in that immaturity is aligned with Theory X beliefs and System I behaviors, whereas maturity is aligned with Theory Y beliefs and System IV behaviors.

Another formulation posits that managerial leaders can be either concerned with production or concerned with people (Blake & McCanse, 1991; Blake & Mouton, 1964). Based on the level and direction of their concern, leaders can be categorized according to specific leadership styles that range from low concern for both people and production (characteristic of an "impoverished leader") to high concern for one and low concern for the other, to high concern for both (characteristic of a "team leader") (Blake & McCanse). For example, a ticket sales manager who is impoverished in this sense may not set sales goals or care about the sales staff's satisfaction. In contrast, a team-oriented sales manager attempts to develop a collegial atmosphere by assisting staff in honing their sales techniques while simultaneously making sales goals clear.

In contrast to trait theories, behavioral theories focus not on personal characteristics but on the actions employed by effective leaders. They explore this central question: What leader behaviors are effective? Yukl (2006) describes 12 leader behaviors in three categories: (a) task-oriented behaviors, such as short-term planning, objective and role clarification, and monitoring of operations and outcomes; (b) relations-oriented behaviors, such as supporting members, recognizing achievements, developing members' skills, consulting members about decisions, and empowering members; and (c) change-oriented behaviors, such as monitoring and adapting to the environment, proposing a vision, encouraging process innovations, and taking risks. Covey (1989) famously identified seven habits of leaders: (a) being proactive by taking early action rather than just letting things happen; (b) beginning with the end in mind by acting toward goals; (c) prioritizing by putting first things first and maintaining balance; (d) creating win-win situations through collaboration and cooperation; (e) communicating effectively by seeking first to understand, then to be understood; (f) synergizing in innovative cooperation with others to align individual and organizational interests; and (g) "sharpening the saw" through continual self-renewal to stay at the top of one's game. Such lists can inform our understanding of our own experience with leaders. When considering who was effective and who was not, we can ask ourselves, Did the leader regularly engage in these behaviors or not? There is a connection between these behaviors and a leader's effectiveness.

SUCCESS STORY

Bill Bradley, Former U.S. Senator and Hall of Fame Basketball Player

William W. "Bill" Bradley is a former three-term U.S. Senator from New Jersey, as well as a hall of fame basketball player and a Rhodes Scholar. Born in 1943 in Missouri, Bradley was a Boy Scout and later an Eagle Scout. He began playing basketball at age nine and spent hours honing his skills in the gym. Having grown to 6 feet 5 inches (1.96 meters) by the age of 15, he scored 3,068 points at Crystal City High School, where he was a two-time high school All-American. The recipient of 75 scholarship offers, Bradley chose to attend Princeton University, where he averaged 30 points per game on the freshman team and was named an All-American in each subsequent season. As a varsity starter, he went on to be recognized as a national player of the year. As team captain, he led Princeton to the Final Four, and despite losing was named the MVP. Bradley scored 2,503 career points for the Tigers and averaged over 30 points per game yet was considered an extremely unselfish player who preferred to pass the ball. As the holder of many Princeton and Ivy League career and season records, he received the 1965 Sullivan Award, becoming the first basketball player to be named the top U.S. amateur athlete. While at Princeton, he also hit .316 as a first baseman on the baseball team and earned a gold medal as the youngest member of the 1964 Olympic basketball team.

After graduating magna cum laude from Princeton in 1965, Bradley attended Oxford University on a Rhodes Scholarship. While attending Oxford, he played a season of professional basketball in Europe for Italy's Olimpia Milano, with whom he won the European Champions Cup. Though he had been drafted by the New York Knicks, accepting the Rhodes Scholarship postponed Bradley's anticipated NBA career for two years. After leaving Oxford to serve in the Air Force Reserve, he joined the Knicks in 1967–68 and graduated from Oxford in 1968 as a Knick. He spent his entire 10-year professional career with the Knicks, with whom he won two championships. During his NBA career, Bradley continued to expand his world view and used his off-court time to prepare him for future opportunities outside sport. After retiring, he was elected to the Naismith Memorial Basketball Hall of Fame in 1982, and the Knicks retired his jersey in 1984. In 2007, Bradley sponsored former teammate Phil Jackson, a championship coach with both Chicago and Los Angeles, into the hall of fame.

At about the time of his retirement from the Knicks, Bradley, then 34 years old, won the U.S. Senate seat from New Jersey that he would hold for nearly two decades. In the Senate, he was highly respected and considered a pillar. Having been re-elected in 1984 and 1990, Bradley left the Senate in 1997, and, after a failed presidential campaign, he exited politics. He has since worked as an investment banker, corporate consultant, corporate executive, and board member of both profit-based and nonprofit organizations. Senator Bradley has also authored six nonfiction books, including *Life on the Run* (1978), *Values of the Game* (1998), and *The New American Story* (2008). He has served as a visiting professor at such institutions as Stanford University and the University of Notre Dame, and he remains an active and respected contributor to the national agenda as a radio host for Sirius Satellite Radio's *American Voices*, which highlights individuals' achievements (Bradley, 2011).

While recognizing the contributions of the trait and behavioral approaches, Yukl and Van Fleet (1992) noted that the complexity of leadership cannot be fully explained by either approach alone. In going beyond the study of leaders' characteristics and behaviors, researchers have attempted to explain the cognitive dimensions of leadership. In short, how do leaders think? These theorists examine such cognitive factors as multiple intelligences and emotional intelligence (Gardner, 1983; Goleman, 1995). Gardner's theory of multiple intelligences (1983, 1999) posits the following intelligences: spatial, linguistic, logical-mathematical, bodily-kinesthetic, musical, interpersonal, intrapersonal, and naturalistic. In this view, individuals with differing intelligences learn differently and thus vary in how they approach problem solving. Cognitive leadership theory aligned with the concept of emotional intelligence suggests that a leader's emotions are contagious (Goleman, 1995; Goleman, Boyatzis, & McKee, 2002). In this view, resonant leaders, who project energy and enthusiasm, influence organizational success not simply through skill and knowledge but also through connectivity. This approach suggests that resonant leadership wielded by emotionally intelligent leaders can drive members' emotions and thereby positively affect organizational outcomes. For example, an enthusiastic marketing manager can use charisma to engage with both clients and staff in pursuit of common goals.

Understanding how leaders and followers think can provide insight into the nature of leadership. Even so, situational and contingency theorists propose that the circumstances surrounding leadership also play an important role. For example, that same charismatic marketing manager may find that the department's success is affected by circumstances beyond his or her control, such as severe time constraints, budget cuts, or new technology that has made the company's product obsolete. Thus investigations of situational factors can reveal additional complexity in each leader–member interaction. Key questions include the following: What situational factors influence leadership? What leadership contingencies exist in response to specific situations? How does a leader choose from these contingencies?

In addition to the previously discussed preference-expectancy theory (Vroom, 1964), prominent theories in this line of thought include those of Fiedler (1967) and House (1971). Fiedler's (1967) contingency theory suggests that any leadership style can be effective if it is applied in the appropriate situation. Depending on position power, task structure, and leader–member relations, Fiedler suggests that either relationship orientation or task orientation can be influential in leadership. In other words, if a leader is powerful and well-liked, and if members have well-defined roles, then this is a very favorable leadership situation, which is clearly not the case if the leader is unliked, has little power, and faces an unstructured task.

House's (1971) path-goal approach presents the leader as a facilitator whose role is to clarify the paths that lead toward achieving individual goals and to align those goals with team goals. For example, the owner of a racing team might provide his or her pit crew with the latest in diagnostic technology in order to produce the most efficient racing machine. Thus this leader reduces roadblocks and increases opportunities for success, which serve as a source of satisfaction and reward. In the path-goal approach, the group or team has a say in setting commonly accepted goals and procedures, and the leader offers guidance and support to each member. Indeed, the individual member is central in the path-goal process. Each member sets individual goals, aligned with his or her abilities, and works with the leader to align those goals with team goals. Thus members' knowledge and perceptions of team goals is also critical. The path-goal leader helps the members find the most effective paths by which to achieve their individual goals, which support team goals, thereby leading to team success. For example, NBA coaching great Phil Jackson was able to merge the goals of individual players (e.g., Kobe Bryant and Shaquille O'Neal with the Los Angeles Lakers; Michael Jordan, Scottie Pippen, and Dennis Rodman with the Chicago Bulls) with the goals and best interests of the team. As a result, if each player achieved his own goals, the team would succeed. The success of this approach is evidenced by Jackson's multiple championships with two different teams.

As the name suggests, integrative theories examine the leadership process by considering multiple elements. Ouchi's (1981) Theory Z extends McGregor's work by merging the collective interests of Japan's paternalistic leadership with the traditional individualism of American leadership. Extending this humanistic approach beyond the individual leader–member relationship to the organizational level, Ouchi suggests that holding values in common increases members' commitment within the organizational culture and, in turn, increases satisfaction, performance, and quality. He suggests that individual responsibility should be combined with collective, consensus-based decision making. In sum, Theory Z fully integrates organizations, individual leaders, and members in a holistic approach to leadership. As an example, consider the growth and success of Nike. Many observers would probably classify Nike co-founder and former CEO Phil Knight as a Theory Z devotee. In fact, Knight has on many occasions expressed appreciation for the Japanese approach to business, and Nike receives high marks for employee satisfaction and organizational commitment (Krentzman, 1997).

Within the context of sport, one prominent integrative theory that addresses the multiple facets of leadership is Chelladurai's (1993, 2006, 2009) multidimensional model of leadership. Chelladurai identifies antecedents such as leader, member, and situational characteristics. As theorists have indicated, leader characteristics include personality, ability, knowledge, and the like. Member characteristics that function as antecedents include factors such as attitudes, skills, commitment, and understanding. Situational characteristics include clarity of tasks, structure, goals and size of the organization, and expectations. Chelladurai also distinguishes various leader behaviors as being required, preferred, or actual. Required behaviors are constrained by situational elements such as organizational structure, group

 Individual commitment to a group effort—that is what makes a team work, a company work, a society work, a civilization work.

Vince Lombardi

Excellence is a journey, not a destination.

Pat Riley

norms, and the task at hand. Preferred behaviors reflect what members would desire in a given circumstance, and actual behaviors are the actions taken by the leader in that situation. Alignment of required, preferred, and actual behaviors leads to improved performance and satisfaction. The model also includes the concept of member transformation as an influential, perhaps omnipresent, process wherein transformational leaders craft the circumstances that facilitate individual and organizational success.

Another holistic approach is offered by Hersey et al. (2008), who integrate leadership theories by weaving together key leadership concepts. More specifically, the theory synthesizes previously conceptualized factors such as member characteristics, leader behaviors, situational and environmental conditions, personality, power, and motivation. Member readiness, for instance, is based upon one's ability (knowledge and skill) and willingness (confidence and commitment). In another example, leadership style is categorized as delegating, participating, selling, or telling, depending on the leader's balance of task-oriented, directive behaviors and relationship-oriented, supportive behaviors. Putting these two factors together, if members are both able and willing, then leaders can relinquish responsibility for decisions and execution; if members are able but unwilling or insecure, then leaders can share ideas and facilitate decisions. If, on the other hand, members are less able but willing, then leaders can explain and clarify decisions; finally, if members are both unable and unwilling or insecure, then leaders can give specific instruction and close supervision. Thus one way to consider a leader's effectiveness is to observe his or her ability to match the appropriate leadership style to members' varying performance readiness (Hersey et al.). A chief marketing officer (CMO) for a large sporting goods manufacturing company (e.g., Adidas, Under Armour) may oversee a marketing and sales staff composed of all four of these member types; in such a case, the CMO will have to be four managers wrapped into one! A CMO who can identify employees' needs in this way and modify his or her leadership behavior to meet them will produce an effective marketing and sales operation for the organization.

Contemporary theories of transactional and transformational leadership focus on both leaders and members and on the relationship between them (Bass, 1985). Burns (1982) identified the transformational and transactional strands of leadership, which focus not on leaders themselves but on the leadership process. Burns described **transactional leadership** as an exchange process built on reciprocity. Transactional leaders use contingent reinforcement through promises, rewards, and punishments. For example, a direct salesperson who exceeds the established sales target (e.g., sells more than 100 tickets in a given period of time) is rewarded with a monetary bonus; in contrast, a salesperson who does not meet the target (e.g.,

transactional leadership—Use of contingent reinforcement through promises, rewards, and punishments.

sells fewer than 100 tickets) is reprimanded, sanctioned, or perhaps terminated.

Transformational leadership, on the other hand, focuses on shared vision, common purpose, leader–member engagement, empowerment, inspiration, mutual understanding, and trust. Bass (1985) expressed the need for the transformational leader to be principle centered in order to avoid the Machiavellian ethical issues (e.g., assuming that ends justify means) that can surface in a distorted pseudo-transformational style. Transformational leadership exhibits the following interrelated facets: (a) idealized charismatic influence, (b) inspirational motivation, (c) intellectual stimulation, and (d) individualized consideration. The dynamic leadership process of transformation aligns with the views put forward by Ouchi (1981), Bass (1985), Goleman (1995), Fullan (2001, 2008), Chelladurai (2006, 2009), and many others in the context of learning organizations. For example, a transformational chief marketing officer might engage the sales staff by soliciting strategies from them, posting inspirational thoughts, providing notes on best practices, offering additional sales training, and meeting with each staffer individually in order to maximize success in pursuit of sales targets.

> **transformational leadership—** Mode of leadership focused on shared vision, common purpose, leader–member engagement, empowerment, inspiration, and mutual understanding and trust.

As with McGregor's Theory X and Theory Y, Burns presents transactional and transformational leadership as mutually exclusive processes. However, successful leadership may emerge from combining the two. Though transactional and transformational leadership are perceived as opposite ends of the leadership continuum, the way in which they can be merged becomes clearer in application. See figure 4.5 for a representation of the transactional-transformational leadership continuum.

The conceptualization of leadership has advanced immensely, and each of the aforementioned theoretical approaches has merit, albeit sometimes with limited unilateral application. Yet each theory also adds to a collective understanding of how organizations, leaders, members, and situations interact in yielding results. Taken in combination, they provide insight into the universal nature of leadership. Based on these insights, it is now time to examine the art of leadership, or some of the strategies that effective leaders can employ.

FIGURE 4.5 **Transactional–transformational leadership continuum.**
From Baker and Nunn 2003.

The Art of Sport Leadership: Strategic Applications

In essence, the art of leadership involves applying the right strategy in the right way. Baker and Nunes (2003) identified the following strategies that leaders can apply in order to enhance their success in sport settings: communication, trust and respect, goal setting, creativity, development, individualization, team building, conflict management, and role modeling. Leaders should value and employ sound communication techniques, which include attending to both verbal and nonverbal content, as well as the emotion, of communication; in fact, superior communication can be practiced and developed as a habit. A leader can facilitate multidirectional trust and respect by valuing members and empowering and supporting them in their activities. Being respectful and trustworthy begets respect and trust in return. Leaders can then trust able and willing members with levels of responsibility and accountability that they expect from themselves. As part of this process, effective leaders should help members set and pursue SMART goals (see discussion earlier in this chapter).

Leaders should also foster creativity in all organizational members by focusing on excellence rather than on the unattainable standard of perfection. Leaders, members, and organizations should not be afraid to make mistakes, but they must learn from them. The pursuit of perfection hinders creativity, whereas the pursuit of excellence—in combination with other appropriate leadership strategies—stimulates creativity and effective risk taking. Similarly, leaders should engage in self-development and facilitate the development of team members; in fact, doing so is essential to the leader's sustained success. As is evident in successful sport teams, an organization accomplishes its goals only through the collective effort of its members. Thus effective leaders build each member's confidence and genuinely care about his or her professional well-being. Such leaders support each individual's pursuit of organizational goals. In this way, individualization is irreplaceable in achieving desired collective outcomes. By connecting motivated, supportive members to each other and to the organizational culture and goals, leaders can use team building to enhance organizational success. Indeed, when members are actively engaged in decision making, social and task cohesion can be enhanced. Putting all of this together, a sport manager who facilitates collaboration, emphasizes the common interests of everyone in the organization, and promotes interactive communication will build a culture where the organization is valued by its members.

Conflict, of course, is unavoidable, but an artful leader can use it to enhance organizational commitment and develop win-win opportunities. Vernacchia, McGuire, and Cook (1996) noted that "conflict is a natural and healthy part of the group process" (p. 46). In addition, effectively addressing conflict can provide a direct path to acceptance as a leader (Maxwell, 2001). Engaging in an inclusive negotiation process yields win-win outcomes wherein the perception of having compromised is minimized by the spirit of collaboration.

In all of this, a leader's use of role modeling can be an extremely effective strategy. If the leader or organization sets an expectation for high energy, enthusiasm, effort, commitment, or any other quality, the leader must model that quality. When

High expectations and belief in people lead to high performance . . . so very often belief creates fact.

Paul Hersey, behavioral scientist and entrepreneur

leaders provide an embedded role model supported by the organizational culture, members rise to meet that expectation.

These strategies, like the theories from which they have developed, are not applicable in every circumstance, for every leader or member, or in every organization. Therein lies the true art of leadership. While some nearly universal insights into leadership have been posited, the leadership process remains both personally and environmentally determined, very diverse, and dependent on an array of antecedents, best practices, and intended consequences. For confirmation of this point, we need look no further than the varied personalities of the successful owners in professional sport, whether in the Premier League, the NFL, or the NBA. Dallas Mavericks owner Mark Cuban, for example, presents a much different study in leadership than the owner of the New England Patriots, Robert Kraft. Both men are good at their jobs, but their approaches are very different.

Consequences of Leadership

Antecedents and the best practices of leaders ultimately produce consequences— the C in the ABCs of leadership. Outcomes of leadership in sport organizations are complicated. Common outcomes include satisfaction, performance, and quality (Chelladurai, 2006; Deming, 1986, 2000a, 2000b; Ouchi, 1981). For example, a high profit margin can be an important corporate bottom line or outcome. Performance outcomes might also include attracting a large amount of sponsorship money or high attendance at games. Quality outcomes might include producing the "best" product, which might be based on various measures (e.g., team championships for a team or sales numbers for a sales department).

Interconnected leaders, members, and organizations are all engaged throughout the system of inputs, throughputs, and outputs; as a result, they all experience outcomes. If those outcomes are balanced, they yield favorable results, such as high satisfaction for individual leaders and members, high-quality output for the organization, and high performance for all constituencies in the leadership process. If unbalanced, they favor one constituency over another. If, for example, a college athletic department is unbalanced in its outcomes, one group of coaches may be very satisfied with their jobs while a larger group may be unhappy with the available resources and extremely unhappy with their teams' win-loss records. The unhappy coaches may be joined by an equally unhappy and larger number of athletes who feel no satisfaction in their participation. Figure 4.6 presents a representation of leadership outcomes.

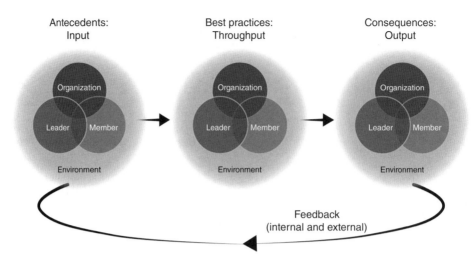

FIGURE 4.6   Leadership outcomes: The ABCs of organizational systems.

Adapted from R.E. Baker and P.H. Baker, 1999, *Professional dominance or personal autonomy: Achieving the win-zone in the decision-making process for athletic inclusion*, Sociology of Sport Conference (Cleveland, OH: North American Society); Adapted from R.E. Baker and P.H. Baker, 1999, *Athletic inclusion: Accommodating athletes with special needs* (Marquette, MI: International Conference on Sport and Society).

Individual productivity and group performance are both important outcomes in sport organizations. They represent outputs measured against organizational goals. Another important outcome is satisfaction, which should be valued on its own, not simply in relation to future productivity (Chelladurai, 2006). At the same time, in maximizing inputs and throughputs, it is essential to attend to satisfaction as an attitudinal outcome related to motivation, since outcomes inform, and at times become, future antecedents in the leadership process. Thus successful collegiate athletic departments produce not only winning teams but also athletes who earn degrees and serve as great ambassadors for the university and the athletic program. In turn, these ambassadors not only help recruit more administrative, coaching, and athletic talent to the school but also become future leaders themselves.

Outcomes should be evaluated, and every outcome can be measured. The key is finding an accurate measure for critical outcomes that are based on the mission and tied to organizational goals. For example, if the mission of a community sport program is to engage a large number of participants, then an important outcome measure would be the number of participants. Organizations and leaders can use outcome numbers to inform and guide planning and decision making. In the same example, if the participation number were low, the community sport program would use all applicable feedback to determine how to evolve in order to achieve its goals. Of course, the organization's goals themselves should also be evaluated in the double-loop learning process in order to ensure that they are appropriate (Argyris & Schön, 1995). Is engaging a large number of participants a feasible goal? Should it be pursued at all costs? What about other desirable outcomes, such as player satisfaction, creation of a safe and enjoyable experience, and player development? This is the essence of leadership—using systems thinking in a learning organization. In fact, this type of data-driven decision making has become the model for many organizations, both in and out of the sport industry (Pyzdek & Keller, 2009). The reason is simple: When organizations assess their attainment of intended outcomes, then use that information as feedback to "close the loop," they increase their effectiveness and their chances of continually succeeding. The NCAA, for example, uses data in the form of the Academic Progress Rate (APR) for member schools not only to promote and measure academic success as an outcome but also to ensure that, when necessary, members are held accountable for not understanding the proper role of education in a collegiate athletic program.

INTERNATIONAL APPLICATION

Jacques Rogge, President of the IOC

Jacques Rogge is slated to serve as the eighth president of the International Olympic Committee (IOC) through 2013 (International Olympic Committee, 2012). He was born in 1942 in Ghent, Belgium. Studying at Ghent University, he received a medical doctorate in 1967 and a master's in sports medicine in 1972 and became a practicing orthopedic surgeon. A well-rounded person, Rogge is known to be an avid reader of historical and scientific literature and a patron of the arts.

In his peak athletic years, Rogge was an accomplished yachtsman who competed in the 1968, 1972, and 1976 Summer Olympics. He also played on the Belgian national rugby union team. Prior to his election as IOC president in 2001, Rogge served from 1989 to 1992 as president of the Belgian Olympic and Interfederal Committee and from 1989 to 2001 as president of the European Olympic Committees, an organization consisting of roughly 50 National Olympic Committees. He became a member of the IOC in 1991 and joined the executive board in 1998.

Rogge was knighted in 1992 and was granted the noble designation of count by King Albert II of Belgium in 2002. In that same year, at the Winter Olympics in Salt Lake City, Rogge became the first IOC president to stay in the Olympic Village. Through Rogge's vision and leadership, new IOC policies have been developed to restrict the complexity and expense of hosting the Olympics and thus facilitate inclusive opportunities for developing countries to host the Games. Rogge has also initiated aggressive anti-doping efforts and increased the IOC's financial reserves fourfold by securing massive media contracts and global sponsorship from the likes of Visa, Coca-Cola, and Omega. In addition, he has promoted the use of sport for development and peacebuilding, championed youth Olympics, and engaged with developing countries. As the leader of the world's premier sporting organization and mega-event, Rogge was listed by *Forbes* magazine in 2011 as the 68th most powerful person in the world.

The Short of It

- Effective leaders communicate their vision to members of the sport organization.
- Leaders who encourage collaboration as part of the organizational culture usually succeed at building members' satisfaction.
- Leaders who exhibit enthusiasm can motivate members to work toward organizational goals.
- Effective leaders come in all shapes and sizes.

Sport Policy and Governance

✓ The components of good governance
✓ How good governance relates to policy
✓ The typical governance structure in high school and college athletics
✓ The three parts of governance structure in professional sport leagues

> That
> government
> is the strongest
> of which every man
> feels himself a part.
>
> **Thomas Jefferson**

The National Collegiate Athletic Association (NCAA) was established in 1906 with a helping hand from U.S. president Theodore Roosevelt. Responding to a rash of deaths in college football games, he convened a meeting of college presidents representing three of the most prominent football-playing schools in the United States at that time (a list that may surprise current readers): Harvard, Yale, and Princeton.

College football had originally been governed by students, and when first played at the collegiate level in the late 1800s it was an extremely violent mishmash of rugby and soccer. In addition, players wore far less protective padding and headgear than current players use. After Roosevelt's initial meeting, the Intercollegiate Athletic Association of the United States was formed to oversee college sport. Initially composed of 62 schools, the group adopted its current name (the NCAA) in 1910.

The NCAA did not name a president until 1951, when Walter Byers was chosen to inaugurate the role, in which he served until 1988. Byers' first duties included managing the college football television contract. This marked a change from the practice that had been followed since the early 1940s, soon after television had been invented and come into popular use for broadcasting college athletic contests; in those days, schools had controlled the rights and decided when they would appear on television. Under Byers, however, it was determined that control and sale of television rights would be better managed at the NCAA level; a concern of Byers and many schools was that a small number of schools would monopolize television time and revenue. Today, however, as the result of a Supreme Court decision (discussed in detail in chapter 7), control of television rights has reverted to the schools, though in practice most of the major (NCAA Division I) conferences act as the television rights agent for their member schools, especially in the major revenue-producing sports of men's basketball and football.

What Is Good Governance?

In its 2010 restatement of the Olympic code of ethics, the International Olympic Committee (IOC) enumerated the major tenets of good **governance** in sport and in the Olympic movement: transparency, accountability, and responsibility (IOC, 2012). Transparency gives stakeholders access to decision making and enforcement in the organization (Parigi, Geeta, & Kailasam, 2004). It also implies that decisions are driven by **policy** and that shared information is readily avail-able. Transparency promotes accountability and encourages involvement by those affected by the governance process. Accountability, in turn, ensures that decisions and actions are subject to oversight, direction, and requisite justification (Stapenhurst & O'Brien, 2012). It involves the obligation to answer for one's actions and the ability to enforce pos-sible sanctions. Accountability provides a foundation for good governance and, along with transparency, promotes responsibility among stakeholders. Shared responsibility integrates leaders, members, and organizations and fosters trust and integrity through accountable actions (Doh & Stumpf, 2005).

> **governance**—Exertion of control or influence over a sport organi-zation or its individual members.
>
> **policy**—Set of rules, ideas, or plans agreed upon by manage-ment or a governing body of a sport organization.

This formulation of good governance is similar to definitions developed by other organizations, such as the United Nations (2012) and the Organisation for Economic Co-operation and Development (2012). These organizations also recog-nize the importance of involving stakeholders in the governance process; in short, democracy is important to good governance. The IOC imposes its code of ethics on all sport federations and organizing committees that participate in the Summer and Winter Olympics. Thus all of these affiliates are spurred to involve their athletes in the governance of their organizations, to evidence concern for their athletes' health in all of their policy making, and to encourage an ethic of constant improvement throughout the organization. In addition, financial records should be audited accord-ing to generally accepted accounting principles, and checks and balances should be implemented to ensure that revenue is distributed evenly (IOC, 2009).

What Is Governance in Sport?

Hums and MacLean (2009, p. 4) note that "sports governance is the exercise of power and authority in sport organizations, including policy making, to determine organizational mission, membership, eligibility, and regulatory power, within the organization's appropriate local, national, or international scope." Sport organiza-tions come in any number of shapes and sizes, and their mission statements also vary. All of this variety affects how policy is made. For example, professional sport teams are governed by their owner or ownership group, managed by execu-tives who handle the business side of the franchise, and led by coaches and player personnel managers who select and direct the athletes on the team. Other for-profit

The first thing you must do to become a great organization is spell out in writing your beliefs and purpose. Write a credo that will be a behavioral guide to every person in your company, from entry-level positions to CEO. This creed, once thought out and formalized, should become as much a part of a company's operation as its product, service, or policies.

Buck Rodgers, author and motivational speaker

organizations manage fitness centers, operate golf and ski resorts, and manage major sports networks such as ESPN, and each of these incarnations has its own governance structure. Athletic departments of public and private high schools and colleges are also considered sport organizations, and, as with larger groups—both amateur and professional (e.g., the NCAA, the National Hockey League, the National Junior College Athletic Association, and Major League Baseball)—they also use distinctive governance and policy structures.

Large sport-related companies such as Nike, Under Armour, and Callaway are managed by a team of executives who oversee day-to-day operations. The team of executives is typically led by a chief executive officer (CEO). Looking over the CEO's shoulder is a board of directors who must be responsive to the many stakeholders of a publicly owned company. The primary stakeholder is the shareholder, but others also have an interest, including the company's employees, its customers, and the community or communities within which it operates. A typical board of directors meets four times a year. At these meetings, the board hears reports from key executives, particularly in regard to the company's finances and budgeting. Most boards also maintain separate committees (e.g., audit, compensation, finance, nominating, and executive) that are composed of board members who are or become experts in their areas.

High school and college sport organizations operate as part of an educational institution. As a result, their primary stakeholders are students and teachers, and alumni and parents come in a very close second. Even though athletic departments operate in a nonprofit environment, they still attempt to make money from the sale of television rights, merchandise sales, sponsorships, fundraising, gate receipts, and other revenue streams that are often similar to those used by professional sport organizations. Indeed, a constant battle may be waged at every governance level over the commercialization of teams and athletes.

Other examples of nonprofit sport organizations include the Young Men's and Young Women's Christian Associations (i.e., YMCA and YWCA), the Catholic Youth Organization, the Boys and Girls Clubs of America, the Jewish Community Centers Association, and the Amateur Athletic Union. These nonprofits, unaffiliated with schools, usually rely substantially on volunteers to manage or coach teams, run tournaments, and administer athletic leagues. Athletic programs are also operated by publicly funded sport organizations; for example, many city, county, and municipal governments operate athletic departments that manage sport competitions, recreation activities, and organized exercise for local taxpayers. These groups also rely on an army of volunteers to coach teams and serve on boards that help with governance issues. In these cases, policy and governance are usually shared by volunteers and a small paid staff of administrators; in addition, elected officials are drawn into the mix when budget issues are negotiated. In fact, fundraising constitutes a major policy issue for both nonprofit and taxpayer-funded sport organizations (Hums & MacLean, 2009).

This chapter focuses on the governance structure of three major areas of sport in the United States: the high school, college, and professional ranks. The chapter's international application discusses the governance of the Special Olympics, and the success story features Ted Leonsis, who is very familiar with various governance structures in sport and business. In reading the chapter as a whole, notice what group or person exercises power and authority in each of the various sport organizations.

Governance of High School Sport

Unlike intercollegiate and professional sports, which are governed at the national level, interscholastic sports at both private and public schools in the United States are governed at the local level (Hums & MacLean, 2009). More specifically, county or district athletic leagues, regional conferences, and state athletic associations set policy for athletes' academic and age eligibility, regulate the length of seasons, set practice limits, and schedule games both in and out of state.

The National Federation of State High School Associations (NFHS) is a rule-making body that wields no authority over eligibility issues for high school athletes, coaches, and schools. The NFHS membership includes the state scholastic athletic associations from all 50 U.S. states and the District of Columbia. NFHS committees promulgate rules that are followed in sports including football, basketball, baseball, and soccer; the committees meet yearly to discuss proposed rule changes. Besides rulebooks, the NFHS publishes information gleaned from participation research involving boys and girls in high school sports and activities around the country. The organization also facilitates national coach education standards and officiating standards and provides information about college eligibility, programs addressing good sporting behavior, injury prevention, and programs aimed at preventing the use of performance-enhancing drugs.

Day-to-day operations at the NFHS are handled by a paid staff that includes an executive director and other executives who handle marketing, communication, financial services, educational services, and legal work. NFHS also maintains a legislative body and a board of directors, as well as a committee structure that handles business not covered under the responsibilities of the board or the legislative council (NFHS, 2012). The executive director is chosen by the board of directors, and all executive directors of the organization have amassed extensive administrative experience in scholastic athletics before being selected for the position (NFHS). Similarly, the committee members gathered by the NFHS to address rule updates all bring extensive experience in high school athletics as athletes, coaches, athletic directors, or game officials.

The state high school associations themselves host state championships for various sports and other activities throughout the academic year. Competitions range from traditional and nontraditional competitive sports to activities such as debate, band, theater, and music. Many of these championships are limited to publicly supported schools, but there are some exceptions in which public and private schools are integrated into a single competition. Many tournaments are hosted at facilities on state university and college campuses. Most of these state bodies are called "athletic associations," but some states (e.g., Virginia, Rhode Island, South Carolina) call their groups "leagues," while others (Maine, Vermont) call them "principals associations," and still others refer to them as "activities associations."

Quick Facts

- The NCAA and NFHS are next-door neighbors; their offices are literally right next to each other in Indianapolis.
- The NCAA moved to three divisions in 1973.
- David Stern has served as commissioner of the NBA since 1984.
- The first commissioner of Major League Baseball (MLB) was federal judge Kenesaw Mountain Landis, who was brought in to clean up the mess created by the betting scandal memorialized in the movie *Eight Men Out*.
- For a time, MLB's National League and American League had separate presidents, both of whom served with the MLB commissioner. These jobs were eliminated in 1999. The current commissioner is Bud Selig, former owner of the Milwaukee Brewers.
- According to the NFHS, girls' participation in high school sports jumped from 294,015 athletes in 1972 to 2,083,040 in 1978.
- More high schools offer basketball for boys and girls than any other sport.
- The National Hockey League (NHL) was formed in 1917 with just four teams, all of which were located in Canada: Toronto, Ottawa, and two teams from Montreal.
- The International Basketball Federation (FIBA) established two new policies in 2010—one on the court and the other in the stands. On the court, FIBA voted to use the rectangular free throw lane found in NBA, NCAA, and NFHS games and thus to do away with the trapezoidal lane that had been a fixture of Olympic and world championship basketball for more than 50 years. FIBA also outlawed vuvuzelas (plastic horns used to produce a loud, monotone note) at basketball events in the wake of their widespread and controversial use at the 2010 World Cup in South Africa.

Governance of Collegiate Athletics

Collegiate athletics in the United States is governed at the national, conference, and school levels. The governing organizations help establish membership rules, academic policies, and eligibility and recruiting policies; they also promote national, conference, and nonconference sport competition between schools.

National Governance

The governing body for athletics at the majority of four-year schools in the United States is the NCAA, which is composed of three divisions known as Division I, Division II, and Division III. Each division represents a category of membership based on how many teams a school sponsors, whether it gives scholarships based on athletic ability, and how it handles certain requirements for academic eligibility. Division I, with 335 members, includes both the Football Bowl Subdivision, whose members participate in the Bowl Championship Series (BCS) and the four team championship playoff (starting 2014-2015), which collectively generate hundreds of millions of dollars, and the Football Championship Subdivision, whose members participate in their own NCAA-sponsored championship. Division II is an intermediate level of competition that offers an alternative to both the commercialized, highly competitive intercollegiate sport offered in Division I and the nonscholarship version offered in Division III. This third level, with more than 440 member schools, constitutes the largest NCAA division. Overall, the NCAA includes more than 1,200 schools, a great majority of whom are also members of athletic conferences formed on the basis of common interests and often (though not always) geographical proximity. These conferences share some governance responsibilities with the NCAA.

Intercollegiate athletics is also home to two other major governing bodies: the National Association of Intercollegiate Athletics (NAIA) and the National Junior College Athletic Association (NJCAA). NAIA schools are similar to those in NCAA Division II. They are permitted to offer scholarships and must also meet certain sport and scholarship minimums. The NAIA's governance structure is also similar to that of the NCAA, in that its Council of Presidents acts as a check on the NAIA president and on the national office staff; the council also approves budgetary policy and any major policy related to academic standards for athletes. An Administrative Council made up of athletic directors and conference executives enacts policy related to championships, awards, rules, and other issues.

The NJCAA, on the other hand, governs a great majority of the two-year schools that participate in intercollegiate athletics. (California has its own community college governance structure, so very few of the NJCAA members are from that state.) The NJCAA maintains a very small staff, based in Colorado Springs, and thus lacks the person power to conduct many of the activities that the NCAA performs in relation to rules education, enforcement, outreach, legislative review, and the like. Many of the committees that conduct NJCAA business are composed of athletic administrators who work with help from the national staff.

The NCAA, in contrast, employs more than 400 full-time staff members who work in a variety of areas, including eligibility, rules compliance, student-athlete health and safety, finance, media, research, and legal and lobbying representation (NCAA, 2012c). The NCAA manages more than 85 national championships conducted in more than 20 sports (NCAA, 2012a). It also negotiates television contracts for the broadcast of many of these championships; the largest of these deals is the contract to televise the NCAA Men's Division I Basketball Championship, which provides a large part of the operating revenue for the NCAA. The organization also employs enforcement personnel to put teeth into its recruiting rules. As part of this effort, legislative staff members help schools, coaches, compliance officials, and high school athletes around the country understand and interpret the very large rulebook that governs the conduct of coaches, players, and athletic department personnel at every level. In keeping with the fact that one staple of good governance is good communication (Hums & MacLean, 2009), the NCAA also publishes brochures to help athletes and their parents understand eligibility requirements.

The NCAA uses a two-level structure of policymaking bodies that act as the primary governance units of the organization. These bodies—the board of directors and the leadership council—handle the NCAA's large policy issues with help from the organization's full-time staff. The board of directors consists of 18 chief executives from schools around the country with an emphasis on schools from the Football Bowl Subdivision. This body of school presidents and chancellors focuses on policy and strategy but also examines and reviews enforcement, budget, and management issues at the many championships conducted by the NCAA (NCAA, 2012b).

The leadership council is a larger body of 31 members, including athletic directors, faculty athletic representatives, and conference executives from around the country—again, skewed toward schools that participate in the Football Bowl Subdivision (NCAA, 2012b). This group's primary objective is to serve as a sounding board for the board of directors regarding policy issues not related to legislation (NCAA, 2012b).

The NCAA holds an annual January meeting, but major policy issues are handled by these two councils. Issues can bubble up from schools, conferences, or outside organizations; they can also be presented directly to the leadership council and the board of directors. Before this structure was established, any change in legislation or major organizational policy had to wait until the annual NCAA meeting.

The Division I governance structure also includes a third policy-making body, called the legislative council, that focuses only on new legislation and potential changes to current NCAA rules and regulations. Divisions II and III each maintain separate governance bodies that deal with policy issues specific to their divisions.

School and Conference Governance

Every school that is a member of a conference also faces another layer of governance structure at that level. Most conferences hire an executive called a conference commissioner, who wields the authority to schedule games, assign referees, negotiate television and sponsorship contracts, and administer postseason championships. The commissioner's duties are prescribed by the conference's schools and their executives, and the commissioner serves at their pleasure. Conferences can negotiate very lucrative television and sponsorship deals that give some of them the ability to hire fairly large staffs, particularly those conferences whose members compose the current Football Bowl Subdivision.

Conference offices maintain staffs to handle a wide variety of tasks that include scheduling games, marketing the conference, hiring conference-affiliated officials, and selling sponsorships for postseason tournaments. For example, see figure 5.1 for information about the Big Ten Conference's governance structure and staff.

The governance of athletics at the school level starts with the university's president and governing board. The tone for athletics is set at these highest levels of every university. In addition, some of a university's most ardent (and wealthiest) alumni take more than a passing interest in athletics (Duderstadt, 2000). The school's athletic history also plays a big part in determining its annual goals and objectives for athletics. Anyone interested in the president's job at the University of Kentucky, for example, will surely need to understand the place occupied by basketball in the

Big Ten Conference

MEMBER SCHOOLS

Illinois	Michigan State	Ohio State	Maryland (as of 2014–2015)
Indiana	Minnesota	Penn State	Rutgers (as of 2014–2015)
Iowa	Nebraska	Purdue	
Michigan	Northwestern	Wisconsin	

GOVERNANCE STRUCTURE

Big Ten Council of Presidents and Chancellors (COP/C)

Presidents from all 14 Big Ten schools

COP/C Executive Committee

Presidents from four Big Ten schools

Conference Office Staff

Commissioner

Deputy commissioner

Chief communication officer

    Associate commissioner of communication

    Assistant commissioner of communication

Senior associate commissioner for television

    Production coordinator and building manager

Associate commissioner of men's basketball

Associate commissioner of championships

    Associate director of championships

    Assistant director of championships

Associate commissioner of compliance

    Associate director of compliance

    Assistant director of compliance

Associate commissioner of governance

Associate commissioner of football and basketball operations

    Associate director of football operations

    Supervisor of officials—football

    Video coordinator

Assistant commissioner for technology

Director of branding

    Associate director for branding

Controller

    Director of accounting

FIGURE 5.1 Governance structure of the Big Ten Conference (Big Ten Conference, 2012).

From www.bigten.org.

school's history. Similarly, a new athletic director at the University of Oklahoma won't have to look far to find a student, alumnus, or employee who wants to know about the football team's prospects.

Some schools, however, view athletics in a different light. At these schools, the president and board are not as involved in athletics, and the athletics budget reflects this fact. Many of these schools belong to NCAA Division III, but this perspective is also reflected in the Patriot League and the Ivy League in Division I. The athletic director at these schools still reports to a vice president or provost, but the communication up and down the governance chain has much less to do with wins and losses (or football revenue) than at a Football Bowl Subdivision school. The governance structure at some of these schools may look the same as for a Division I school, but policy discussions at committee meetings and board of directors meetings will leave athletics to the athletic director.

The athletic director is the executive charged with primary responsibility for the intercollegiate sport enterprise on college campuses. At some schools, the AD reports to a dean or vice president, perhaps with occasional access to the president. Depending on the school's size, staff members reporting to the athletic director may include associate and assistant athletic directors who handle the administration of individual teams and departments (e.g., marketing, finance, development), as well as managers who run athletic facilities. At smaller schools with tighter budgets and less emphasis on athletic revenue, coaches may double as administrators; the men's lacrosse coach, for instance, may also serve as the facilities director and the sports information director for lacrosse. At a large Division I school, on the other hand, the football program may employee a staff that is larger than some Division III athletic departments and enjoy a much bigger budget as well.

For each team, the coach is the policy maker, strategist, and governance executive. Coaches also supervise assistant coaches, trainers, weight and conditioning personnel, sports information staff, and, of course, the team itself. For an example, see figure 5.2, which presents the staff of a Division I athletic department.

Governance of Professional Sport

Governance of professional team sports in the United States is shared between league offices, owners, and players unions and associations. The league office is typically administered by a commissioner selected by an ownership committee or by a vote of all owners in the league. The commissioner is granted powers by a league constitution that also outlines the basic parameters of how competitions are conducted, who can own a team, what disciplinary powers are wielded by the commissioner, and other aspects of the league not covered in the **collective bargaining agreement (CBA)**.

collective bargaining agreement (CBA)—Document governing items such as pay, benefits, and working conditions for professional athletes who have agreed to the terms with representatives of team owners in their sport.

The CBA is negotiated by a league or owner representative and a union representative designated by the players. It governs relationships between owners and players for the

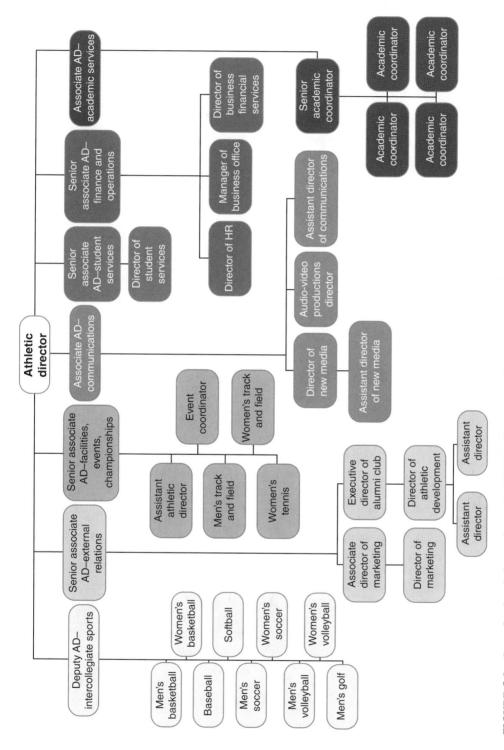

FIGURE 5.2 Organizational chart of a typical NCAA Division I athletic department.

SUCCESS STORY

Ted Leonsis, Chair and CEO of Monumental Sports & Entertainment

Photo courtesy of Monumental Sports & Entertainment.

Ted Leonsis was born to Greek immigrants and raised in Brooklyn. Today, he is chair and CEO of Monumental Sports & Entertainment, which owns the NBA's Washington Wizards, the NHL's Washington Capitals, the WNBA's Washington Mystics, the Verizon Center, and the Baltimore-Washington Ticketmaster franchise. Monumental also operates two other sport facilities: the Kettler Capitals Iceplex, where the Capitals practice, and George Mason University's Patriot Center.

Leonsis' business interests do not end with sport. He founded Snag Media, invests in many new media enterprises, and serves on several corporate boards, including those of Groupon, American Express, and Rosetta Stone (Washington Capitals, 2012). Leonsis also publishes a blog in which he focuses on his interest in sport but also comments from time to time on business, entrepreneurship, technology, and anything else he wants to discuss. In 2010, he published *The Business of Happiness*, in which he outlines six strategies that he has used to become a successful businessperson and a very happy father and husband. In the book, he discusses the "double-bottom line," whereby executives focus on doing the right thing as well as making profit.

Leonsis got his start in business with Redgate Communications, which he sold to AOL in 1994, whereupon AOL hired him as an executive. He remained closely involved with the company, serving in various roles, until retiring from AOL in 2006. His success with Redgate and AOL enabled him to purchase the Washington Capitals from Abe Pollin in 1999. He had been a minority partner of Pollin's in Washington Sports and Entertainment until he and Monumental Sports purchased the entire operation in 2010.

As one of the most innovative owners in professional sport, Leonsis has made himself available to fans literally all the time. His blog, Ted's Take, and his thousands of e-mails have given him a connection with his fan base that few owners enjoy. Of course, it doesn't hurt that the Capitals have become one of the best teams in the NHL, having compiled a league-best record of 54 wins, 15 losses, and 13 ties in 2010. Leonsis' use of new media has been imitated by other franchises in the NHL and NBA, and his embrace of blogging (both his own blog and those of bloggers who cover his teams) has proven to be a shrewd public and media relations move.

In the world of organizational governance, Leonsis occupies many positions that enable him to affect policy. His position as majority owner at Monumental gives him similar status in shaping policy there as he enjoys with his charitable foundation. As one of 30 owners each in the NHL and NBA, he can help shape policy in those two professional leagues by building coalitions with fellow owners.

length of the agreement. CBAs typically cover player compensation, injury protection, free agency rights, the rights of the union and management in the bargaining relationship, grievance procedures, and other issues pertaining to salary, benefits, and working conditions. Thus the two most important written documents that outline policy and governance issues are the league constitution and the current collective bargaining agreement.

Another form of professional sport is a tour. Some popular examples are the Ladies Professional Golf Association (LPGA) Tour, the Professional Golfers' Association (PGA) Tour, the Women's Tennis Association (WTA) Tour, the Association of Tennis Professionals (ATP) World Tour, the Grand Prix racing series, and the National Association for Stock Car Auto Racing (NASCAR) series. Golf, tennis, and racing are lucrative professional sports that generate considerable money for athletes, television partners, tour-stop sponsors, and many charities. Each tour establishes requirements for staging events, rules of competition, distribution of prize purses, and participant requirements.

Golf and tennis players are much more involved in the governance of their tours than are the drivers in NASCAR, whose tour is governed by an executive team and structure that is heavily influenced by NASCAR's founders, the France family (Ross & Szymanski, 2008). NASCAR also controls several regional tours and international stops in Canada and Mexico. Appeals from drivers and racing teams are handled by a separate racing commission composed of 32 volunteers; the commission includes NASCAR executives, former drivers, presidents of racing tracks, and executives from other motorsports (Aumann, 2010). NASCAR also operates a research and development department that helps the executive team set policy for car specifications and safety requirements. NASCAR has been criticized for its top-heavy governance structure, but that structure has also been defended as necessary for a sport as expensive as stock car racing. The up-front capital expense of forming a racing team of drivers, maintenance and pit crews, maintenance facilities, spare parts, and transportation to and from more than 30 tour stops may require a limit on democracy in order to be viable as an enterprise.

 Management Insight

The players unions in the NHL, the NBA, MLB, and the NFL did not always wield the power they enjoy today. Indeed, players' ability to affect policy in these leagues was minimal during the infancy of professional sport in the United States. In fact, owners were offended when players in each of these leagues first attempted to organize.

The trail to today's more powerful players organizations was blazed by a number of pioneers who were instrumental in the growth of these unions. Here are a few examples: Bob Cousy of the Boston Celtics (NBA); John Mackey of the Baltimore Colts (NFL); Jack Kemp of the Buffalo Bills (NFL); Ted Lindsay of the Detroit Red Wings (NHL); and Marvin Miller, who served as executive director of the MLB Players Association after working for the United Steelworkers. Without the sacrifice of these early union organizers, players today would not possess the current policy-making power they enjoy in the form of collective bargaining agreements.

INTERNATIONAL APPLICATION

Special Olympics

Through the leadership of founder Eunice Kennedy Shriver, the Special Olympics has grown into a nonprofit sport organization that facilitates participants' development and stages events in some 200 locations around the globe. The organization's mission is to provide physical training, coaching, and competitive opportunities for intellectually challenged athletes. These athletic opportunities are also designed to change attitudes among the general population about people with intellectual challenges and to provide participants with the confidence to become productive members of society (Special Olympics, 2012).

The first Special Olympics competition, held in Chicago in 1968, was billed as the International Special Olympics Summer Games, and the organization now offers competitions in both summer and winter sports around the world; for example, Special Olympics locations include Austria (1993), Ireland (2003), China (2007), and South Korea (2013).

The Special Olympics is governed by a board of directors who are selected by Special Olympics regional directors worldwide. Two board members must also be related to Special Olympics founder Shriver; the Joseph Kennedy Foundation provided the seed money to start the Special Olympics in the 1960s, and Shriver felt that the inclusion of these two directors would help preserve the organization's sense of its history. The CEO of the Special Olympics can also be a board member, but the bylaws call for a lead director to be appointed to mitigate conflicts, apparent or actual, that might accompany the CEO's board involvement.

The board oversees the executive team, which includes the CEO, the chief financial officer, a marketing executive for development, general counsel, and several other managers. This executive team must also manage each of the Special Olympics regional offices: Africa, Asia Pacific, East Asia, Europe Eurasia, Latin America, Middle East–North Africa, and North America. Each regional office has its own president, as well as a regional leadership council that advises the regional president on management, financial, and governance issues.

The board and the executive team are advised by many committees composed of experts in sport, intellectual disability, business, and government, as well as members of the International Association of Chiefs of Police, who help with the Torch Run Executive Council. The Torch Run itself is a major fundraising and marketing activity for the Special Olympics around the world.

The ATP, LPGA, PGA, and WTA all use boards to govern their tours and oversee policy changes. Tournament sponsors are also given a place at the table, as are the professional managers who compose the paid executive staff of each tour. For example, the WTA board is composed of three directors who represent the players, three who represent the tour stops, one from the International Tennis Federation, and the CEO of the WTA, who is analogous to the commissioner in the NBA or NFL. The governing board for the LPGA includes six independent directors, seven player representatives, the LPGA commissioner, and the president of the LPGA Teaching and Club Professionals. The LPGA commissioner handles day-to-day operations of the tour, but the board oversees policy changes and governance issues.

The Short of It

- Sport governance is the exercise of authority in sport organizations.
- High school sports are governed by a national rule-making body called the NFHS and by state associations responsible for, among other things, eligibility requirements.
- Collegiate sports are governed by the NCAA, the NAIA, and the NJCAA.
- Professional team sports are governed by commissioners, players associations, and team owners.

Sport Venues, Event Management, and Building Operations

In this chapter, you will learn the following:

✓ How to differentiate between the roles of event manager, operations head, and facility director

✓ Major components of risk management

✓ The importance of building systems into the operation of a sport facility

✓ Three major stages of a sport event

> Every sporting tournament should have sporting excellence as its aim. Anything else betrays the spectators, the television viewers, the athletes, and sport itself.
>
> **Simon Barnes**, reporter for *The Times*

In preparation for the 1984 Summer Olympics, Peter Ueberroth was named president of the Los Angeles Olympic Organizing Committee (LAOOC) in March of 1979. The job would require Ueberroth to hire a team of executives to manage all of the Olympic venues, every Olympic event, and all other operations of the world's largest exhibition of sport. Ueberroth would also bear the burden of finding private sources to fund the Games. In addition, though he did not know it when he accepted the job, the Soviet Union would be skipping the Olympics this time around. (The United States, at the behest of President Jimmy Carter, would boycott the Moscow Olympics in 1980 to protest the Soviet war in Afghanistan, and the Soviets would return the favor in 1984.) The Soviets' absence in 1984 would eliminate the high drama typically associated with competition between U.S. and Soviet athletes in events such as basketball, track and field, and boxing. Ueberroth was also cognizant of the financial burden that the 1976 Olympics in Montreal had placed on taxpayers there, and he would not receive any financial help from the Los Angeles city government or California taxpayers.

The 1984 Games were staged in 27 stadiums and other facilities located in three states. To save money, the organizing committee secured the use of many college athletic facilities in the Los Angeles area, and some of them had to be upgraded to meet the standards for major international competition. Each facility was home to multiple events on multiple days, which required a massive number of volunteers and paid operations staff members. The preliminary rounds for soccer were held at four sites, two of which were outside of California—the campuses of Harvard University in Massachusetts and the U.S. Naval Academy in Maryland. Ueberroth and his management staff also had to figure out how to come up with a secure way to produce and distribute seven million tickets.

Another major undertaking was the Olympic Village, which would serve as home to 10,000 athletes and coaches even as the competition venues would be filled with hundreds of thousands of spectators. The athletes and coaches would have to travel from the Village to their respective venues many times during the two weeks of the Games. Not only was transportation a major issue, but also Ueberroth was responsible for the Olympic participants' security from the day they arrived until the moment they stepped on the plane to leave after the closing ceremonies. The memory of the terrorist attack at the Munich Games in 1972 served as a stark warning for the manager of each Olympic venue and to the operations staff for each event. One of Ueberroth's many success stories was the ability to coordinate forces from the U.S. Immigration and Naturalization Service, the Federal Bureau of Investigation, the Los Angeles Police Department, and local police units into a well-managed security apparatus for the Los Angeles Games (Ueberroth, 1985).

Meeting this diverse array of challenges required a unique approach, and Ueberroth used a new sport management technique that had not been tried at previous Olympic Games. He appointed a commissioner to manage and run each of the 23 Olympic sports (Ueberroth, 1985). In addition, in order to pay for many of the facility upgrades and cover early operations costs, Ueberroth became very involved in arranging sponsorships and negotiating the television broadcast rights for the Games. In fact, his leadership and management skills in this area drew the attention of Major League Baseball (MLB), which hired him as its commissioner soon after the conclusion of the Olympics.

Granted, most sport venue managers don't have to run a Summer Olympics, most event coordinators will not be called on to manage an opening ceremony involving thousands of athletes from all over the world for an international television audience numbering in the millions, and most concession managers will not be responsible for feeding thousands of hungry athletes and spectators with diverse culinary tastes from around the globe. Even so, professionals who work in venue management, event management, and building operations must all grapple with certain fundamentals in order to give their customers an enjoyable day at the ballpark, stadium, arena, or whatever the venue may be. Those fundamentals form the focus of this chapter.

Venues

Sporting events can be staged in facilities of all shapes and sizes—from the Maracanã stadium featured in this chapter, which at one time had room for 200,000 fans at a World Cup soccer match, to a high school gymnasium that is home to the school's boys and girls basketball teams. This section of the chapter discusses the historical development of sport venues and lays out the different types of facilities where sporting events are held. Along the way, the section addresses venue design features, as well as the functions of the facility or venue manager, the operations manager, and the event coordinator or manager.

Historical Background of Sport Venues

The concept of venues for sport can be traced back to ancient Greek and Roman times, where sport venues were built for staging footraces, horse races, and chariot races around an oval track. In ancient Greece, the site of some horse and chariot races was called a **hippodrome** (John & Sheard, 2000); in modern usage, the term hippodrome refers to horse racing tracks, which can be found in Argentina, Canada, Russia, Sweden, Belgium, Germany, Great Britain, and literally

hippodrome—Originally, an oval track used by the ancient Greeks for horse or chariot racing; currently, a sport venue for horse racing.

stadium—Originally, an area in ancient Greece or Rome usually hollowed out of the side of a hill, where athletics competitions were held while spectators watched from the hill. Today the term connotes a large venue where you will find soccer, football, cricket, or baseball games.

palaestra—Indoor rectangular structure used by the ancient Greeks for training in the sports of wrestling, boxing, and athletics.

arena—Originally, a flat, circular area at the base of an ancient Greek or Roman amphitheater, covered with sand and used for gladiatorial contests; currently, an indoor entertainment venue where spectators can watch a sporting event (e.g., basketball, ice hockey, volleyball, boxing, wrestling).

all over France. In ancient Athens, the "Olympic" **stadium** was hollowed out of the side of a hill, and the remaining hill portion was used for spectator seating. For boxing and wrestling, the ancient Greeks used indoor venues called **palaestras**, which were square or rectangular structures with high ceilings usually supported by four large columns. In Rome, the Colosseum and the circuses, including the Circus Maximus, were built for spectators to view the various gladiators, be they human, animal, or a combination of the two. The Colosseum still stands today in downtown Rome as one of the most popular tourist spots in Italy (Gaffney, 2008). The Colosseum's oval shape was replicated for the many bullfighting **arenas** found in Portugal, Spain, southern France, Mexico, and South America. In fact, in some areas of Europe (e.g., Arles and Nimes, both in France), bullfights are still staged in ancient stadiums built during the Roman Empire.

The shapes of today's arenas, coliseums, palaestras, and stadiums are affected by the playing dimensions of the games or sporting events viewed in the facility. Stadiums used for soccer, rugby, lacrosse, and American football usually take the shape of an elongated oval built around the rectangular field on which the sport is played. Modern ballparks built for "ball and bat" sports such as baseball, softball, and cricket are shaped differently to account for the different dimensions in their playing fields. Arenas used for indoor ice hockey, volleyball, and basketball usually require an oval design to bring more spectators close to the ice or court. The Indianapolis Motor Speedway, built for the modern version of the chariot race, holds 250,000 spectators who watch cars moving at speeds above 200 miles (320 kilometers) per hour. Churchill Downs, a modern hippodrome in Louisville, Kentucky, serves as home to the Kentucky Derby and features stands in the home stretch and an infield area without seats—all very similar to many horse racing facilities around the world.

Outdoor sports such as golf, snowboarding, and skiing have their own unique venues. Since golfers, skiers, and snowboarders can't participate in their sports in stadiums or arenas, they use the natural or redesigned topography of the "course" as the setting for their unique athletic endeavors, and ski resorts and golf clubs usually bring in temporary grandstands to accommodate their sporting events. Tennis, however, despite being another "resort sport," can be played in stadiums that are very similar to the indoor arenas used for basketball and volleyball. Popular examples of the large tennis stadium can be found at the homes of the U.S. Open (Arthur Ashe Stadium in New York), the French Open (Stade Roland Garros in Paris), and the Wimbledon Championships (Centre Court at the All England Lawn Tennis and Croquet Club in London).

The 21st-century stadium has been dramatically upgraded from the facilities built at the end of the 19th century. Those stadiums contained room for the competitors and spectators but offered little in the way of modern conveniences, such as wide concourses, multiple concession areas, media space, and shelter from the elements

(Masteralexis, Barr, & Hums, 2012; Horrow & Swatek, 2011). As the industrial age brought more and more businesses and people into close proximity, professional sport became an entertainment alternative for a greater portion of the population (Gems, Borish, & Pfister, 2008; John & Sheard, 2000). Teams and leagues sprouted up in Europe and the United States in football, soccer, rugby, baseball, and cricket. In addition, organizers began to promote competition in basketball and ice hockey by using large convention centers and concert halls as sport venues. Once the world recovered from World War II, interest in professional sport rose sharply, stadium and arena construction followed, and improvements were made in design, technology, architecture, and engineering (Kitchin, 2012). Just as marketing firms recognized the business opportunities available in the sport industry, architectural and engineering firms began to develop this area as a specialty in their disciplines (Horrow & Swatek).

From the 1950s into the 1980s, many large stadiums were built in the United States to house both professional baseball and professional football teams at one site. However, because the two types of field are shaped so differently, these multipurpose facilities left many spectators far from the action. Many franchises also moved their stadium or arena from the city to the suburbs (Ammon, Nagel, & Southall, 2010). The Baltimore Orioles organization and its design partners made a groundbreaking decision to reverse both of these trends in building Oriole Park at Camden Yards, a baseball-only facility in downtown Baltimore. The result was a much more fan-friendly venue that provided better sight lines for spectators and promoted development in the surrounding area (Horrow & Swatek, 2011). The model of a baseball-only facility has since been followed by a number of communities, including San Diego, Cleveland, Washington, Philadelphia, Miami, and Detroit.

Venue Design

Venue design must fit both the mission statement and the budget of the facility owners. For example, in terms of mission, a sport facility that will be used for physical education and free play at a middle school or elementary school certainly does not have the same need for spectator seating or revenue-producing amenities as a facility that will host the opening ceremonies of the Summer Olympics or the Super Bowl. Furthermore, school gymnasiums usually serve multiple purposes—for example, basketball and volleyball practices and games, physical education classes, large school gatherings, and, in inclement weather, practice sessions by outdoor sport teams. In similar fashion, many church gymnasiums serve both as a gathering place for the congregation on days of worship and as a home for the church's basketball and volleyball teams. Revenue generation at these venues is intended only to reduce expenses.

Operators of modern-day outdoor facilities can choose between grass and some very effective artificial surfaces. Though the initial expense of an artificial surface is prohibitive for some communities and amateur sport organizations, such facilities can pay for themselves with additional usage over the long run (Horrow & Swatek, 2011; Robinson & Sgarzi, 2010). Outdoor facilities can also be designed for nighttime sporting events with the addition of lights, and new technology can be used to reduce light dispersion into neighboring communities.

The primary concern of every architect designing a sport facility is to determine the composition of the required playing surface and provide enough space to play the chosen sport safely. For example, a high school basketball court must measure at least 84 by 50 feet (about 25.6 by 15.2 meters). In addition, the gymnasium walls and the first row of seats must be far enough from the sideline to allow space outside the court boundary for players to run after loose balls and for event organizers to situate the scorer's table and team benches. Furthermore, the ceiling must be high enough for length-of-court basketball passes and volleyball play. With such concerns in mind, it is a good rule of thumb to review architectural plans with coaches or physical education instructors.

Venue design must also fit the capital budget and satisfy the desires of the venue owner. For example, planners need to determine whether the facility will be used for multiple sports and how much spectator space is needed; to help answer this second question, they can use attendance figures for the home team and for the league in which it plays. If the venue owner also plans to sell food and drinks at events, the architectural plans should include sufficient kitchen and concession space. For a larger facility with more spectator space, more bathrooms will also be needed.

Another feature of modern stadiums and arenas is premium seating, which includes both club-level seating and the luxury suite or "box." Today's venue owners generate a large revenue stream from corporate customers and high-income sport fans by building comfortable areas that offer access to more food, better service, multiple televisions, and semiprivate bathrooms (Masteralexis et al., 2012; Cagan & deMause, 1998; Horrow & Swatek, 2011; John & Sheard, 2000; Kitchin, 2012). Early adopters of this concept include Joe Robbie Stadium (now Sun Life Stadium) in Miami and the Palace of Auburn Hills in the suburbs of Detroit (Ammon et al., 2010; Horrow & Swatek, 2011). The concept was quickly copied by franchise owners all over the world (e.g., Wembley Stadium, Emirates Stadium) and by college athletic administrators across the United States (John & Sheard). The first luxury boxes were not built close to the action, but now in many arenas and stadiums they are located very close to, and sometimes on, the field or court.

Since 1990, building design in the United States must also comply with the requirements of the Americans With Disabilities Act (ADA), which requires wheelchair accessibility, seating for fans who use wheelchairs, and a certain number of doors, exits, and entrances built to ADA standards. An ADA-compliant building also provides a required number of accessible toilets built with grab bars and sufficient space for use with a wheelchair, as well as parking spots reserved close to the facility for visitors with a disability (U.S. Department of Justice, 2010). Other countries have passed similar legislation that affects sport facilities—in the UK, Disability Discrimination Act 2005; in Australia, Disability Discrimination Act 1992; in Germany, the Equal Opportunities for People With Disabilities Act of 2001; and in Spain, the Spaniards With Disabilities Act of 2003 (Paramio, Campos, & Buraimo, 2012).

Venue Operations

Every sport venue—no matter its size or whether it is operated as a nonprofit, a public facility, or a for-profit enterprise—must have an operations staff to make the building function for users. This section outlines the responsibilities that venue owners and managers meet in order to manage a sport facility in today's sports entertainment marketplace.

Venue Engineering, Security, and Maintenance   Any sport venue must be built and located in such a way that it can serve the purpose for which it was built. If that purpose is to provide a place where two teams can play soccer while 20,000 fans watch, then the facility must actually be able to accommodate that number. In addition, the building must be safe for players and fans, and the operations staff must be able to provide an enjoyable experience for all who use the facility.

Ultimately, responsibility for daily maintenance falls to the facility manager, but many arena and stadium operators also hire an operations manager, who reports to the facility manager and is responsible for ensuring that the building functions as intended. The facility manager also manages individual events or hires an event coordinator to do so. Most facility managers handle the facility's daily schedule and negotiate with promoters who bring in events.

The operations manager is responsible for all of the working systems in the building, including electrical, plumbing, lighting, sound, and telecommunication. Operations and event managers must report to the facility manager, and maintaining open lines of communication between these three managers is key to operating a functional building. The amount and variety of work that must be done is daunting. The building must be kept clean from debris, which is a full-time job when spectators and concessions are added to the mix. The playing surface must be regularly maintained—grass mowed, wood floors cleaned and waxed, artificial surfaces repaired and maintained. Spectator seating areas must be regularly inspected and cleaned, particularly after an event. Indoor buildings must be equipped with effective HVAC (heating, ventilation, and air conditioning) systems throughout the offices, the competition area, the restrooms, and the concession areas. When the system breaks down, the operations manager and staff must be able to get it repaired in a timely fashion.

Of course, any modern sport facility must also be equipped with a power system sufficient to operate the building for all of its intended purposes. At the height of an athletic event, the facility must provide a functional lighting system, scoreboard, video board, LED signage, and access to electrical power for members of the media. The operations manager of a large facility may also need space for crews to park television production trucks near or inside the building, as well as sufficient power outlets to operate cameras around the building.

The venue's court or field also needs a reliable lighting system, which must be sufficient to accommodate a full house of spectators. The operations manager must maintain the lights and know how to quickly repair them, particularly during an event. The lighting system may also dictate whether a facility can be used for televised games, since guidance for television lighting standards is provided by sport governing bodies, such as the International Federation of Association Football (FIFA), the National Basketball Association, the Premier League, and the International Olympic Committee. Local building codes also require emergency generators and safety lighting throughout the building (John & Sheard, 2000).

SUCCESS STORY

Barry Geisler, General Manager of the Patriot Center

Photo courtesy of Rafael Suanes.

Barry Geisler serves as general manager (GM) of the Patriot Center, the multipurpose facility on the campus of George Mason University in Fairfax, Virginia. Geisler has held this position for more than 20 years since starting his career as an assistant GM.

During any given year, the Patriot Center conducts a wide variety of events. Its major tenants are the men's and women's basketball teams of George Mason, but Geisler also books entertainers (from the Jonas Brothers to Bruce Springsteen), boxers, high school graduations, circuses, and even professional bull riders. In 1990, the NCAA Men's Volleyball Championship was held at the Patriot Center, and Barack Obama made an appearance there during the 2008 presidential campaign.

In 1985, the Patriot Center became the first major on-campus arena in the United States to be managed by a private firm. The management firm was Washington Sports and Entertainment, which owned the Washington Wizards. The management company that Geisler now reports to is Monumental Sports and Entertainment, founded by Ted Leonsis, who is featured in chapter 5. Monumental also manages the Verizon Center and the Kettler Capitals IcePlex.

Geisler started out in the facilities business as an administrative aide at the Coliseum in Oakland, California, before becoming an event coordinator for the Long Beach Convention and Entertainment Center, where he worked for a little more than two years. He received an undergraduate business degree in finance from the University of California, Berkeley, and holds a master's in sport management from the University of Massachusetts Amherst. Geisler developed an interest in sport at a very young age. He can remember attending Knicks, Mets, Yankees, and Rangers games with his family, but he became truly hooked on sport at the age of 17 when he attended the Summer Olympics in Montreal.

If the venue is an outdoor facility, the staff faces particular challenges in maintaining the playing surface. Grass must be grown and maintained with expert care, and the field must be lined for football, soccer, rugby, lacrosse, or whatever game is to be played. Arrangements must also be made to protect the field from the elements. The field should be built in such a way that water drains away from the playing and spectator areas. Space must be provided for storage of tarps to cover the field, lawn mowers, and other needed equipment—both to maintain the playing area and to play the sport itself (e.g., football goalposts, soccer goals). The facility's plumbing system also falls under operations; water is needed not only for the field but also to operate toilets and sinks in bathrooms. Expertise in this area is very important, and someone with that expertise must be present when spectators are in the building.

Another part of the operations manager's brief is building security. He or she is responsible for ensuring security for the workforce, any visitors, and vendors who enter the building on non-event days (risk management for events themselves is discussed a little later in the chapter). For example, the operations manager establishes and enforces procedures for accepting deliveries to the facility. How will truckers and other delivery people be cleared to enter the building and store their inventory in a secure location? The operations manager must ensure a secure perimeter. He or she must also evaluate whether the building is big enough to warrant a full-time security staff or at least a security director who can staff up for big events. A safe and secure building will have fewer intruders to potentially interfere with maintained areas and there won't be unsupervised individuals in the facility, which also makes daily maintenance easier.

Accounting, Finance, Marketing, and Promotion   Even at a nonprofit sport venue, the facility director must tackle certain fundamental business functions. For example, a schedule of events must be planned and negotiated with potential users of the facility, and the facility manager must maintain a master calendar of building events. He or she must also draw up a budget outlining the costs of running the facility, the payroll for full- and part-time facility employees, and any revenue projected from venue operations.

If the facility uses a promotions apparatus to encourage spectators to attend events, then it must also establish a ticket-selling operation, a ticket-taking system, and an accounting system for the resulting revenue. These functions are usually overseen by a full- or part-time ticket manager; at larger facilities, the manager oversees a staff with its own offices.

If the facility's mission is to turn a profit, the facility manager or business manager must promote the facility as a viable location for sporting events. Doing so involves developing a marketing strategy and, in the case of large facilities, hiring a marketing manager. The operation will also need a website to promote the facility, give information about upcoming events, and provide an online mechanism for buying tickets. Another avenue of promotion involves sponsored signage, which advertisers have decided makes good business sense due to the heavy spectator traffic and sizable television audience associated with many sport venues (Masteralexis et al., 2012; Cousens & Bradish, 2012; Horrow & Swatek, 2011). Sponsored signage is usually handled by the marketing manager, who may also find that advertising partners are interested in buying space on the venue's website. The advertising signs displayed around the building are serviced by the facility's maintenance staff. The signs must be visible to both the television audience and the building's spectators, but this visibility must be achieved in a manner that does not interfere with the competition or endanger fans.

It is typically the facility or business manager who negotiates contracts with vendors, promoters, sponsors, leagues, and teams. A contract should clearly spell out the terms of the agreement, taking into account each party's responsibilities. Contracts with vendors should spell out delivery dates. Contracts with teams and leagues should specify agreed-upon game dates and terms for how the building will be set up for their events. Contracts with event promoters must indicate building setup and how the group will be paid. Contracts for outdoor games must address

Quick Facts

- The largest outdoor stadium in the world can be found in Pyongyang, North Korea. It seats 150,000 spectators for national team soccer matches and national celebrations. The world's largest indoor arena, the Gwangmyeong Velodrome, is located in South Korea; it accommodates 30,000 fans. An arena seating 50,000 people is scheduled to open in 2014 in the Philippines.

- The Shanghai International Circuit hosts Grand Prix races with a seating capacity of 200,000.

- The Tokyo Racecourse, the world's largest horse track, can host 223,000 spectators. The world's second-largest horse track, the Nakayama Racecourse, can also be found in Japan, in Chiba City. It has space for nearly 166,000 spectators.

- Another name for the Indianapolis Motor Speedway is the Brickyard. This name comes from the fact that the speedway track was renovated in 1909 with 3.2 million bricks, each of which weighed 9.5 pounds. All but 1 yard of bricks at the start/finish line have been paved over during the course of renovations through the years.

foreseeable issues involving the weather. A savvy facility manager can transfer some of the financial risks inherent in these sporting events to the other party—for example, by giving the promoter of an event a percentage of ticket revenue, which gives the promoter some responsibility for ensuring that a large crowd attends the event. Mediation and arbitration clauses can also be used to reduce litigation expenses in the case of a disagreement between parties.

The facility manager is also charged with maintaining relationships with various stakeholders in the community. Developing contacts with leaders from local schools, businesses, and governments helps raise the sport venue's profile in the community (Shonk & Bravo, 2010), and these contacts may lead to new events at the facility or new sponsorship opportunities. In addition, the facility manager should attend events hosted at other facilities in order to keep an eye on the competition, learn about new operational practices, and discover innovative design ideas. The manager can also look to many national and regional organizations for help in learning about new methods and growing the venue's business.

Event Management, Risk Management, and Crowd Control

Each event that the facility manager chooses to host will be limited only by the size of the venue, the creativity of the event coordinator's staff, the event's budget, and the performance of the athletes. This section of the chapter outlines the steps in the life of an event and attends closely to two key considerations that help determine an event's success: risk management and crowd control.

Event Management

Every sport event can be divided into three major stages—pre-event, event, and post-event (O'Connor, 2012). Stage 1 (pre-event) includes the idea, the feasibility study, negotiation, the work plan, and staffing. Stage 2 involves managing the actual event, and Stage 3 (post-event) includes clean-up and evaluation (O'Connor).

The life of an event begins at the idea phase, which should be discussed by the operations staff, the facility director, and the event coordinator. The next step is a feasibility discussion to address perceived costs of the event, whether the venue can hire the right people to host this particular event, and whether or not there is room on the master calendar for the date and time suggested. In many cases, sufficient temporary staff are not available because of competing events in the area. The event coordinator must estimate the event budget and the number of staff needed to safely manage the event. The facility director then determines whether there is sufficient negotiating room with the promoter to make a profit.

Once the event coordinator, operations staff, and facility manager have determined that they can indeed host this event—and do so in a way that ensures its quality—they or their staffs should devise a plan that outlines personnel needs, timelines, and a preliminary budget (Pedersen, Parks, Quarterman, & Thibault, 2011). Those involved in producing the event should also draw up a production schedule, operational checklists, and a contact sheet of key individuals involved in the event. Planning and communication are key. The event coordinator must develop a good working relationship with the facility's operations staff, as well as the part-time staff and volunteers who will work the event. When event staff are well managed, no employee's time gets wasted, and no responsibilities overlap. The operations staff may need to manage some of the part-time employees and volunteers hired for the event, and supervisory responsibilities must be clearly spelled out. Various problems can be prevented through effective training, which should include a short walk-through with all supervisory staff for the event and a comprehensive training program for volunteer and temporary staff (Masteralexis et al., 2012).

While strategizing for the event, the event coordinator should develop an emergency contingency plan with the operations manager. An experienced operations manager working for a topflight facility director will already have several possible plans from which to choose, depending on the event (Lussier & Kimball, 2009). For example, a well-developed plan for an outdoor event takes into consideration scenarios for moderately bad weather and for very bad weather. Event coordinators can turn to many sources in order to monitor the weather. The coordinator should also put a plan in place for handling injury to fans or athletes; this plan should address issues such as the location of the ambulance that will be parked outside for a football game, the procedure for summoning medical personnel onto the field in the event of a serious injury, and staff assignments for accompanying an injured fan or athlete to the hospital if necessary. The coordinator also needs a plan for evacuating the stadium in the event of a fire. The plan should assign key personnel to assist with the evacuation and contact the nearest fire station. It should also include a schedule for checking all fire extinguishers in the building on a regular basis. Staff members at large facilities should conduct fire and ambulance drills on a regular basis.

Management Insight

On Veterans Day in 2011, the USS Carl Vinson served as the venue for a men's basketball game between the University of North Carolina and Michigan State University. This aircraft carrier may be familiar for two reasons. It was the location of a speech given by President George W. Bush proclaiming the end of the Iraq War; it was also the vessel used to bury Osama bin Laden at sea.

As you might imagine, this unique sport facility presented many challenges in event management. Some of the issues faced by the planners were basic. For example, would the game be played on the carrier deck or below deck? This problem was solved by building two courts; the below deck would be used in the event of bad weather. Other issues involved spectators—specifically, how many could this facility accommodate, and how would they be transported to the game? In addition, since the game was nationally televised, planners faced another major logistical issue in the need to accommodate the television equipment. Security was also a challenge, not only because the game was played on a military vessel but also because President Barack Obama and his wife, Michelle, would be in attendance. Planners came up with a unique approach to security, which also prevented ticket scalping, by putting a picture of each authorized attendee on his or her ticket. Thus all ticket holders were prescreened. Production costs for the game were split by ESPN and a nonprofit company called Morale Entertainment (Bishop, 2011). Logistics were handled by the United States Secret Service and the U.S. Navy in conjunction with ESPN, Morale Entertainment, and the two schools.

The event coordinator must also determine during the planning stage whether the event warrants media coverage; in cases where it does, a good working relationship with the local media can facilitate maximum publicity. If the event will be televised, accommodations must be made for production trucks, cameras, and the many wires needed for power and transmission; the operations manager helps production companies who need power for their production trucks. Reporters will also need to file stories from the event, so a plan must be in place to accommodate their need to power their laptops and access Internet connections and phone lines (Schultz, Caskey, & Esherick, 2011). Planners must also arrange staffing for concessions, and it is the event coordinator's job to estimate the expected crowd's size and tastes. Concession needs vary with the event; for some events, retail kiosks are set up inside and outside the facility. If planners decide to serve beer and wine, the operations manager secures the necessary licenses.

Even when the event has ended, the job of the operations and event staff is far from finished. For one thing, the exit of all attendees—media, spectators, and competitors—must be supervised. After they have left, the building must be cleaned. In fact, depending on the event, planners may need to hire additional staff just to clean the building after the event; if so, a plan must be put in place for when and where the cleaning crew will arrive, and a supervisor must be assigned and sufficient time budgeted to hold a quick informational session for the clean-up crew. Depending on the facility, the crew may also need to be credentialed by the security manager.

The final stage in event management is to evaluate the event, and each part of the event process has to be examined. When possible, it is a good idea to solicit opinions from fans who attended the event, perhaps through the use of new media such as Facebook and Twitter. Useful feedback can also be obtained from supervisory personnel, other employees, coaches, team staff, and game officials. Once the event has been evaluated, it is imperative that the facility director, operations manager, and event coordinator meet to determine what can be improved, which staff members did their jobs, which ones did not, and which employees should be commended.

Risk Management

Identifying and managing risk constitutes a major responsibility of the facility manager, the operations manager, and the event coordinator. In a sense, risk management can also be considered a responsibility of coaches and officiating crews; to a certain extent each of the aforementioned are responsible in some way for the safety of the players. And if a game gets out of hand, players are much more likely to be injured.

In the context of sport and the venues in which it takes place, risk refers to the potential for damage to property, equipment, the venue's business, or people—both during an event and on non-event days (Masteralexis et al., 2012). Two themes run through all discussions about how to handle this critical area: communication and training. In other words, the risk management policy created by the event manager and other planners must be communicated to everyone who will be employed (full- or part-time) by the facility.

To manage risk effectively, you must do the following:

1. Identify
2. Assess
3. Repair
4. Avoid
5. Insure
6. Communicate
7. Train
8. Reidentify and reassess

An attitude of safety must pervade the management suite at the facility, and facility design should also reflect a concern for risk management. If management identifies design flaws that increase risk, they must be resolved or minimized as much as possible (Robinson, 2010). If the venue makes use of volunteers during events, they need training in risk management. In fact, this type of training is extremely valuable for sport management students who intern at a sport facility; more generally, the nuts and bolts of facility management form a great skill set to add to your toolbox before you graduate. Proper training also helps prevent mistakes that can result in expensive lawsuits.

Despite all precautions, it is simply a fact that a stadium or arena seating thousands of people will be the scene of accidents. Therefore, even before construction is completed, the facility and its parking areas should be covered by an insurance policy written with the intended use of the building in mind. It is also a good idea to consider insurance that covers certain types of business loss. For example, when hosting a major outdoor event, it might be worth the cost to insure the event against cancellation due to a catastrophic storm (Masteralexis et al., 2012).

Every building should also be thoroughly mapped to determine potential problem areas for spectators, athletes, and employees. For example, most stadiums and arenas include a large number of stairs, and it is critical to keep them clear and clean. A spilled beer on a staircase in the upstairs level needs to be quickly identified and mopped. More generally, good risk management requires supervisors to be vigilant and ushers and vendors to be well trained. Each area and each activity should be thoroughly examined by someone trained in managing risk. Managers at every MLB stadium, for instance, are aware of the danger posed to fans by foul balls, and those in charge of every National Hockey League arena know the risk to fans when a fast-moving puck sails over the boards. To reduce such risks, screens or fencing should be placed in critical areas to protect the fans who face the greatest risk of being hit. Other ways to inform fans of these dangers include warning signs, cautionary language on tickets, and public address announcements, all of which can help create a safer environment that benefits everyone involved (Puhalla, Krans, & Goatley, 2010).

Crowd Control

Crowd control begins with building design. The Colosseum, for example, was built with a large number of entrances and exits—an approach that can be both a negative and a positive. At the end of a sporting event, the number of exits directly affects the speed at which your building empties; on the other hand, a large number of entrances can be a security problem, a staffing problem, and a ticket-taking problem. Certain questions arise: On off-days, can you secure the building's entrances? And when you do host events, can you be certain that only those with proper credentials or tickets enter the facility? Other considerations arise inside the facility. Wide concourses enable easy access to seats, bathrooms, and concession areas. In contrast, poorly lit bathrooms, bad plumbing, and a too-small number of entrances to seating areas create crowd management nightmares.

Signage can be a big help in handling crowd control. Entrances and exits must be clearly marked, restrooms and first-aid stations clearly identified, and signs pointing out the facility's various seat locations easily spotted. The building should also include maps of the entire facility to enable visitors to find their seats, locate concessions, and find the nearest exit or first-aid station.

 Ninety-five percent of our customers will take up 5 percent of your time. Five percent of our customers will take up ninety-five percent of your time. It is our challenge to make the 5 percenters happy. The other ninety-five percent are easy.

Barry Geisler, general manager of the Patriot Center at George Mason University

Effective crowd control also requires good communication and training. The facility's full-time staff will be familiar with the building and current standard operating procedures, and it is very important to instruct part-time employees and volunteers in crowd control as well. Problems can be prevented by conducting a pregame briefing for all food vendors and ushers; the meeting should outline the size of the anticipated crowd, highlight management concerns about this particular event, and update experienced workers with any new information relevant to the event. Ushers, in particular, should know the locations of bathrooms and first-aid stations and be familiar with the facility's first-aid policy. All employees should know how to summon security if a problem arises.

Some crowd control issues at sport events can be anticipated. For example, security concerns may arise when two longtime rivals play for first place at the end of the season, since rival fans will be sitting close to each other. Separating the two groups is a good idea, but sometimes this can't be done due to space issues or external ticket brokers. At arenas and stadiums where alcohol is served, fans sometimes drink too much, and night games usually bring more alcohol-related problems than day games. In addition, sport sometimes causes emotions to run high, and alcohol can fuel the fire. Effective risk and crowd management strategy in this area includes limiting the number of drinks one can buy and closing the tap after a certain point in the contest; for example, at MLB games, no beer is served after the 7th inning (Mulrooney & Styles, 2005). The facility should also have an ejection policy for unruly fans, and it must be communicated to the staff, who must also know how to implement it.

ORGANIZATIONS FOR SPORT EVENT AND VENUE MANAGERS

http://aausports.org	Amateur Athletic Union
www.essma.eu	European Stadium & Safety Management Association
http://fsoa.org.uk	Football Safety Officers Association
www.iaks.info	International Association for Sports and Leisure Facilities
www.iavm.org	International Association of Venue Managers
www.ifma.com	International Facility Management Association
www.olympic.org	International Olympic Committee
www.ises.com	International Special Events Society
www.nacda.com	National Association of Collegiate Directors of Athletics
www.naia.org	National Association of Intercollegiate Athletics
www.ncaa.org	National Collegiate Athletic Association
www.nfhs.org	National Federation of State High School Associations
www.njcaa.org	National Junior College Athletic Association
www.rlgsoa.co.uk	Rugby League Ground Safety Officers Association

The Maracanã

One of the most famous sport venues in the world is located in downtown Rio de Janeiro. The Maracanã, as it is called by locals, was built more than 60 years ago to celebrate Brazilian ingenuity and to host the 1950 World Cup. Guidebooks list this facility as the most popular building in South America and the second-most visited tourist site, trailing only the Christ the Redeemer statue overlooking Rio.

In the championship game of that 1950 World Cup, the largest group of spectators in the history of team sport saw the home team upset by Uruguay. Paid attendance was listed at 175,000, but there were reports of 199,000 or even 205,000 fans, and the FIFA president said that he was sure there were 220,000 people in the Maracanã on that fateful day in Brazilian soccer history.

The official name for this iconic venue, Estádio Jornalista Mário Filho, honors the man viewed by many as the greatest Brazilian sport journalist. Construction of the stadium was begun in 1948, and even though the World Cup was played there in 1950, the venue was not completed until 1960. The grounds are also home to a track-and-field facility seating 5,000 spectators, a large indoor arena, and an Olympic swimming and diving facility.

The Maracanã's rich history also includes other classic soccer matches, such as Brazil versus Paraguay in 1969 and Brazil versus Colombia in 1977. It was the scene of Pelé's first

and thousandth goals, and fans there have also been thrilled by the play of other greats, including Garrincha, Romário, Ronaldo, and Zico. When Garrincha died, his remains were brought to the hallowed grounds of the Maracanã, where thousands of Brazilians could pay their respects to their *fútbol* star. The four local club teams in Rio—Vasco da Gama, Botafogo, Flamengo, and Fluminense—still play many of their regular season games at the stadium.

The venue also hosts events other than soccer matches. In 1980, Pope John Paul II celebrated Mass at the stadium. Concerts have been staged there by iconic musicians, including Madonna, Paul McCartney, Frank Sinatra, and Tina Turner. The 2007 Pan American Games used the Maracanã grounds to host its opening and closing ceremonies, as well as soccer, water polo, and volleyball contests.

The stadium and other athletic facilities on the grounds are managed by the Superintendency of Sports of Rio de Janeiro State. It employs more than 1,300 people, and its schedule is set to remain busy in the coming years. The Maracanã was selected by FIFA as the home for the championship game of the 2014 World Cup. It will also be used for the 2016 Summer Olympics, the 2013 FIFA Confederations Cup, the 2015 Copa América, and the 2016 Paralympic Games. In order to prepare for these high-profile events, the stadium has been given an expensive upgrade that includes a new sound system, new lights, and other modern conveniences. By 2016, the Maracanã will be the sixth venue to host both a World Cup and an Olympics.

PA Photos

When staff are being trained in this area, they should also be trained in customer service. Indeed, crowd control and customer service go hand in hand. You want every customer to enjoy the event, to be impressed with the venue, to feel comfortable there, and to want to return. One unruly patron, however, can make life miserable for those sitting nearby.

The Short of It

- Coordination between all of the major venue departments helps ensure great events for fans and athletes.
- Building design plays an important role in planning for events.
- Volunteers and temporary workers must be trained properly by facility and event managers.
- Iconic facilities such as the Maracanã become living museums to sport around the world.

CHAPTER 7

Sport Law

Junial Enterprises—Fotolia

In this chapter, you will learn the following:

✓ Where laws come from
✓ How the concept of negligence affects sport managers
✓ The elements of a contract
✓ Important federal legislation that affects the sport industry

> Baseball is almost the only orderly thing in a very unorderly world. If you get three strikes, even the best lawyer in the world can't get you off.
>
> **Bill Veeck**, former owner of the Chicago White Sox

Ed O'Bannon, a former UCLA basketball player, was playing a video game one day when a sport law question popped into his head. The image he saw on the screen looked like him. The number was the one O'Bannon had worn at UCLA, and the player was left-handed and built like O'Bannon. His question was simple: Why am I not compensated for the use of my likeness in this video game? He was many years out of UCLA; he had played professionally in the National Basketball Association and in Europe, and NCAA eligibility was no longer a concern. So why didn't the company selling the video game pay rights fees to the identifiable players in the game? Should UCLA, and other schools, reap all of the benefits of licensing deals? Did all players who signed waivers in college necessarily believe they were signing away publicity rights for the rest of their lives? Would that really be fair?

O'Bannon was joined by other former college athletes who shared his questions; together, they filed an antitrust lawsuit in federal court naming EA Sports, the National Collegiate Athletic Association (NCAA), and the Collegiate Licensing Company as defendants. The plaintiffs included Naismith Memorial Basketball Hall of Fame members Bill Russell and Oscar Robertson. As of this writing, the judge has ruled on several motions, most of which have benefitted the plaintiffs, but the verdict is yet to come.

O'Bannon's lawsuit involves many institutions intimately involved in the sport industry, and the case illustrates the fact that sport management, like all areas of our lives, sometimes requires an understanding of basic legal principles. In fact, the practice and study of law as it relates to sport has become a specialized area. Many law firms have established sport-related practices, and most sport organizations hire a general counsel or at least put an attorney on retainer for frequent legal advice. This chapter covers some basic concepts to help you better understand how laws are made, what a contract is, what a tort is, how to define negligence, and how certain federal laws have affected the world of sport. It also briefly discusses intellectual property—a key area for sport managers (and player agents) in the 21st century, since it involves such issues as sporting goods manufacturers' patent rights, trademark protection for team names and logos, and broadcast rights.

The U.S. Legal System

When America's founding fathers sat down to form a government—after they had taken the momentous step of declaring independence from England and fighting a war to indicate that they were serious—they clearly were not interested in bestowing power on one branch of the new government or on one person within that government. Instead, they wanted a government that could accomplish the people's business without centralizing power and tyrannizing the public. Their solution was to create a constitution equipped with many checks and balances to prevent any branch from duplicating the role of the English king under whom they had served before declaring their independence. Specifically, Madison, Jefferson, Franklin, and the rest of the founders established three branches of government—a legislature (the U.S. Congress) to enact laws, an executive (the president) to execute those laws, and a judiciary to interpret the laws and rule on the constitutionality of the executive branch's actions.

To further dilute the power of the legislature, the founders divided it into two groups called the Senate and the House of Representatives. In the Senate, two members are elected by each state, regardless of a state's population size; in the House, members are elected by voters in congressional districts throughout each state, and the number of representatives from any given state depends on the size of its population. Legislation proposed by one body must also be approved by the other before it reaches the president to be signed into **law**. If the president vetoes it instead, Congress can override the veto by means of a two-thirds vote in each of the two legislative bodies. When Congress creates a new law, it can also empower a government agency to create regulations for enforcing the law; the Federal Communications Commission, for example, was created to manage the television, radio, and telephone industries. This chapter discusses two examples of legislation greatly affecting the sport industry: Title IX of the Education Amendments of 1972 and the Americans With Disabilities Act of 1990. (The Sports Broadcasting Act of 1961, discussed in chapter 9, was also groundbreaking for the sport business.)

> **law**—Regulation established by a state, local, or federal government, or a decision passed down by a court of law, that acts as a principle of behavior for individuals or legal entities.

The U.S. Constitution established the Supreme Court as the highest court in the land. The Supreme Court has the power to review decisions made by the lower federal courts as well as decisions made by each state's highest court. The "Supremes" can also review actions taken by the other two branches of government. Decisions made by the Supreme Court have a similar effect on behavior as legislation. For example, in *Federal Baseball Club v. National League* (1922), the Supreme Court granted an antitrust exemption to professional baseball.

As a further check on the power of the federal government, each state was given the power to form its own legislative, executive, and judicial branches. Each of the 50 states has its own constitution, and a state legislature has the power to pass laws that govern the behavior of those who live and work in that state. Each state also elects a governor who wields executive power, and the state judiciary has the ability to say what the law is in that state and to rule on the constitutionality of actions taken by the other two branches.

U.S. Tort Law

Like many areas in the law of the United States, tort law can be traced back to English common law. The writ of trespass was developed by local judges empowered by kings to compensate victims of assault and battery by force of arms, victims of armed robbery, and those whose land was unlawfully occupied. Part of the rationale for establishing this ability to recover was to preserve the peace. The noble class was concerned that victims would take the law into their own hands to recover property or inflict retribution for injuries suffered at the hands of alleged "trespassers" (Kionka, 2005). Today, state courts attempt to use the common law to deter antisocial behavior, compensate victims for wrongful acts, provide effective rules that can be administered fairly, and give victims the opportunity to achieve some form of public justice in a court of law.

tort—Wrongful act, which does not involve contract law, where there has been an injury. With a specific act, coupled with a specific injury, the law permits the injured party to be compensated.

A **tort** is a "civil wrong, wherein one person's conduct causes a compensable injury to the person, property, or recognized interest of another, in violation of a duty imposed by law" (Kionka, 2005, p. 4). Modern torts can be classified as intentional, unintentional (negligence), and strict liability. Most tort cases are brought under a theory of negligence. Here are a few examples from the world of sport:

- Football coach—failure to instruct the team in how to properly tackle in order to reduce the chance of neck or head injury
- Recreation league baseball coach—failure to warn the team about the hazards of sliding into a base headfirst
- Middle school basketball coach—failure to properly condition the athletes
- Elementary school gym teacher—failure to properly supervise the class
- College ice hockey coach—failure to provide athletes with proper headgear
- School district—failure to provide education or certification programs for all coaches involved in a contact sport
- Minor league baseball team—failure to provide adequate backstop and fencing behind home plate for foul balls and wild pitches

Intentional torts typically fall into one of the following categories: assault and battery, false imprisonment, intentional infliction of emotional distress, defamation (libel or slander), invasion of privacy, destruction of property, or willful conversion of property. One prominent example can be found in a lawsuit filed by former University of Alabama coach Mike Price against *Sports Illustrated* and its publisher, Time, Inc. *Sports Illustrated* published a story characterizing the newly hired coach's behavior at a golf tournament in Pensacola. Price objected to much of the story and filed a US$20 million defamation lawsuit in 2003, and the two parties settled the matter for an undisclosed amount in 2005 (Associated Press, 2005).

The third type of tort, strict liability, protects consumers against defective products, such as a poorly made football helmet or the inferior manufacture of a basketball goal. When injury results from proper use of such a product, the manufacturer can be held "strictly liable" for all damages caused by provable defects.

As these examples suggest, sport managers should include tort law, and negligence in particular, in any employee training program. Athletic directors, coaches, and sport facility managers who take the time to learn up-to-date procedures, new safety methods, and common-sense knowledge passed on by other administrators put themselves in the best position both to prevent accidents and to demonstrate to a judge that they exercised reasonable care to ensure the safety of those in their charge.

Negligence actions brought by plaintiffs in tort claims include four major elements (Kionka, 2005):

- A *duty* or standard of care was owed to the plaintiff.
- That duty or standard of care was *breached*.
- There was an *injury*, damage, or loss.
- A *connection* can be made to the injury, loss, or damage caused by the breach of duty.

Since tort law is governed by state law, the court's concern is the standard of behavior in the state where the alleged tort occurred. In cases involving the sporting world, sport managers are held to the standard of care that would be provided by a reasonable sport manager in a particular locale. In other words, what course of action would be taken by someone with the typical knowledge, experience, and perception that accompanies his or her particular position in that part of the country?

When a court finds that a duty of care has been violated by a defendant, the judge can award damages to the party winning the lawsuit (i.e., the plaintiff). Those damages may involve compensation for the wrongful act or failure to act. If the court finds that the plaintiff was wronged but did not prove the suffering of quantifiable harm, then nominal damages may be awarded. The court is also permitted to award punitive damages, above and beyond compensatory damages, when the conduct of the defendant or defendants is so egregious that it is deemed necessary to send a clear signal to punish the behavior and deter others from engaging in it. When calculating damages, the court looks at economic loss (e.g., medical bills), mental pain and suffering, physical pain suffered, physical impairment or disfigurement resulting from the injury, and even consequential damages suffered by a spouse or child (Kionka, 2005).

One form of negligence complaint that is extremely important to sport managers involves facility law. For example, athletic directors at the high school and college levels manage arenas, stadiums, and fields. Professional sport teams and tours (e.g., NASCAR) manage and own large and expensive facilities. At various levels—high school, college, and professional—managers rely on revenue received from members of the ticket-buying public who attend games, events, and exhibitions. In turn, when managers of these facilities open their property to customers, they have a duty to provide a safe environment. Paying customers are classified as invitees, and this designation establishes some responsibility on the part of the facility manager to keep stairways safe and well lit, to provide security that prevents and controls unruly behavior on the part of other fans, and to properly maintain the facility so that fans can watch the event in relative comfort.

Managers of certain venues face particular obligations. For example, sport managers who own or operate a baseball facility must also provide reasonable protection for fans who could be hit by foul balls, particularly in the area behind home plate. Similarly, sport managers in ice hockey must provide reasonable protection against hockey pucks that leave the playing area (Sharp, Moorman, & Claussen, 2010).

More generally, facility owners and managers must inspect their premises for potential safety hazards. They must repair those areas if they are accessible to the public during a game or used by vendors or employees during working hours. They must also warn all parties who might happen upon the danger (Champion, 2004).

U.S. Contract Law

Sport managers tend to be involved with many contracts during their tenure in the business—contracts for employment, contracts with vendors, game contracts with other teams, contracts with sponsors, and player contracts. All of these necessitate at least a passing knowledge of contract law. Of course, if you have a lawyer on staff or a law firm on retainer, the safest option is to have a professional review all contracts before you sign them. The terms of any contract should be preserved in writing. Oral contracts are enforceable, but sport managers can save themselves trouble, time, and attorney fees if they get each agreement in writing.

Contract law is governed by the relevant state legislature and the common law as defined by the state judiciary. There is also a code of conduct in business transactions called the Uniform Commercial Code or UCC (2011), which is the product of many years of work between the American Law Institute, the American Bar Association, and the National Conference of Commissioners on Uniform State Laws. The UCC is very helpful when looking for guidelines related to contract law and commercial transactions. The UCC has been adopted in some form in all 50 states and the District of Columbia. This set of guidelines has been a big help in standardizing commercial transactions that involve entities in multiple states; it has been called one of the most important developments in American law (American Law Institute, n.d.).

A **contract** is a promise or set of promises between two or more parties or individuals that involves either required action or a requirement that one of the parties refrain from doing something. A contract contains four major elements—an offer, an acceptance, consideration, and performance (Rohwer & Skrocki, 2010). An offer is a promise conditioned either upon some future act by a party or parties to that promise or upon one of the parties refraining from some act in the future (Byrne, 2005). Here is an example from the world of sport. Imagine that you are the

contract—Agreement between two or more parties that is enforceable by law.

athletic director at the local high school. A hot dog vendor calls you up and says, "I will supply you with 200 hot dogs for your football game on Saturday if you pay me 25¢ per hot dog." This vendor has made a promise to sell you a certain number of items at a suggested price.

This *offer* is not yet an enforceable contract. In order to reach that point, an *acceptance* must follow; that is, the party to whom the offer was made must manifest some measure of assent to the terms of the offer (Byrne, 2005). If you immediately tell the vendor that you think the offer is fair and you want the hot dogs, then a contract has been created. In other words, you have agreed to an exchange of value, in which you as the athletic director are exchanging an agreed-upon amount of money for the vendor's agreed-upon number of hot dogs. This exchange of value is the *consideration*, which is necessary to form a binding agreement (Byrne).

If, however, you tell the vendor that you do want the 200 hot dogs but will pay only 20¢ each, rather than 25¢, then you have made a *counteroffer*, and the vendor must now decide whether to accept your counteroffer. In both of these examples, you as the athletic director made a promise. In the first example, you promised to buy the hot dogs for 25¢ each and to accept delivery of those hot dogs at an as-yet unspecified time and place. Your counteroffer is also a promise but with the caveat that you will pay the vendor only 20¢ per hot dog. In making this counteroffer, you rejected the first offer; thus a contract will be formed only if the vendor accepts these new terms.

There is another important requirement of a legally enforceable contract. Both parties to the promise must have the *capacity* to contract. If, for instance, the hot dog vendor negotiated with the football team's 15-year-old quarterback, the court

Management Insight

Have you ever wondered why so many college football games are televised? It may seem that every network carries at least one game on Saturdays in the fall and that the sports networks carry three or four. This phenomenon resulted directly from a U.S. Supreme Court case decided in the 1980s. Prior to this decision, the NCAA decided which games were televised, and it severely limited the appearances of many teams but also divided the revenue on a fairly equal basis among all Division I schools that did appear on television. However, because an NCAA committee had determined that television adversely affected attendance across the country, the organization established a policy that permitted only one game to be televised in each television market. In this model, schools and conferences did not negotiate with the television networks; the NCAA itself did the talking (Roberts & Weiler, 2004).

All of this changed with the Supreme Court's decision in *NCAA v. Board of Regents of the University of Oklahoma* (1984). The Court ruled that the NCAA's practice constituted a restraint of trade and that it could no longer limit TV games in each market. As a result, it could no longer prevent a school like Notre Dame from televising *all* of its games! The floodgates had been opened.

would not be inclined to enforce the contract since it would have been made with a minor (i.e., someone under the age of 18). The court might also ask why the vendor would think that a minor had the authority to negotiate on behalf of the school. Lack of capacity can also occur when one of the parties is mentally or emotionally challenged or is under duress when the offer or acceptance is communicated (Rohwer & Skrocki, 2010).

More generally, when interpreting a contract, courts look to the ordinary meaning of the language in the contract. They also examine the entire contract in order to determine the contextualized meaning of a particular section being contested.

When one party to a contract engages in wrongful conduct, that party has committed a breach of contract. In the hot dog example, a breach of contract would occur if the vendor did not supply hot dogs, supplied only half of the contracted number of hot dogs, or supplied hot dogs that were not sanitary. It would also occur if the athletic director did not pay the vendor the agreed-upon price for the hot dogs. In any of these examples, one of the two parties to the contract would have failed to perform an important condition of the contract, and it is only through *performance* of the promises laid out in the contract, by both parties to the contract, that the terms of the deal are fulfilled.

In the case of a breach, three basic remedies can be sought in a court of law: damages, restitution, and specific performance. If the breach was not significant (if, say, the vendor provides 196 hot dogs instead of 200), the court may award nominal damages. If, on the other hand, the breach results in significant injury, the court may award large compensatory damages. Punitive damages, which are sometimes awarded in tort cases, are generally not awarded in breach-of-contract judgments. Restitution is a remedy designed to prevent unjust enrichment on the part of one of the parties to a contract. For example, if the athletic director paid the vendor for the hot dogs, then found out that the hot dogs were unsanitary, the judge could require the vendor to return the money paid for the hot dogs (restitution) and also award compensation for the athletic director's inability to offer hot dogs for sale at that football game.

Specific performance is usually awarded to a plaintiff in cases where monetary damages would not provide an adequate remedy. Examples include contracts for the transfer of land, contracts where the damages are difficult to estimate or ascertain, contracts involving goods that are of a sentimental or aesthetic value, and cases where the defendant is unable to compensate the plaintiff due to a lack of sufficient assets. Specific performance cases may arise when a sport fan contracts for "one of a kind" memorabilia (e.g., autographed baseballs, jerseys, or game-worn uniforms). For example, a basketball jersey bearing Michael Jordan's number is not the same as a jersey worn and signed by Michael Jordan. A collector who did not receive the jersey of the type promised does not want his or her money back. The collector wants an authentic Michael Jordan jersey, worn by the superstar, and signed by him. In this case, forcing the seller to return the purchase price does not compensate the buyer as effectively as demanding specific performance (providing the buyer with a jersey like the one promised).

Title IX

When Richard Nixon signed the Education Amendments of 1972 into law, he and many others, both in and out of Congress, had no idea how dramatically it would affect women's athletics in the United States. The law has led to staggering increases in girls' participation in high school sport, women's participation in intercollegiate athletics, and the number of women's teams on college campuses all over the United States. A year before the enactment of Title IX, there were 300,000 female high school athletes; in 2002, there were 2.7 million (Roberts & Weiler, 2004).

Title IX provides that no person shall, on the basis of sex, be excluded from participation in, be denied the benefits of, or be discriminated against in any education program that receives federal financial assistance (Education Amendments of 1972). The legislation is enforced by the U.S. Department of Education (ED), which, along with its Office of Civil Rights (OCR), has promulgated regulations that add teeth to the law enacted by Congress. Under Title IX regulations, individuals and organizations can file claims with the OCR, which can also investigate on its own.

Title IX requires each athletic department at the high school or college level to provide male and female teams with substantially equal accommodations in the form of equipment, supplies, locker rooms, practice and game facilities, medical and training facilities, and housing and dining facilities. Schools must also provide comparable staffing—coaches, tutors, trainers, and medical personnel. In addition, college programs are examined to determine the relative financial aid expenditures for each group. The regulations also require that equal opportunity be provided for teams of both sexes in the scheduling of games, practices, and away tournament participation (Hogshead-Makat & Zimbalist, 2007).

A three-pronged test is used to evaluate whether an athletic department has met the interests of the underrepresented group. This test was the product of a policy guideline issued by ED's Office of Civil Rights called the Clarification of Intercollegiate Athletics Policy Guidance: The Three-Part Test (Hogshead-Makat & Zimbalist, 2007). The first prong compares the ratio of male and female students enrolled with the ratio of male and female students participating in athletics. The second prong examines whether the school has a history of complying with Title IX or a trend of improving opportunities for the underrepresented group over a period of time.

The triumph can't be had without the struggle. And I know what struggle is. I have spent a lifetime trying to share what it has meant to be a woman first in the world of sports so that other young women have a chance to reach their dreams.

Wilma Rudolph, Olympic gold medalist

The third prong examines whether the athletic department has met the interests and abilities of its underrepresented group through its programs.

The Supreme Court has also provided an avenue for individuals to sue under Title IX. Specifically, the court's decision in *Franklin v. Gwinnett County Public Schools* (1992) permits plaintiffs to sue for compensatory and punitive damages and injunctive relief.

ADA

The Americans With Disabilities Act of 1990 (ADA) was passed by Congress to prevent discrimination against people with a disability who attempt to use public accommodations or public services. The act provides protection to athletes and spectators with a disability in many sport settings. For example, buildings must provide wheelchair access and appropriate viewing areas if they are used for public sporting events. In addition, an athlete who proves that he or she has a disability cannot be prevented from participating in an event unless that participation would fundamentally alter the event or involve an unreasonable expense on the part of the event's sponsor or the facility's owner or operator.

One of the more prominent ADA court cases involved professional golfer Casey Martin's attempt to use a golf cart during a PGA event due to a circulatory problem in one leg that made it impossible for him to walk the 18 holes of the tournament each day. The Supreme Court ruled that the location of the tournament was a public place (thus ADA applied) and that Martin's use of the golf cart would not substantially alter the rules of golf or give him an unreasonable advantage over other golfers in the tournament (*PGA Tour, Inc. v. Martin*, 2001).

In response to the ADA, sport managers must provide access to their facilities for spectators with a disability, be conscious of this duty when building new athletic facilities, and provide people with disabilities with access to recreational and athletic programs. Academic accommodations must also be made for athletes with demonstrated disabilities in the classroom or in standardized testing. NCAA academic regulations spell out applicable guidelines for coaches, athletes, and athletic departments. Public and private high schools must also comply with ADA guidelines and court decisions supporting such accommodations, particularly in the area of age eligibility rules. Schools must also make reasonable accommodations regarding a student's known academic disabilities (Wong, 2010).

Intellectual Property

Intellectual property is a "commercially valuable product of the human intellect, in concrete or abstract form, such as a copyrightable work, a protectable trademark or a patentable invention, or a category of intangible rights protecting commercially valuable products of the human intellect" (Garner, 2009, p. 881). This area of law has grown in importance with the explosion of revenue opportunities in television and radio rights, Internet rights, merchandising, and new designs of sport products such as running shoes, football helmets, and sport drinks.

For example, a unique sport drink recipe, a safer kind of football helmet, and a lighter type of basketball shoe can all be protected under patent law, which is a busy part of the intellectual property domain. Federal patent law governs the process by which inventors secure patents, which give the inventor exclusive rights for 20 years to exploit the invention in the marketplace.

Media rights—television, radio, or Internet—related to a sporting contest are owned by the home team. In many conferences and leagues, teams bundle their rights to negotiate a collective deal with a network or networks to enhance the value of the package to the group as a whole. The NFL commissioner, for example, negotiates with television networks on behalf of the entire league. Similarly, the commissioner of the Atlantic Coast Conference negotiates on behalf of member schools for television rights to football and men's basketball. If a television network buys those rights, it can prevent others from televising anything other than highlights or news clips of games that fall under the contractual agreement.

A trademark, for the sake of this discussion, is a unique symbol used by a sport organization to identify its team, league, or other group or business. In the United States, the Lanham (Trademark) Act (1946) governs this area of law. Under that legislation, a team can register its mark and prevent others from using it or a mark that is overly similar to it. The act gives both college and professional sport teams the right to trademark their name and logo. Even unique phrases can be trademarked, as the NCAA has done with the "Final Four" and "March Madness." These trademark rights have brought tremendous licensing revenue to teams and conferences; indeed, the market registers in the tens of billions of U.S. dollars for licensed and trademarked products related to the National Football League (NFL), Major League Baseball (MLB), the National Hockey League (NHL), NASCAR, Formula One, the National Basketball Association (NBA), and collegiate athletics.

Another branch of intellectual property is the right of publicity based in state law. This right to profit from one's likeness grew out of right-to-privacy protections; it grants athletes the ability to protect and market their name, image, and likeness. This property right has netted many athletes very large endorsement deals from advertisers around the world (Roberts & Weiler, 2004). The players unions for the NHL, MLB, the NBA, and the NFL also bundle these individual publicity rights into large deals for the benefit of their members. Michael Jordan, Peyton Manning, and LeBron James have all made more money through endorsement deals than they have received from the professional teams paying them to play their respective sports. Under NCAA rules, athletes are not permitted to profit from their image or likeness. However, once they are no longer playing for their school, can that school continue to profit from the athlete's likeness or image? This is the crux of the O'Bannon court case discussed at the beginning of this chapter.

Dispute Resolution—Negotiation, Mediation, Arbitration, and Litigation

Like all businesses, sport businesses have their share of disputes. Some can be resolved quickly, whereas others take years to play out in court. Major disagreements are resolved by means of four main mechanisms: negotiation, mediation, arbitration, and (the final option) litigation. Each method has its strengths and weaknesses, but clearly the most contentious and expensive method of resolving a business argument is to slug it out in a court of law. The other three methods are part of an approach known as alternative dispute resolution (ADR), and a sport manager who can use them to resolve disputes without going to court will save the organization both time and money.

Negotiation

This method of resolving disputes is no more difficult than making a phone call or sending a letter offering to sit down and discuss the issues. Almost every dispute can be solved in this manner if the parties are willing to engage in a frank discussion. Negotiation takes many forms. It might involve a boss sitting down with an employee to work out a more acceptable arrangement or the owner of a sport franchise scheduling a meeting with the owner of the construction company building a new stadium.

The advantage here is that the parties themselves are sitting across from each other and talking about the issues. No legal fees are paid, no depositions are taken, and no third parties are brought in (a tactic that sometimes escalates the tension). Thus this method is the preferred first step. Negotiation can always give way to the other three steps, but a well thought out negotiation, a sincere desire to resolve a problem, and a meeting of all parties involved in the dispute might just save the individuals or companies on both sides considerable money that is better used in running their respective organizations.

Mediation

When negotiation fails, or the parties reach a stalemate, some business executives find it worth trying to jump-start negotiation and stave off litigation by hiring a third-party facilitator called a mediator. Many contracts call for mediation in the event of a dispute, and some even point the parties to a particular mediator or mediation firm.

Mediators interview both parties and build a plan to bring closure to the disagreement. The interviews help the mediator identify pressure points and emotional issues affecting the dispute. The mediator may either bring the parties together in order to propose options or send each party an array of possible solutions before meeting as a group. A skilled mediator uses good psychology and communication skills to bring the parties to the conference table to hash out an acceptable end to the dispute. Mediators who have the skill of reading personalities and issues can sense how close or far apart the parties are.

DeMaurice Smith, Executive Director of the NFLPA

DeMaurice Smith was elected to serve as executive director of the National Football League Players Association (NFLPA) in March 2009. He replaced Gene Upshaw, whose death in 2008 after 25 years in the position left a vacuum of leadership in the union. Smith was one of four candidates vying for the position; he won unanimously on the first ballot.

Born and raised in the Washington, D.C., area, Smith attended Cedarville University in Ohio, where he was a member of the track-and-field team for four years and became an All-American during his senior year. He then earned a law degree from the University of Virginia in 1989.

Smith brought an impressive resume to his new post. A member of the D.C. and Maryland bar associations, he has extensive experience in both private and public law practice. He was an assistant U.S. attorney for almost 10 years and served as counsel to the assistant attorney general. While working in private practice as a partner for the D.C. firm Patton Boggs, Smith worked in white-collar criminal defense and tort liability. He has represented many Fortune 500 companies. He has also taught trial advocacy at the law schools of American University, George Washington University, and the University of Virginia.

Smith took over the NFLPA at a crucial point in its relationship with the National Football League. Owners had voted to opt out of the most recent collective bargaining agreement and locked the players out of NFL facilities. Fans were greatly concerned that the impasse would affect the regular season, but the parties eventually reached an agreement to avert the loss of regular season games. Two tough issues lingered—testing to deter the use of human growth hormone by players and a proposed increase in the regular season from 16 to 18 games—but these issues did not affect the start of the season. As Gene Upshaw did, Smith also faces continuing challenges from retired players who want to be included in decisions about revenue, pension benefits, and health insurance.

You can learn more about the NFL, the NFLPA, and union–management relations in general at the following websites:

www.nfl.com	National Football League
www.nflplayers.com	National Football League Players Association
www.nlrb.gov	National Labor Relations Board
www.dol.gov	U.S. Department of Labor

Mediation is a paid service, but the cost pales in comparison with the expenses involved in a lawsuit (e.g., attorney fees, transportation costs, copying fees, telephone calls, research). A skilled mediator also has the advantage of being an outsider. Sometimes a person with fresh eyes can see a solution that the two parties had not even thought about. A third party also can take some of the emotional baggage out of the room in order to help the parties look at the problem in a more intellectual way.

One downside shared by both mediation and negotiation is that neither guarantees a resolution. A mediator cannot force the parties to agree, and negotiations may go on and on and on . . .

Arbitration

The Federal Arbitration Act of 1925 was passed by Congress to facilitate the relationship between employees and management in an increasingly industrial and unionized United States. Today, 90 percent of labor–management contracts call for an arbitrator to resolve disputes between the parties, and arbitration is viewed as an acceptable mode of resolving disputes in all of the collective bargaining agreements in current professional sport in the United States (e.g., in the NHL, the NBA, the NFL, MLB, and the related unions). The benefits are numerous: An arbitrator is perceived as a neutral party, his or her decision is enforceable in a court of law, the process is flexible, most arbitrators assigned to labor contracts have expertise in that area, the arbitration process is efficient and final, the process is confidential, and the parties usually come out of it feeling much less antagonism toward each other than if they were walking out of a courtroom after the culmination of a lawsuit (Szalai, 2007).

ALTERNATIVE DISPUTE RESOLUTION

Here are some resources for learning more about alternative dispute resolution. Each of these websites provides information about mediation or arbitration and offers resources for those who want to handle disputes out of court.

www.adr.org	American Arbitration Association
www.aaauonline.org	American Arbitration Association University
www.campus-adr.org	Campus Conflict Resolution Resources
www.tas-cas.org	Court of Arbitration for Sport
www.fmcs.gov	Federal Mediation and Conciliation Service
www.iamed.org	International Academy of Mediators
www.arbitration-icca.org	International Council for Commercial Arbitration
www.nafcm.org	National Association for Community Mediation
www.mediate.com	General informational site for arbitration and mediation

🌐 INTERNATIONAL APPLICATION

Court of Arbitration for Sport

The International Olympic Committee has created two entities that are now used to settle sport-related disputes through either arbitration or mediation. The International Council of Arbitration for Sport (ICAS) is the administrative and financing authority overseeing the Court of Arbitration for Sport (CAS). The CAS was the brain child of former IOC general secretary Juan Antonio Samaranch and Judge Kéba Mbaye of the International Court of Justice at The Hague (Reeb, 2006). Samaranch recognized that the growth of international sport had created a need for dispute resolution. Mbaye was already involved with international dispute resolution at The Hague, and the two men started a process that led to the establishment of the CAS in the summer of 1984. In the early 1990s, the ICAS was created to add a level of independence from the IOC and to protect the rights of the parties involved.

The ICAS is composed of twenty members selected by the International Olympic Committee, the Association of National Olympic Committees, and the International Sports Federations for the Summer and Winter Olympic Games. Four of the twenty must be selected with an eye toward representing the interests of athletes, and another four must be selected as independent members. ICAS members are high-level jurists who are appointed for a four-year term that can be renewed (Reeb, 2006). Each member of the ICAS must pledge his or her independence and take an oath of confidentiality. The most important function of the ICAS is to appoint the mediators and arbitrators who compose the CAS. The CAS, in turn, is made up of two divisions: the Ordinary Arbitration Division and the Appeals Arbitration Division. The ICAS selects at least 150 arbitrators, who must have legal training and a recognized competence in sport.

The CAS is charged with resolving disputes, resolving appeals of previous CAS panel decisions, and settling appeals from other disciplinary bodies or tribunals of groups (e.g., FIFA or UEFA) designated by its charter. The CAS also offers advisory opinions if asked to do so by the IOC, one of the International Sports Federations, a National Olympic Committee, an Organizing Committee for the Olympic Games, or one of certain other associations recognized by the IOC. The CAS can also be asked to mediate a dispute between two parties. In such cases, the mediator identifies the issues, facilitates a dialogue between the parties, and proposes a solution or several possible solutions. The mediation process is not binding on the parties; either party can terminate the mediation at will, and the process includes many safeguards to ensure confidentiality. The costs incurred for the mediation process or for arbitration must be borne by the parties involved, though in some cases the prevailing party may be reimbursed by its adversary.

The list of arbitrators and mediators contains many highly respected persons from around the globe. Americans on the list include former U.S. Secretary of State Henry Kissinger; Alan Rothenberg, a former executive for four NBA teams; Gary R. Roberts, dean and professor at the Indiana University Law School; David Askinas, CEO of USA Taekwondo; and Anita DeFrantz, who has been involved for many years with the U.S. Olympic Committee.

The majority of cases brought before the CAS involve doping issues. A typical doping case results from a positive test for a banned substance in a blood or urine sample collected from an athlete during or after an event. The International Sports Federation governing that particular sport then bans or suspends the athlete from competition, and the athlete's appeal is heard by the CAS due to an arbitration clause in the federation's bylaws. In many cases, the home country's sport federation is also a defendant in the proceeding because that sport federation had to honor the international ban and suspend the athlete as well. An athlete might challenge a doping ban on procedural grounds or offer evidence that explains the presence of the banned substance in his or her system.

Litigation

This method of resolving disputes is considered the option of last resort—and for good reason. For one thing, trying a case in open court is more contentious and more expensive than the various methods of alternative dispute resolution. Attorney fees escalate due to the preparation needed to get ready for a battle before a judge or jury. Tension between the parties also tends to rise as depositions are taken and witnesses are cross-examined. Indeed, many friendships have ended before a trial even begins. For these reasons, alternative dispute resolution—whether in the form of negotiation, mediation, or arbitration—is a better way to preserve an important relationship.

Even so, in some situations the finality imparted by a trial makes it the necessary method for resolving a dispute. Once a judge or jury rules, that ruling carries legal weight. Indeed, in some cases the mere threat of litigation brings the parties to the negotiating table.

The Short of It

- A contract involves an offer, an acceptance, and an agreed-upon exchange of value. The parties to the contract must have the legal capacity to make such promises.
- Negligence is an important concept for sport managers to understand. What would a reasonable sport manager do in the same situation?
- Sport managers should understand alternative methods for resolving disputes without going to court. Negotiation, mediation, and arbitration can save money for sport organizations.
- Trademarks, copyrights, and patents are important ways to protect intellectual property that can be marketed by sport businesses.

CHAPTER **8**

Sport Marketing

Photo courtesy of George Mason Athletics.

In this chapter, you will learn the following:

✓ The four Ps that make up the marketing mix
✓ What makes sport marketing unique
✓ The purpose and process of developing a marketing plan
✓ How marketers use knowledge of consumer behavior

> The aim of marketing is to know and understand the customer so well that the product or service fits him and sells itself.
>
> **Peter Drucker,**
> management consultant

Some 45 million women tune in weekly to watch a National Football League (NFL) game on television (Vega, 2010). More women watch the Super Bowl than the Academy Awards. The number of women engaged in fantasy football leagues has recently doubled, and women now account for 44 percent of NFL fans (Dosh, 2012; Gentilviso, 2010). Increased interest in the NFL among women has resulted in increased sales of NFL-related women's apparel, which have more than doubled in recent years (Lefton, 2010). One reason for the rising number of female NFL fans is the league's commitment of US$10 million to a marketing campaign geared toward women. Thus the NFL is both responding to women's demands and attempting to increase their demand for NFL-licensed products.

The apparel marketing campaign, which uses the tagline "NFL Women's Apparel, Fit For You," was initiated in 2010 to promote an array of NFL-licensed women's products, including apparel, Longaberger baskets, scented candles, nail polish, yoga mats, flip-flops, and garden accessories (Gentilviso, 2010; Lefton, 2010; Vega, 2010; Weprin, 2010). Hundreds of licensed companies produce these and other products that represent all teams and come in a wide range of styles and sizes. The products are sold online at the NFL's website and in major retail outlets (Weprin). The NFL has even piloted a store exclusively for women. Apparel remains a top choice with women, and it is perhaps no surprise that the jersey of Troy Polamalu, half of whose 875,000 Facebook fans are women, is the top seller among women (Rovell, 2011).

The NFL's efforts to capture active, family-oriented, female fans from 20 to 40 years old consists largely of television commercials, as well as several print advertisements. The print ads, with taglines such as "Who Says Football Isn't Pretty?" and "Finally. Love Your Team Without Looking Like You're On It," appear in magazines such as *Shape, InStyle, People,* and *Sports Illustrated* (Vega, 2010; Weprin, 2010). The league has also targeted the valued female market through a dedicated website at www.nfl.com/women (Dosh, 2012). Though the NFL trails Major League Baseball and Collegiate Licensing Company in licensed product sales, its effort to market to women has succeeded in improving not only the league's reach but also its revenue. Their growing female market also makes the already-attractive NFL even more appealing to potential advertisers and sponsors.

This campaign by the NFL illustrates clearly that strategic sport marketing is crucial to the business of sport. In fact, marketing is a central component of most sport enterprises. It can be a multifaceted undertaking, and it is critical to success. Speaking generally, **marketing** includes the activity of "selling or purchasing in a market" or the process of promoting, selling, and distributing a product or service; in the aggregate, marketing involves the functions implicated "in moving goods [or services] from producer to consumer" (*Merriam-Webster Unabridged Dictionary*, 2012). One professional organization for marketers, the American Marketing Association (2012), defines marketing as "the activity, set of institutions, and processes for creating, communicating, delivering, and exchanging offerings that have value for customers, clients, partners, and society at large." Within this broader field, of course, **sport marketing** applies basic marketing principles to the sport industry. Pitts and Stotlar (2002) have defined sport marketing as "the process of designing and implementing activities for the production, pricing, promotion, and distribution of a sport product to satisfy the needs or desires of consumers and to achieve the company's objectives" (p. 79). Shank (2005) has characterized sport marketing as "complex and dynamic" and noted that it involves applying marketing principles both to and through sport (p. 3).

> **marketing**—Activities, institutions, and processes for developing, communicating, distributing, and exchanging things that are valued by consumers.
>
> **sport marketing**—All activities designed to meet the needs and wants of sport consumers through exchange processes.
>
> **marketing mix**—Combination of four elements influencing marketing decisions: product, price, place, and promotion (the four Ps).
>
> **product**—Any commodity or service directed toward consumers.

The Marketing Mix

The **marketing mix** includes four elements that are central to the marketing process: product, price, place, and promotion. These elements are well established in the industry and are universally known as the four Ps.

Product

The **product** is any commodity or service that an organization directs toward consumers. Pitts and Stotlar (2002) have defined a sport product as "any good, service, person, place, or idea with tangible or intangible attributes that satisfy consumer sport, fitness, or recreation related needs and desires" (p. 180). As Mullin, Hardy, and Sutton (2000) have noted, the "sport product is inconsistent from consumption to consumption" (p. 117). In other words, in the sport industry, the product can take the form of goods, services, or even an event itself. For example, sporting goods include apparel, footwear, equipment, and licensed products related to all kinds of sport and fitness. Sport services might include, among many others, such diverse activities as event security, facility management, advertising, and player agent representation. The essential components affiliated with sport activities, goods, and services are considered to be the core sport products—whether it be a tangible good (e.g., a basketball), an intangible service (e.g., coaching), or an event (e.g., an NBA contest). Games and events are sport products that are made up of the competition itself, as well as related activities such as concessions, cheerleading, pep band music, and other entertainment. Sport marketers rarely control the core product; rather, they should focus on the many aspects and extensions of the core product, including the game experience. The core product, then, is just one part of an assemblage of products (Mullin et al.).

Licensed and branded products abound in sport. Branding serves as a way to differentiate products; at the same time, as a reflection of differentiation, branding is an end in itself. Brands can be identified in names, logos, images, trademarks, designs, and any other intellectual property. For example, Nike is a recognized brand, its "JUST DO IT" a recognized motto, and its swoosh symbol a recognized logo. Licensing sport product brands is "a contractual method of developing and exploiting intellectual property by transferring rights of use to third parties without the transfer of ownership" (Mullin et al., 2000, p. 140). Licensed products are produced by independent entities, who provide royalties, or licensing fees, in return for the right to use the brand. For example, the United States Olympic Committee (USOC) uses licensing agreements that provide returns on the sale of licensed Olympic merchandise. This commercial use of USOC's intellectual property yields significant revenue for the group through licensing agreements that, for example, allow a licensee to refer to its product as the "official" one (e.g., car, sport drink) of the USOC. Similarly, the licensing of collegiate athletic products yields considerable revenue.

All products, including sport products, pass through a life cycle (Shank, 2005) that includes four distinct stages: introduction, growth, maturity, and decline (Mullin et al., 2000). Some might consider product development to be a stage as well. In any case, once a product is developed, the introduction phase requires significant up-front investment while producing relatively small returns. The growth phase is marked by a rapid increase in sales. In the maturity phase, product sales stabilize, as does the industry segment in general. In the decline phase, sales begin to steadily decrease.

Sport marketers must recognize where a product is in its life cycle in order to use different marketing strategies as needed. For example, Tiger Woods, once justifiably considered the best golfer in the world at the maturity stage of his personal product life cycle, entered a decline phase and was dropped by several sponsors. As of this writing, Woods' recent victories raise the possibility that he is returning to top form, and the shape of his full career arc is thus yet unknown. In marketing terms, his branding will be reinvented, with a different focus than his original brand. In contrast, Under Armour has been in the growth phase and could be interpreted as entering the maturity phase, although its recent slowdown might be a result of the worldwide economic downturn, which interrupted its growth phase, rather than a reflection of a move to the maturity phase. More generally, many international sporting ventures—as well as certain fantasy sport, adventure sport, and sport diplomacy products—appear to be in the introduction and growth stages of the product life cycle.

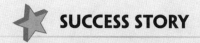

SUCCESS STORY

Kevin Plank, Founder of Under Armour

Under Armour is a Baltimore-based company best known for its introduction of formfitting, moisture-wicking, high-performance athletic apparel designed to provide compression, regulate temperature, and enhance performance when worn under sportswear. Kevin Plank, who played college football, founded the company in 1996 as part of his quest for an alternative to the sweat-soaked cotton shirts traditionally worn by athletes. Inspired by the material and performance of compression shorts, Plank used moisture-wicking fabric for shirts and, later, other apparel. Guided by its overarching mission, "to make all athletes better through passion, design, and the relentless pursuit of innovation," Under Armour has evolved into a sport industry success story.

Under Armour products were originally marketed to football players but are now targeted to a broader consumer base across a wide range of sports. The company now supplies a wider range of sportswear and casual apparel—including lines aimed at youth and women—and offers apparel designed specifically for either cold weather (ColdGear) or hot weather (HeatGear). Since 2006, it has also produced footwear. Under Armour continues to expand its target markets and product lines; for example, in 2010 the company offered its first line of basketball shoes. Under Armour's branded performance apparel, footwear, and accessories are sold worldwide. Its technically advanced products are worn by men, women, and youths at all levels of competition, as well as consumers who live active lifestyles but are not engaged in competitive sport.

Under Armour has used emotive advertisements featuring athletes to brand its products with a unique logo and an emotional catchphrase: "Protect this house!" (Under Armour, 2011). Consumer identification with Under Armour has been reflected in the company's skyrocketing sales. In 1996, Under Armour sold about US$17,000 worth of products; by 2006, its revenue exceeded US$467 million, and it continues to grow. Clearly a major player in the American sports apparel market, Under Armour became a publicly traded company in 2005 (its stock is traded on the New York Stock Exchange). Kevin Plank remains with the company as its president, chief executive officer, and board chair.

While Under Armour engages in product development, manufacturing, marketing, and distribution, it generates revenue primarily through wholesale distribution of its products to retailers. Under Armour opened its first company retail outlet in 2007, but its products are offered in more than 20,000 other retail stores. Most of these stores are located in North America, but Under Armour is a global brand. Though its global headquarters is in Baltimore, it also maintains a European headquarters in Amsterdam, as well as offices in Denver, Hong Kong, Toronto, and Guangzhou (China).

In response to retirements and resignations, Under Armour has undergone changes in executive positions; it has added a new chief operating officer, chief supply chain officer, and senior vice president of human resources. In addition, the recently hired president of Under Armour International strategically drives the company's expansion into selected markets by bringing the brand to consumers from diverse sociocultural backgrounds around the globe. Throughout the development of this corporate strategy, Plank has provided the vision and served as the consistent leader at the top of the organization, and he has declared that "Under Armour is deeply committed to continued international growth" (Canada Newswire, 2012).

Price

Product **price**, though seemingly simple, is actually a complex concept. Price is the value of a product, where value is a quantitative measure. It can also be seen as the worth placed on that product, either quantitatively or emotionally. Ultimately, of course, price is the amount that consumers are willing to exchange for the product— its cost. Whether purchasing a ticket to an NFL game, a pair of shoes from Nike, a set of golf clubs from Callaway, a membership at Gold's Gym, or the marketing services of Octagon, consumers in the sport industry pay a price for a chosen product. Thus price is influenced by both producers and consumers—producers establish what price they are willing to accept for the product, and consumers establish what price they are willing to pay for it.

In developing a pricing strategy, one must consider both internal and external factors. Internal factors involve the nature of the product itself, including the cost of producing it, and the elements of the marketing mix that the organization uses to pursue its mission and objectives. Thus the company itself is clearly influential in developing a pricing strategy, but so are its competitors and their pricing strategies, which constitute external factors. Other external pricing factors include consumers' considerations, such as product quality, service availability, company image, perceived bargains, and so forth. Pricing strategy is also influenced by the overall external climate, which includes such elements as broader economic conditions, governmental regulations and laws that establish parameters within which pricing can be decided, and the ever-changing state of technology.

price—Cost of a product or the value or worth placed on a product (either quantitatively or emotionally).

law of demand—Dynamic in which consumers demand less of a product as its price increases but more of the product as its price decreases.

law of supply—Dynamic in which producers decrease production as price decreases but increase production as price increases.

At the heart of pricing lies the concept of supply and demand (see also chapter 10). Demand refers to the relationship between the price of a sport product and the quantity or amount of the product that consumers are willing to purchase, whereas supply refers to the relationship between the price of a product and the quantity or amount of the product that suppliers are willing to produce and distribute. In general, the **law of demand** predicts less consumer demand for a product as its price increases and more demand as its price decreases. The **law of supply** holds that producers will decrease production as prices go down and increase production as prices rise. A surplus of a product reflects a high price that leaves consumers less willing to purchase the product and producers more willing to produce it. Conversely, a shortage of a product indicates that consumers are willing to purchase more at the price than producers are willing to produce. Market equilibrium, the price at which supply and demand are in balance, is established when producer and consumer interests are both met. For example, if nearly 170,000 people are willing to pay between US$200 and US$2,000 to attend the Daytona 500, and if the event organizers are willing to sell tickets at those prices, then market equilibrium is achieved, and all tickets are sold.

Place

Place is also referred to as distribution. The focus here is on how the product is distributed to the consumer, or how the consumer is brought to the product, and on the marketing channels and methods used in this process. Sport products—whether activities, goods, services, events, or pieces of information—are made available to consumers when, where, and how they are desired through the selected distribution channel. This movement can be facilitated by intermediaries, such as wholesalers, retailers, agents, direct mailers, and Internet-based distributors. For example, a sporting goods manufacturer may use a distribution network through which the product, say, a basketball, is sold to a wholesaler, who then distributes it to retail outlets. The advantage for consumers is that they can seek out and purchase basketballs, as well as other sport products, from these retail outlets. Wholesalers distribute various products from various manufacturers to retail outlets, where consumers can readily access the products, whether they are basketballs or running shoes. In addition, whether through intermediaries or direct distribution, many sport products nowadays reach consumers through online outlets. Distribution systems thus allow consumers to easily access products when, where, and in the form they choose. Of course, each intermediary involved in the distribution process increases the cost of the product. For example, a ticket broker charges a fee to distribute game tickets to interested consumers, thus increasing the cost of the ticket.

> **place**—How a product is distributed to consumers or how consumers are brought to the product; also known as distribution.

In positioning each sport product, producers must decide how to distribute it. Intensive distribution involves offering the product in as many places, at as many times, and to as many people as possible. For example, intensive distribution of a pair of running shoes would make them available in specialty shoe stores, in general department stores, in discount stores, via Internet outlets, and through as many other outlets as possible. Selective distribution, in contrast, involves offering the product in limited locations and quantities. For example, in a selective distribution system, those same running shoes might be made available through a specific retail chain and thus would not be as widely available as with intensive distribution. Another approach—exclusive distribution—would see the running shoes available in only one location or in a very limited quantity in very restricted locations. If the product is an athletic event, extensive distribution might include stadium seating, broadcast television, radio coverage, online streaming, and other news media. Distribution of the event could also be more selective; for example, the product could be made available only through live seating and select pay-per-view cable outlets as defined by television contracts. The event's organizers might even pursue exclusive distribution via live attendance only. In determining the distribution system for a product, the sport organization must consider many factors—among them, the organization's objectives, the product itself, the targeted consumer, the general environment, and the promotions to be employed.

Promotion

Promotion is the process of informing, persuading, and influencing the product-purchasing attitudes and actions of potential consumers (Boone & Kurtz, 1992). In sport marketing, the term *promotions* includes many activities designed to stimulate consumers' interest, awareness, and purchase of the sport product (Mullin et al., 2000). In addition to affecting the organization's image, effective promotions increase consumers' awareness of the product's availability, sales, and distribution locations. Promotions are guided by objectives.

The **promotional mix**—which includes advertising, promotions, publicity, and personal selling—is the strategic combination of promotional methods that an organization can use to meet its promotional objectives. As part of the mix, advertising informs and sways consumers through paid exposure. An advertising message is created and controlled by the organization. Advertisements can be made *for* sport organizations or *through* sport. For example, producers of sport products as varied as WNBA apparel and an Ironman Triathlon can develop advertising campaigns and purchase exposure opportunities through various media outlets. Possibilities include television, magazines, the Internet, billboards, and other signage. Similar to advertising, product placement has become an alternative form of paid advertising. For example, an apparel manufacturer might pay to have its logo or product placed in plain sight in a video game or motion picture.

promotion—Process of informing, persuading, and influencing the product-purchasing dispositions and activities of potential consumers.

promotional mix—Strategic combination of promotional methods, including advertising, promotions, publicity, sponsorship, and personal selling, used to help an organization meet its promotional objectives.

Another element in the promotional mix involves sponsorships and athlete endorsements, which are frequently employed by sport-related and non-sport-related companies alike. In a sponsorship relationship, the sponsor provides resources in some form to the sponsee in return for some form of benefit (Lough, 2005). Benefits to sponsors vary based on their objectives, which influence the terms of sponsorship agreements (Daniels, Baker, Backman, & Backman, 2007). Benefits might include an enhanced corporate image or hospitality and sales opportunities; whatever the benefits, they should align with the organization's mission. Examples of sport sponsorship abound, such as the Tide detergent company sponsoring a NASCAR race car or a local retailer sponsoring uniforms for a Little League Baseball team. Athlete endorsements are also common and lucrative. For example, Michael Jordan has long endorsed Hanes apparel, and Tiger Woods (despite being dropped by Gatorade, AT&T, and Accenture due to very public indiscretions) earned more than US$70 million in endorsements in 2010 (Freedman, 2010).

I like to think of sales as the ability to gracefully persuade, not manipulate, a person or persons into a win-win situation.

Bo Bennett, businessman and entrepreneur

The promotional mix also includes publicity, which differs from advertising in two ways: (1) it is free, and (2) the organization is not always in control of the message. For example, if a blogger writes about a product, say, a minor league baseball game, the league and the teams involved may have little influence over what the blogger says. Despite this dependence on a third party, organizations do attempt to manage or at least influence publicity through the use of public relations, community relations, sports information, and media relations departments. For example, a college volleyball team involved in providing community service to a local elementary school might highlight that activity through the department's sports information office in pursuit of positive publicity. The team might even pitch, or sell, the story for public distribution.

Direct personal selling—a presentation to potential consumers for the express purpose of making a sale—is another key element in the promotional mix. Direct selling is the link between the producer and the consumer. Sales communication with the consumer most often includes conveying the benefits of the product. Direct selling involves prospecting for clients, approaching prospective clients, and developing relationships with clients. These tasks can be undertaken in person, via telephone, or even via collective media such as the web; in fact, online and new media advertising and sales are becoming critical in the promotional mix for sport products. For example, many sport organizations connect with potential consumers via Facebook and Twitter.

Quick Facts

- Sport advertising amounts to approximately US$30 billion dollars annually.
- At least a dozen companies spend between US$103 million (Southwest Airlines) and US$278 million (Anheuser-Busch) annually to advertise on television during sport programming in the United States (Madkour, 2009).
- Over a two-year period, all but one of those dozen companies (Ford at –2.3 percent) increased its spending on sport television advertising by anywhere from 2.9 percent (Chevrolet) to 140.8 percent (Visa).
- At least 100 companies spend more than US$24 million each annually on sport television advertising in the United States.
- Countless companies in more than 40 industry segments engage in sport sponsorship at a national level in the United States.
- Star athletes' endorsement deals often outpace their salaries. For example, in Major League Soccer, David Beckham earned US$5.5 million in base salary, plus a percentage of team revenue, but he received an estimated US$40 million annually through endorsements (Plunkett, 2010).
- At 78 million strong, baby boomers are still a driving segment in many areas of the U.S. sport market.

What's Unique About Sport Marketing?

Marketing is a complex undertaking, and sport marketing is even more complicated due to certain unique characteristics of sport. For example, sport products are perishable, often intangible. Sport can also engage consumers' emotions; it is subjective and thus reflects the diverse experiences and perceptions of each consumer. In addition, sport is generally unpredictable, even volatile, which makes marketing it a more challenging task. And, as Mullin et al. (2000, p. 9) have noted, the complexity of marketing both *in* sport and *through* sport creates a unique marketing application:

> Sport marketing consists of all activities designed to meet the needs and wants of sport consumers through exchange processes. Sport marketing has developed two major themes: the marketing of sport products and services directly to consumers of sport, and marketing of other consumer and industrial products or services through the use of sport promotions.

Marketing *of* a sport product, say, a licensed NFL football jersey, can be done through the NFL's website, through television advertising, or via personal sales at a sports apparel store in a shopping mall. The marketing of sporting goods and services includes everything from ticket sales to agent representation. At the same time, the marketing of nonsport products *through* sport is also commonplace in the form of sponsorship deals and athlete endorsements. For example, Tide detergent sponsors a NASCAR race car and has its brand image emblazoned on the car and on the driver's suit.

At its core, of course, success in sport marketing depends on attracting consumers, but sport consumers are extremely varied in their consumption patterns and motivations. For instance, consumers who are engaged as sport participants often respond to different motives than those who are engaged as spectators. This means that the better a sport organization understands its prospective consumers, the more successful it can be in strategically applying its marketing mix. Therefore, it is crucial for sport marketers to grasp consumer behavior in sport.

Consumer Behavior in Sport

Consumer behavior is what consumers do when searching for, buying, using, and assessing sport products. Sport consumers—both participants and spectators—can be distinguished based upon their levels of involvement and commitment. Involvement can be behavioral, cognitive, or affective; in other words, it can be active, knowledge based, or emotional (Mullin et al., 2000). For example, a sport participant might actively engage in running marathons, read and think about race strategy, and get emotionally charged by the activity. In contrast, a runner might be actively involved due to health requirements but detached in terms of emotional and cognitive engagement. Similarly, a spectator might or might not be actively engaged in cheering on a team, understanding strategy and player tendencies, and investing emotionally in the action.

consumer behavior—What consumers do when searching for, buying, using, and assessing sport-related products.

True fans, as consumers, are often seen as not only involved but also committed. Commitment refers here to sport consumers' willingness to spend time, money, and

> *Our DNA is as a consumer company—for that individual customer who's voting thumbs up or thumbs down. That's who we think about. And we think that our job is to take responsibility for the complete user experience. And if it's not up to par, it's our fault, plain and simply.*
>
> **Steve Jobs**, founder of Apple

energy on sport-related consumption. Committed fans consider sport consumption interesting and important in their lives. These involved and committed sport consumers can come to identify with the sport product if their involvement becomes central to their sense of self. For example, if a participant says "I'm a volleyball player" and perceives herself as such, then her identity is intertwined with her sport consumption. Identification often occurs with a team; for example, an involved and committed sport spectator may be a self-identified fan of the Indian Premier League's Delhi Daredevils cricket franchise. Sport marketers seek to influence consumers' identification as both participants and fans because individuals who identify in this manner are more likely to regularly purchase products related to that identification. Thus consumer loyalty may reflect an investment made up of high levels of involvement, commitment, and even identification. The sport industry thrives on fan loyalty, which is more prominent in sport than in most industries, thus allowing sport marketers to use their knowledge of consumer loyalty in pursuing their marketing objectives.

Sport marketers attempt to persuade prospective consumers to purchase sport products, attend sport events, participate in sport contests, and use sport-related services. In order to efficiently achieve desired results, sport marketers use market research, which is compiled to help marketers understand their prospective consumers—who they are and how, when, and where they consume sport products. Sport marketers use research to identify consumers' common characteristics, interests, and patterns of consumption. They often begin by using the process of **segmentation** to divide large, heterogeneous groups of prospective consumers into smaller, more homogeneous groups with common needs, characteristics, interests, and behaviors.

segmentation—Process of dividing large, heterogeneous groups of prospective consumers into smaller, more homogeneous groups whose members share common needs, characteristics, interests, and behaviors.

To obtain this useful information, sport marketers conduct both demographic and psychographic consumer research (Pitts & Stotlar, 2002). Demographic segmentation addresses factors such as income, education, marital status, location, age, gender, ethnicity, religion, and occupation. Psychographic segmentation examines consumers' lifestyles, interests, opinions, likes, and dislikes. For example, if marketing strategies that use new forms of media reach a predominantly young demographic whose members have a reasonable amount of disposable income, then a skateboard, BMX, or snowboard company might want to use those media to reach potential customers. Segmentation thus allows sport marketers to separate consumers into subgroups for analysis, thereby helping their companies acquire new consumers and retain existing ones.

target market—Market segment chosen on the basis of gathered market data to support efficient marketing.

positioning—The process or activities that help to shape how a product is perceived by the target audience.

One primary purpose of using segmentation is to implement target marketing, which allows a sport organization to pursue its marketing objectives efficiently. An organization establishes a **target market** based upon a set of useful segmentation data gathered via market research. Key factors in strategically targeting a market segment include the segment's size and projected growth. While large segments are often desirable, bigger is not always better if the sport organization is seeking a market niche or smaller group with common interests. Sport marketers must also consider a segment's accessibility—that is, the organization's ability to reach the segment via appropriate channels, be they traditional or innovative. Low accessibility can make the segment less desirable, whereas high accessibility may allow the organization to open new segments. For example, NBA basketball, which was once a geographically limited product, can now be broadcast globally via streaming Internet video.

Sport marketers' success depends on their ability to measure a segment's size, accessibility, purchasing power, and other relevant traits. For example, should the organizers of a sporting event seek to attract the enormous baby boomer segment, which controls half of America's discretionary income, they can use market research and segmentation to identify and market directly to the prospective consumers within that segment. Effective research thus enables sport marketers to enhance the success of their strategic sport marketing decisions by gathering useful information not only about prospective consumers but also about their product, their competitors, and the market itself. As a result, sport marketing research has itself become a sport product, and many sport market research companies gather and analyze sport industry and consumer data.

Positioning

Positioning a sport product begins with the targeted market segment—more specifically, how the product is perceived by the target audience. A given sport product, for example a sport tour to a major college football bowl game, might be positioned differently for current students than for alumni. In addition, though the target market is critical to positioning strategy, all sport products must also be positioned in the overall sport marketplace. Leagues and teams, for example, position themselves with fans. For years, the Dallas Cowboys have embraced their image as "America's Team," thus positioning themselves as having broad geographic appeal. Likewise, athletes position themselves to build their personal brands. For example, Shaun White's positioning has branded him as a likeable, new age, All-American superstar in the alternative sports of snowboarding and skateboarding. Sporting goods manufacturers also position their products. Ping, for instance, is viewed as a high-quality brand of golf club by its target segment. Similarly, sport service providers position their services in relation to their targeted segments. One such provider, Collegiate Licensing Company (a division of IMG), is positioned as the premier product licenser in college sports. Developing a relationship between the brand and consumers is essential for sport marketers; in building this relationship, public relations and communication skills are critical, and thus they must be learned by students who are interested in this area of sport management.

Business has only two functions—marketing and innovation.

Peter Drucker, management consultant

Public Relations and Marketing Communication

Public relations is an ingredient of the marketing mix that encompasses such associated elements as community relations, media relations, sports information, and sport communication. It promotes the development of positive relationships between the sport organization and the people it affects—that is, its various publics. As you might imagine, success in this type of work requires strong communication skills, such as writing and speaking ability. Communication is a process wherein senders and receivers share meaningful messages (Parks, Quarterman, & Thibault, 2007), and the components of communication include the sender (or source), the message, the delivery channel, and of course the receiver. This process can occur at the interpersonal level, in groups, and with the masses.

In communicating with various publics, two modes of public relations exist: one-way and two-way. One-way communication focuses on the flow of information from the sport organization to the public; it does not involve seeking input from the public. This type of communication is practiced both by publicity offices, which seek to garner public attention, and by public information offices, which

> **public relations**—Use of effective communication to promote the development of positive relationships between the sport organization and the people it affects (its various publics).

seek to provide service and inform the public. Two-way communication, in contrast, involves interaction between the sport organization and its publics. This exchange process is at the heart of marketing. If sport marketers are to influence consumers' behavior, they must initiate an exchange process by employing effective communication skills through the marketing mix. Seeking input and feedback from various publics can inform sport organizations about public opinion and may allow them to influence the public as well.

Sport Marketing Plans

Ultimately, the purpose of sport marketing, in either its immediate effects or its long-term influence, is to increase the revenue of the sport organization by strategically employing the marketing mix in alignment with the organization's marketing objectives. With this in mind, sport marketing plans and the actions they prompt should be driven by the organization's mission. Sport marketers implement marketing plans to maximize their success; the plan describes for in-house staff, or for a client, how a product will be marketed. Stotlar (2001) identified the following components that any sport organization should include in its marketing plan: (a) executive summary, (b) introduction, (c) situational analysis, (d) target markets, (e) marketing objectives, (f) marketing strategies and tactics, (g) implementation and control, and (h) summary.

INTERNATIONAL APPLICATION

Worldwide Reach of the NBA

During the 2010–2011 season, the National Basketball Association (NBA) offered programming in 37 countries or international regions (NBA, 2012). Given its global branding as the pinnacle of professional basketball, perhaps the NBA should be called the International Basketball Association. In fact, basketball is one of the most popular U.S.-based sports on the international level, and the NBA, also based in the United States, actively embraces its international prospects. This effort has been extremely successful in establishing an international presence for the league, which is in the process of generating a growing fan base around the world.

As part of this effort to expand its global reach, the league has used new technologies. For example, the league's website is accessed daily by millions of users, more than half of whom are located outside of the United States (Hoopedia, 2011a). The league also boasts web destinations tailored to Latin America (e.g., Brazil, Panama), Europe (e.g., France, Germany, Spain, the United Kingdom), and Asia (e.g., China, Japan). In addition, more than 95 percent of the NBA's marketing partners have a presence through the website.

The NBA has also partnered with the International Basketball Federation to operate a global basketball development program called Basketball Without Borders (BWB), which uses the sport as a vehicle not only to encourage the development of basketball skills but also to spur positive social change. Since 2001, the program has served thousands of aspiring players from more than a hundred countries who have been coached by hundreds of NBA players and staffers. BWB operates in Europe, the Americas, Africa, and Asia.

Of all the NBA's activity around the world, its work in China is a model of the league's international success. More than 300 million people play basketball in China, more than 80 percent of young Chinese males consider themselves basketball fans, and 40 percent identify basketball as their favorite sport. In China, NBA games are watched by more than 30 million viewers per week, and the NBA website attracts more than 3 million page views per day. In addition, NBA products are sold in more than 20,000 locations across China, and the inaugural NBA China Games, held in 2004 in Shanghai and Beijing, attracted more than 29,000 attendees. The event also drew major sponsors, including Budweiser, Coca-Cola, Disneyland, Kodak, and Reebok.

The NBA's relationship with Chinese basketball dates back to 1979, when the Washington Bullets (now Wizards) played two exhibition games in China against the Chinese national team. Under the leadership of NBA Commissioner David Stern, the league has since established offices in Hong Kong, Beijing, and Shanghai; built relationships with multiple Chinese broadcast partners; conducted many grassroots basketball events; and seen several players from China, including star Yao Ming, play for NBA teams. The NBA's first television exposure in China came in 1989, and China Central Television now airs many regular season NBA games, as well as the league's all-star game and post-season games. With assistance from key sponsors, the league has also staged coaching clinics, in-country games, and NBA player appearances in China.

In 2008, the NBA formed NBA China with US$253 million from strategic partners that included ESPN, the Bank of China, Legend Holdings Limited, the Li Ka Shing Foundation, and China Merchants Investments. NBA China's mission is to conduct all of the league's business in Greater China and work with the State General Administration of Sports and the Chinese Basketball Association to grow basketball and the NBA brand. As a result, the NBA has enjoyed constant increases in telecasts, strategic marketing partnerships, and product distribution. For example, the league has partnered with Reebok to offer apparel, shoes, and accessories throughout China at locations that include more than 150 direct NBA and Reebok outlets. In fact, China is Reebok's (and Spalding's) top market outside of North America (Hoopedia, 2011b). Other marketing partners in China for the NBA include Adidas, Coca-Cola, Budweiser, Nutrilite (an Amway brand), Nokia, Homenice Wood, China Mobile Communications Corporation, Li Ning Company Limited, and Red Bull. Many of these partners are actively engaged in China through multiple channels, including retail, promotions, sponsorship, and media programming.

Though it comes first in the document, the executive summary is usually written last. It must succinctly describe the sport product and its advantages. It should also provide a financial overview that includes projected revenue, profits, and return on investment. Following the executive summary, a table of contents guides readers to the introduction, which describes the sport organization, including its mission and any unique elements. Next comes the situational analysis, which examines the relevant environment, or climate, including economic conditions, technological trends, competitors, consumer characteristics, and other external factors. The next section identifies target markets, assesses prospective consumers, and addresses the demographic and psychographic data used to segment the consumer base. The following section covers marketing objectives, which provide direction for the marketing plan on the basis of information such as market share, revenue, sales, and product positioning. The plan then describes what strategies will be used and how they will be implemented through tactical use of the marketing mix. The next section provides details about implementation and control, such as initial and operational costs, public relations, and other general parameters of operation, as well as necessary monitoring and evaluation. Finally, the summary reiterates the sport organization's mission and, as a synopsis, concisely connects it to each element previously outlined in the plan.

Pitts and Stotlar (2002) identify multiple steps that sport marketers should take in the planning process. First, they must align the plan's purpose with the sport organization's mission, taking into consideration the core sport product and its extensions. They can identify key factors that should influence the plan by conducting a SWOT (strengths, weaknesses, opportunities, threats) analysis. Marketers should also analyze and segment the market, then brand the product in order to position it in the target market. Packaging the sport product involves presenting the product in the most attractive way to the target market. For example, packaging could include offering highly desired benefits to attract sponsors or highly desired tickets to attract affluent event attendees. Then, once the product is priced, marketers identify the promotional activities that will best persuade consumers to choose the product. Marketers must also plan product distribution in a way that ensures consumers' access to it. Finally, marketers evaluate the marketing plan's effectiveness (Pitts & Stotlar).

The Short of It

- The marketing mix includes the four Ps: product, price, place, and promotion.
- Sport products include both goods (e.g., apparel) and services (e.g., agent representation), as well as sporting events themselves.
- Many factors influence the complex process of pricing a product.
- A good sport marketing plan aligns with the organization's mission and goals and describes the marketing strategy.
- Segmentation, based on appropriate market research, allows sport marketers to target specific consumer groups.
- Sport marketers seek to understand consumers' behavior—that is, the ways in which consumers buy, use, and assess sport products.

Sport Media

In this chapter, you will learn the following:

✓ How the sport media industry has been transformed by the Internet
✓ How Twitter and Facebook are used by sport communication managers
✓ The influence of media companies such as Fox and ESPN
✓ The use of sport team websites for e-commerce and the dissemination of information

> I always turn to the sports pages first. They are full of man's accomplishments. The front pages record only man's failures.
>
> **Earl Warren**, former Chief Justice of the U.S. Supreme Court

By any standard, Arn Tellem is one of the more successful agents in professional sport. He has represented some of the most successful athletes in the world and currently represents a few pretty good players in the National Basketball Association (NBA). These days, one of Tellem's jobs is to advise players about media and promotional strategy, and this task has grown more complicated with the advent of new forms of communication. For example, Tellem must now consider whether the player should write a blog—and, in fact, whether the player would have something to say that would interest anyone in reading the blog in the first place.

One of Tellem's clients is Pau Gasol, an all-star power forward for the Los Angeles Lakers who grew up in Spain. Since Gasol speaks both Spanish and English, he and his representatives may decide that he should publish the same blog in both languages. Facebook also provides a great opportunity for media-savvy athletes to interact with a large audience. Pictures are a big part of Facebook, and since Gasol travels to many parts of the world, he finds compelling photo opportunities during both the season and the off-season. At the same time, athletes (and sport management students!) should be careful about what they post on Facebook; pictures and content should be suitable for an audience of all ages. Also, it is important to be careful when discussing teammates, coaches, management, and fans. Electronic posts leave a permanent record, and one misstep can lead to embarrassment for the athlete or team. Another new social media tool that can be used by athletes and sport agents is Twitter, which allows a person to easily send brief messages and pictures to a large following; managed correctly, these "tweets" can help an athlete and agent create a marketable and sustainable brand. Facebook and Twitter both provide opportunities for a large number of fans to interact with Gasol and other athletes, which creates a deeper relationship between these athletes and their fan base.

We have come a long way, then, from the days when newspapers, magazines, and radio broadcasts were the only modes of coverage for sport personalities and sporting events. **New media** such as Facebook, Twitter, and YouTube enable athletes such as Pau Gasol to speak directly to their fans, without the filter of a sports reporter. In addition, when an athlete speaks in this manner, the message can easily be transmitted not just to a local audience but worldwide.

Sporting events themselves are also widely distributed via the Internet. The National Collegiate Athletic Association's (NCAA's) annual basketball tournament is streamed over the Internet and to mobile devices for free. NBA fans who live in the Middle East can watch games on the Al Jazeera network. And if you love cricket but live in the United States where coverage is scarce, you can now watch the best in the sport via the ESPN3 streaming service. You can also tune in to YouTube, where the Indian Premier League (IPL) broadcasts all of its contests. Similarly, if you are a fan of the English Premier League (EPL), you can watch your soccer team from many locations around the world, either via the Internet or on a local sports network that has purchased the rights to show the league's games. On an even larger scale, the Summer Olympics and Winter Olympics have become worldwide media extravaganzas that draw thousands of members of the media from around the world. The same is true of the World Cup. In fact, the viewing audiences for these events almost defy the imagination, as millions of viewers watch their country's athletes via television or online streaming. At the same time, the viewing experience has been made that much more enjoyable by leaps in technology. ESPN has launched a 3-D channel, and CBS/TBS has televised recent NCAA Final Fours in 3-D and in high definition (HD); in fact, for many people, HD televisions are now a must-purchase item. As explained in the finance and economics chapters of this book, revenue from television has dramatically affected both college and professional sport.

> **new media**—Communication used by individuals and sport entities that includes digital media such as blogs, websites, YouTube, Facebook, podcasts, Twitter, DVDs, and CD-ROMs but does not include print and analog broadcast media (e.g., print newspapers and magazines; traditional television and radio).

This chapter discusses how the sport media have evolved from the classic image of a reporter with his or her trusty notepad to an expansive array of options, including 3-D and HD television, the World Wide Web, sports talk radio, Twitter, podcasts, streaming to smartphones, YouTube, and satellite-enabled coverage of events around the world. This discussion addresses how these changes have affected sport, athletes, fans, and members of the media themselves. You will learn about the many job opportunities available to students who want to make their way in the sport media industry. You will also learn about the skills needed to succeed in this era of new media.

Sport managers in today's industry interact with the media in many settings. For example, college athletic departments hire sports information directors (SIDs), who arrange media conferences for their coaches and players. They also interact with newspaper, radio, video, and online reporters who want to interview a coach or star player. SIDs also send out media releases to announce an event or trumpet a milestone accomplished by one of the school's athletes, coaches, or teams. Another common position is a community relations director. For example, when a professional team or league wants to publicize a community event, its community relations director contacts members of the media to talk about what the group will be doing for the benefit of a local school or boy's and girl's club. Public relations (PR) staff at companies such as Nike and Under Armour plan media conferences to announce developments such as releasing a new product or signing a star athlete to an endorsement deal. Major governance organizations (e.g., the International Federation of Association Football [FIFA], the International Olympic Committee

JOBS IN SPORT MEDIA AND SPORT COMMUNICATION

Reporter for a newspaper sports page or website

Website editor for a professional league or team

Community relations director for a sport club

Sports producer for a television network

Media relations director for a sport governing body

Sports information director for a college athletic department

Public relations manager for a sporting goods manufacturer

Sports editor for a newspaper

Broadcaster for a television sports network

Director of publications for a sport governing body

Director of communication for a sport governing body

Blogger for a local or national sports website

Media relations manager for a professional team or league

Director of communication for a nonprofit sport organization

[IOC], the NCAA) also hire communication professionals to interact with the sport media; these same professionals also write stories for use on their group's own website—for example, outlining a new policy or highlighting a major accomplishment.

As these examples suggest, properly prepared sport management graduates can now find media careers in various sport enterprises and in collegiate and professional sports in a variety of capacities. Many of these positions had not even been conceived of just a few years ago; certainly, the sport media have come a long way!

History of Media in Sport

The newspaper sports "page" had humble beginnings in the form of the "Sporting Olio" (i.e., sporting miscellany page) published in the *American Farmer* in Baltimore in 1825 (Stevens, 1987). The first sport periodical was the *American Turf Register and Sporting Magazine*, which was launched in 1829 (Stevens). Soon thereafter, another periodical, the *Spirit of the Times*, appeared, and other magazines followed, including the *Knickerbocker*, the *Southern Literary Messenger*, and the *New York Sporting Magazine*. These publications focused on horse racing and also allotted some space for other sports, such as boxing. In the 1840s and early 1850s, coverage of baseball, a popular new team sport, was begun by the *New York Clipper*, the *New York Times*, the *New-York Tribune*, the *New York Sun*, and the *New York World* (Kirsch, 1989). The *Clipper* baseball writer Henry Chadwick also published an annual baseball guide that included statistics and the rules of the game (Stevens).

Two more sport magazines started publication during the 1880s—the *Sporting Life* and the *Sporting News* (Bryant & Holt, 2006).

During this general time period, newspapers came to recognize the importance of the sports page in attracting advertisers. Joseph Pulitzer, publisher of the *New York World*, set up his own sports section in 1893 (Schultz, 2005). The section had its own writers and editors, and its creation coincided with both a drop in the cost of newsprint and the development of a better form of type (Linotype) for use in printing; as a result, the sports section provided a useful tool for advertisers looking to reach male readers. This period also saw the development of sport-centric coverage in newspapers and magazines in England, Italy, France, and Belgium (Mandell, 1976). The sports page, then the sports section, became bigger and bigger and included more and more sports in the daily coverage. This phenomenon involved a mutually beneficial relationship between the growth of sport media and the growth of the sport industry itself, as more press coverage begat greater public interest in sport, which in turn fed into more sport coverage (Mandell; Bryant & Holt, 2006).

During this expansion of sport coverage in newspapers, Guglielmo Marconi invented a wireless device that could transmit telegraphic signals over great distances. Marconi patented the device in 1896 and demonstrated the new invention during the America's Cup sailing races in 1899. He was signed as a correspondent by the *New York Herald* and reported live from the race on a boat in which he followed the contest between the *Shamrock* and the *Columbia*. Another invention of the time, the motion picture, also helped popularize sport to a larger audience through newsreels of sporting events shown to audiences at movie theaters.

In 1906, Thomas Edison's colleague R.A. Fessenden became the first person to speak over the airwaves via radio. Fifteen years later, radio was used for the first time to broadcast a boxing match between Jack Dempsey and Georges Carpentier. Major White, who was at ringside, spoke via telephone with J.O. Smith, who was across the street in a hut. Meanwhile, Smith broadcast the conversation over the WJZ airwaves during the fight. In 1921, baseball was presented via radio for the first time in the form of a playoff game between the New York Yankees and the New York Giants. Across the Atlantic Ocean, cricket was covered by BBC (British Broadcasting Company, now British Broadcasting Corporation) radio in the early 1920s, but concern arose that listeners might find it boring (Williams, 2011).

One of the pioneers in these early days of sports radio was Graham McNamee, who broadcast the World Series and nine other sports, as well as the Democratic and Republican conventions (Barber, 1970). Other groundbreakers included Ted Husing, Bill Munday, and Harold Arlin. By 1927, CBS was on the air with 16 radio stations. In 1928, NBC established a radio network that spanned the United States from coast to coast (ProQuest, 2009).

The newspaper industry was none too happy about radio's popularity or the new advances in production and transmission that made it cheaper and easier to broadcast sporting events. Radio broadcasters reacted similarly to the development of television in the 1930s and 1940s. Indeed, inventors were experimenting with what would become the modern-day television as early as the 1920s. During the 1936 Summer Olympics in Berlin, images were broadcast over the airwaves to large halls in the German cities of Leipzig, Potsdam, and Berlin (Davies, 2007). In 1937, the Wimbledon Championships were televised to a few thousand homes in London. The first cricket match ever televised was put on the air by the BBC in June 1938, when viewers were treated to a match between England and Australia (Williams, 2011). In 1939, television was introduced to those attending the World's Fair in New York; in that same year, a college baseball game between Princeton and Columbia was televised to viewers who reported having trouble seeing the ball during the telecast (Davies).

By 1952, five million U.S. homes had televisions, and the sport of boxing was proving to be ideally suited to the medium, since the ring was small and there was no ball for the viewer to follow. As a result, both NBC and CBS developed weeknight boxing telecasts that took advantage of the sport's popularity. Baseball was the first team sport to make use of television (Davies, 2007). By 1960, some 46.5 million U.S. homes had television sets, and the large-market teams in baseball were using this fact to their advantage , selling broadcast rights to their home games. The invention of videotape permitted the stockpiling of games and the rapid production of programs, and the invention of the portable video camera improved the quality of televised sporting events thanks to tighter camera angles on the action.

The lucrative potential of sports television led the National Football League (NFL) commissioner to lobby Congress for an antitrust exemption in order to collectively negotiate national television deals for his league without being deemed in violation of provisions of the Sherman Antitrust Act. The resulting legislation, the Sports Broadcasting Act of 1961, enabled the league office to wield greater leverage than an individual team could in negotiating with the competing television networks. It also provided protections for professional hockey, baseball, and basketball and was therefore critical to the escalation of rights fees paid to these leagues.

The first Super Bowl was televised in 1967 by both CBS and NBC, and in 1970 ABC came up with the concept of *Monday Night Football*. Clearly, football was growing in popularity as a televised spectator sport. In 1979, a new network, dedicated to sport, came on the scene and changed the entire landscape of sport media. Over the next 30 years, ESPN would become a cash cow for its parent companies (ABC, then Disney), drawing large fees from cable networks, as well as advertising revenue that has continued to grow. During that period, the network has added ESPN2, ESPNU, and ESPN3 (formerly ESPN360). The network has created signature shows, including *SportsCenter* and *Outside the Lines*, as well as new events, such as the X Games and the ESPY Awards. It has also created ESPN restaurants and begun to purchase rights for athletic events overseas, thus establishing beachheads in Europe, Asia, and Australia.

The 1980s brought a decrease in regulation, as well as the globalization of media businesses, the fall of the Berlin Wall in 1989, and the opening up of markets in Yugoslavia, Russia, China, and India. In addition, the European Economic Community welcomed new members Greece, Portugal, and Spain in this decade, bringing its membership to 12 countries. Changes also continued to mark the television industry. By 1990, cable television accounted for 60 percent of the market in the United States, and cable subscribers could now watch networks such as the BBC, BET, CNN, ESPN, HBO, TNT, and USA. Furthermore, ESPN was not the only one of these networks to offer sports programming. TNT presented a full schedule of Atlanta Hawks and Atlanta Braves games, CNN provided regular sport news reports, and sports programming also appeared on BET, HBO, and the BBC. At the end of the 1980s, another phenomenon in sport media was introduced, as sports talk radio became the staple of the New York City radio station WFAN (Gullifor, 2006).

The 1990s saw the creation of large media companies capable of competing on an international stage. International markets became more accessible. For example, the European Union was formed in 1993 and has come to include 27 member nations that serve as a common marketplace for sports media distribution. During the 1990s, Disney acquired ABC and all of the ESPN properties, Viacom and CBS became one company, and Time Warner merged with Turner Broadcasting. Meanwhile, the Fox Network, owned by Rupert Murdoch's News Corporation, became the fourth major broadcast network. ESPN launched the ESPN Radio network in 1992 and *ESPN The Magazine* in 1998 (Bryant & Holt, 2006). ESPN also launched its own website in 1995, and the floodgates opened. Major sport media companies followed with their own websites, as did athletes, teams, leagues, and governing bodies.

Cable television operators themselves also faced new competition in the form of direct-broadcast satellite services. In the United States, two companies, DirecTV and Dish Network, began to compete with cable providers for subscribers around the country. Satellite transmission technology continued to improve, eventually permitting people all over the world to watch the same sporting event at the same time. With this capability established, satellite companies started trying to grab market share by offering sport packages that featured, for example, contests in the NFL (now available as the NFL Sunday Ticket), the English Premier League, UEFA Champion's League, and the NCAA men's basketball tournament.

Traditional Media in the 21st Century

Traditional media have survived the assault on their existence from the Internet—as of now! As advertisers have followed customers to sport content on the web, this migration has inevitably led to changes in the newspaper and magazine industries. For one thing, the web's enabling of e-commerce has wreaked havoc on the classified ad business upon which newspapers used to depend. In addition, the number of radio and television stations has grown, which has increased the pressure on each station to protect its bottom line. In 1976, 962 television stations were being operated in the United States; by January 2009, that number had grown to 1,759. Growth has also been dramatic in the number of niche television networks, including sports networks, that compete with other television, radio, and print media companies for advertising dollars.

In contrast, the number of radio stations has remained relatively the same over the last 10 years; however, the number of sports radio stations doubled between 1998 and 2008. Traditional radio must also compete for listeners with Internet offerings and with the satellite radio networks Sirius and XM, which launched separately in the early 2000s but are now both operated by the merged company Sirius XM Radio. Its business model relies not on advertisers but on subscribers.

Newspapers and Magazines

The traditional sports reporter from the local newspaper can still reach an audience with stories about local teams and sport personalities. The difference lies in the fact that the audience has become much more mobile. As a result, the great majority of today's newspapers in the United States maintain an online presence that is coordinated with their regular print newspaper; stories online can be updated after the morning paper has been delivered. Breaking news can be posted to the website by reporters as the news is happening, and readers can access these stories with their PCs, mobile phones, tablets, and laptop computers. In fact, many young people have become so comfortable with the Internet that they don't even think about buying the hard copy of a newspaper or magazine; instead, they look for their sporting news on the web. A further problem for the old media business model is the creation of search engines as well as popular classifieds and dating websites; all of these businesses have siphoned off advertising dollars from the newspaper business (McArdle, 2009).

These pressures, though substantial, have not killed off the newspaper or magazine; indeed, many Americans still read the sports page every day in the local newspaper or, for a national take on the sport scene, in *USA Today*. In addition, *Sports Illustrated* remains a popular magazine, and a number of others—including *ESPN The Magazine*, *Golf Digest*, *Fitness*, *Field & Stream*, *Golf Magazine*, *Car and Driver*, and *Motor Trend*—all still have at least a million subscribers (Madkour, 2009). The challenge in the 21st century, then, is to put together a business model to attract advertising revenue that was lost to the explosion of the web and cable television; as part of that model, magazines must maximize their presence on the web. The magazines just mentioned are national in scope, but they can still provide an opportunity for college sports information directors and communication directors for professional sport leagues to suggest compelling stories about, for example, athletes and coaches who are having a particularly good year. And since sport magazines need writers, they present opportunities for sport communication students to develop their skills during internships and perhaps find full-time employment down the line.

Newspapers have also attempted to interest local readers by covering more high school athletes and local contests. For example, the *Washington Post* employs several reporters who cover only high school sports; it also dedicates a section of its website called AllMetSports to video, statistics, and stories about high school athletics. This hyperlocalism is in part a response to the plethora of websites devoted to sport on the national and international levels; in this environment, certain media outlets have decided that they are better off focusing on local content (Schultz, Caskey, & Esherick, 2010). This trend provides another opportunity for sport management students to work part-time or fashion an internship based on the need to cover local games. Through this work, students can develop their writing skills, learn what it is like to write a story on deadline, and learn how to film and post video clips of high school games, since many local newspapers and television stations like to post short interviews with high school players and coaches.

Just as modern-day newspapers have had to adjust to the new era of video and the Internet, reporters themselves have had to learn new skills to adapt to the 21st-century media market. Today's sports reporters are adept not only at writing compelling stories but also at operating a video camera, uploading video to the newspaper's website, posting stories from the field to the web, sending tweets to their followers, and doing research via smartphone while moving to cover another story. Sport management students can start developing these skills while still in school. Many internships with media companies can start you down this path of learning skills that will help you stand out when applying for jobs in sport communication.

Radio

In the United States, sports talk radio has become a popular medium for discussing everything about sport on both the local and national scales; in fact, from 2002 to 2012 the number of sports talk stations grew a staggering 64 percent (Ourand, 2012). Many sports radio programs have been syndicated to a national audience; one example is ESPN's *Mike & Mike in the Morning*, which features former NFL player Mike Golic and veteran sport journalist Mike Greenberg. The show, heard daily all over the United States, is syndicated to many local ESPN affiliates and shown live on the ESPN2 television channel. The two Mikes interview athletes and coaches with a focus on the New York area, but they also talk about news events on the national level. In the New York market, Mike and Mike compete with the nation's first sports talk station, WFAN. Other U.S. cities that are also home to this type of sports talk radio include Boston, Buffalo, Dallas, Orlando, Omaha, and Philadelphia (Dempsey, 2006).

Sports talk radio is much more popular with men than with women, and this split brings with it a certain type of advertiser. Research has also shown that sports talk radio is much more likely than other formats to attract affluent listeners (Dempsey, 2006). Specifically, market research conducted by a magazine that covers the talk radio industry found that the sports talk radio audience was 77 percent male, that two-thirds of the audience had either attended or graduated from college, and that the audience was ethnically diverse (Harrison, 2011). Sports talk radio is also popular because of the call-in segments that are often included. This interactive component permits listeners to vent about their local teams, and some call in so often that they become local personalities themselves. High school, college, and professional teams also contract with sports talk stations to broadcast their games. Since many of these broadcasts are streamed, you can often listen to your favorite play-by-play announcer talk about your favorite team on your personal computer, laptop, tablet, or smartphone.

With this media landscape in mind, sports information directors for university athletic departments and communication directors for professional teams should establish close relationships with sports talk radio personalities and producers. When athletes and coaches are interviewed on these programs, they may be asked to stay on the air afterward and answer questions from listeners. Savvy sport communication professionals anticipate this scenario and brief their coaches and athletes before they go on the air. Preparation is also important for students who want to work in sports talk radio. Clearly, sports talk listeners love sports, and sport management students who want to be on the air should be as knowledgeable about sports as their listeners are (Dempsey, 2006). Thus hosts of sports talk radio programs should follow both local and national sports. They should also go to sporting events and develop relationships with local athletes, coaches, college SIDs, and media relations directors for local professional teams.

Television

Most of the changes in sports television in the early 21st century have been beneficial to the teams and leagues that derive revenue from televised events. Advances in transmission technology and the change from analog to digital have opened up space not only for HD channels but also for more sports networks. Many of these networks are carried by satellite services such as DirecTV and Dish Network (United States), BSkyB (United Kingdom), Zee TV (India), Austar (Australia), Star (Hong Kong), and Sky PerfecTV! (Japan). Cable television operators have launched their own sports networks, as have professional leagues (e.g., NBA, NFL, Major League Baseball, the National Hockey League) and some college conferences (e.g., Big Ten Network, MountainWest Sports Network). Several teams have also formed their own television networks; for example, the Longhorn Network was formed by the University of Texas in partnership with ESPN. The world-renowned football clubs Barcelona and Real Madrid also have their own television networks.

Such networks often feature former players and coaches as studio experts or color commentators for games. They have also hired a large number of former reporters to fill on-air positions requiring skill and experience in sport communication, reporting, and news gathering. These networks also need sport managers with sales experience, since developing a marketing strategy to attract advertisers is a key part of their business model. In addition, their production arms need producers, directors, camera operators, statisticians, studio producers, writers, copyeditors, and graphic designers. Working for any of these networks can help you develop valuable skills that are needed in community, media, and public relations positions with sport teams, leagues, federations, and other governance organizations.

Television rights deals are discussed in great detail in the finance and economics chapters of this book, but it is worth mentioning here how important television has become to professional and college sport. Indeed, revenue from television deals has been as revolutionary as the Internet for the sport industry, and it has given fans a huge buffet of televised events to choose from.

> *The manifold influence of television is today the single most important element in sports—money, fan interest, new fans, public acceptance. Today, football games are moved around to get them on television. The play-off games in baseball, as well as the World Series, are scheduled in order to be on television on weekends.*
>
> **Red Barber**, from *The Broadcasters*

Quick Facts

- The first sporting event ever televised was a 1939 baseball game between Columbia University and Princeton University.

- The top-grossing sport movie of all time, with more than US$250 million in ticket sales, is *The Blind Side*. The top sport movie franchise is the *Rocky* series composed of six installments in which Sylvester Stallone portrays fictional boxer Rocky Balboa; the series grossed more than US$560 million.

- In the early years of radio, some baseball owners did not allow broadcasting of their games because they were concerned that fans would stay home to listen rather than buy a ticket and attend. A version of this practice continues in the NFL today: The league can enforce a television blackout if an NFL regular season game is not deemed a sellout within 72 hours of game time.

- The CBS television network paid US$390,000 for the rights to televise the Rome Olympics in 1960.

- Comcast-NBC will pay US$4.4 billion for the rights to broadcast the 2012 and 2016 Summer Olympics and the 2014 and 2018 Winter Olympics (McCarthy, 2011).

- Ronald Reagan began his media career as a radio announcer for University of Iowa football games.

- In October 2009, 88 million Americans logged onto a sport-related website at least once.

- A then-record 106.5 million people watched the CBS broadcast of the New Orleans Saints winning the Super Bowl in 2010, according to Nielsen Media Research (Bauder, 2010). The record was broken again in both 2011 and 2012, as viewership surpassed 111 million viewers in each of those years.

- The cost of a 30-second television advertisement during the Super Bowl was US$55,000 in 1969, US$675,000 in 1989, and US$3 million in 2009.

New Media

Traditional sport media were often symbolized by a male reporter with a hat, a pencil, and a shorthand pad watching a sporting event or interviewing an athlete after an exciting win. The new media, in contrast, can be described as all things audio, video, and online. The effect is almost kaleidoscopic: Twitter, YouTube, smartphones, HDTV, bloggers, tweeters, reporters, broadcasters, and journalists with multiple skills. As a result, students interested in this field need to bring more to the table than just being a good writer. They must also be able to post videos to the web, operate a camera, tweet every day, blog every day, and so on. In fact, you may never have had so much fun getting exhausted!

The Internet and Websites

The Internet has had a huge effect on the sport industry, and no one has been more deeply affected than the print media. Newspaper sports pages have lost readers and advertisers to sport-related websites, such as those offered by ESPN, Yahoo!, Sports Illustrated, AOL's SportingNews, and Fox Sports. However, many former print reporters have moved online to work for these websites. Such changes have caused pain in the lives of some reporters, but they have also created new opportunities for those who are versatile enough to tell their stories online, in print, and on television.

Internet sport media have an advantage over print media in that their chosen medium can create interactivity between the writer and the fan; indeed, they are now working on a 24-7 news cycle that provides nearly continuous breaking news from the world of sport (Masteralexis, Barr, & Hums, 2012). Websites have also made creative use of online polls, chat rooms, and e-commerce. In fact, e-commerce is to new media as the classified section was to old media—it pays the bills! Web media practitioners can also link other related content to a site and post video, audio, and pictures from an athletic contest that is in progress or has just ended. Sports information directors at colleges can post stories and videos on Facebook, then link them to the school's athletic department website. During a contest, fans can go to websites for real-time information (e.g., scores), and sports reporters can post comments to the web or tweet them and receive tweets from fans. Video of spectacular plays can be posted before the event is over. All of these possibilities provide opportunities for sport management graduates who have developed the requisite skills through internships, summer jobs, or practicums.

Websites can also be used to capture the international market. For example, Real Madrid's site has five versions: English, Spanish, Japanese, Arabic, and Indonesian (Pedersen, Parks, Quarterman, & Thibault, 2011). The NBA has created multiple websites, each in the appropriate language, for markets in Africa, Greece, Germany, India, Italy, Spain, the Philippines, France, and Brazil (National Basketball Association, 2012). Thus sport managers who can speak multiple languages and possess solid writing skills may find opportunities with Real Madrid, the NBA, and many other sport enterprises. Other leagues that reach out to fans worldwide include Major League Baseball (MLB), the NFL, the IPL, and the EPL.

Every major college athletic program maintains a web presence that provides statistics, rosters, biographies, and results for all of its athletic teams. These sites also include advertisements for local and national businesses; just as colleges make use of video to attract fans, they also use their websites for e-commerce. These sites are part of the reason that working in your college's sports information office can provide a great opportunity for you to develop key skills. College programs at all levels have an online presence for their athletic programs, and that means they need people to write stories and post scores and video highlights. Schools also produce short video clips of news stories, and many games are streamed online. Interns in sports information offices also interact with members of the media, which offers a great chance to develop your interpersonal skills. These offices also create media guides for each of their teams to provide background information for reporters and

Advances in computer technology and the Internet have changed the way America works, learns, and communicates. The Internet has become an integral part of America's economic, political, and social life.

Bill Clinton

recruiting information for high school athletes, and working on these guides can help you hone your writing skills and learn how to produce and price such a publication.

Professional sport teams and leagues have also made great use of the Internet. Possibly the most innovative of the leagues in this regard is MLB, which has created an Internet group called Major League Baseball Advanced Media (Swangard, 2008; Horrow & Swatek, 2011). Combining all of the league's sites under the league's control has proven to be a brilliant move that has generated additional web traffic and growth in e-commerce (Swangard). Each team's site offers substantial opportunities for e-commerce. For example, fans can buy hats, T-shirts, and jerseys, as well as signed memorabilia from current and past players; it is also easy for them to buy tickets and watch highlights of recent games. The sites also provide fantasy league resources, mobile apps, and plenty of statistical information, as well as blogs posted by players and even cheerleaders. Fans can also find abundant news content that is created by each team's media relations staff and updated regularly, and external sport media members can find contact information for each team.

Streaming Video

The capacity of websites to stream video highlights as well as entire sporting events has opened up another channel for advertisers and fans; this development has been enabled by technological advances that have made the experience more rewarding for fans (Masteralexis et al., 2012). For example, golf fans can not only watch an HD telecast of the Masters; they can also, much like an on-site spectator, follow their favorite golfer around the course online or just focus on one hole and watch all of the golfers come through. Basketball fans who do not like the choice of games during the early rounds of the NCAA tournament can open up the laptop and watch, free of charge, whichever game *they* choose. Cricket fans are also in luck, as ESPN3 has signed a multiyear deal with the IPL, thus allowing fans in the United States to watch the best batsmen from Australia, England, India, Pakistan, and other countries. During the Winter Olympics, cross-country skiing fans can watch all of the events rather than depending on NBC to broadcast bits and pieces. These sites and others like them provide opportunities for sport managers to drive revenue, offer sponsorship opportunities for international businesses, and create jobs for sport management graduates who bring the requisite skills.

Here again, MLB provides a good example. Baseball fans who subscribe to MLB. TV can watch video streams of more than 2,000 games over the course of a season, including 150 spring training games. Those who subscribe at the premium level can select the home or away audio version of games, access a digital video recorder to play back highlights, and watch more than one game at a time. The service also allows MLB teams to create deeper relationships with fans and gives their cable television sponsors an opportunity to reach consumers who are online. Sport management students should keep an eye on the movement of video to the web, which can drive revenue in many ways, including ticket sales, merchandising, and sponsorship. High-quality video content that is exclusive and creative can attract fans to team's websites and keep them there longer, which is highly attractive to potential sponsors.

College basketball conferences face a different challenge. Many do not have big television rights deals with national networks, so they offer fans online streaming of their games. For example, the Horizon League, which features a 2010 and 2011 NCAA men's basketball championship finalist in Butler University, streams all of its men's and women's games online. The league uses a multi-camera shoot and, when it doesn't have a dedicated announcing team, it melds the radio broadcast with its online streaming video. As a result, parents and fans who can't attend a game are able to watch online, wherever in the world they happen to be. The quality of this technology has steadily improved over the years to the point where these streams are now quite good—not television, exactly, but a satisfying viewing experience for the price. Such productions can be managed through companies such as CBS Sports, PrestoSports, Sidearm Sports, and Neulion, who provide services that include streaming content for many college athletic department websites. This type of service is an example of a technological advance in sport media that has created jobs for those who possess the skills necessary to produce these games and post them to the web. Sports information offices at many colleges provide internship opportunities for students to assist in filming and producing these games.

YouTube is also used by sport organizations to promote their contests, post packaged video, and show great performances by their athletes. University sports information directors and their staffs do this all the time, and it represents another great opportunity for student interns to learn how to produce and post a high-quality video clip. Marketing departments for schools and professional teams upload highlights of recent games on a dedicated channel that they have set up on YouTube.

Social Media: Twitter and Facebook

Twitter and Facebook have become very popular ways to meet new friends and stay in touch with large groups of people via the web. These social media have also been adopted by college athletic departments, athletes, coaches, and leagues to reach out to current fans and create a dialogue with new ones. They can be used by ticket managers to announce upcoming game schedules to potential ticket buyers. They can also be used to send traffic back to the school's website. Facebook allows teams to post pictures and video, as well as links to stories that may be of interest to fans. It can also be used to connect fans with sponsors, promote one-time events sponsored by a team or league, and promote specific products (Masteralexis et al., 2012).

Twitter allows sports reporters to post news, share links to interesting stories, follow athletes and teams they cover, and promote their own publisher or network. For example, ESPN writer Bill Simmons has been a very popular member of the Twittersphere. Many athletes and coaches also use Twitter to stay in touch with their fans, and college football and basketball coaches use it to contact recruits.

One of the most prolific users of Twitter as a coach is the University of Kentucky men's basketball coach, John Calipari. He has millions of followers and counting. Shaquille O'Neal of NBA fame has also been an active Tweeter, even in retirement, as have NBA MVP LeBron James, tennis great Rafael Nadal, and the world-famous cricketer, Sachin Tendulchar from India. However, the athletes with the largest Twitter following are both footballers (soccer): Kaka and Renaldo had several million more followers than James, O'Neal, Nadal, or Tendulchar (Laird, 2012).

Twitter is also a great way for sport managers to solicit feedback from their customers or fan base. For example, if Nike introduces a new running shoe, its marketing staff can tweet a request for specific opinions about the shoe's design and functionality. Similarly, an event manager at a sport venue can solicit immediate feedback about a halftime show or time-out promotion (Masteralexis et al., 2012).

Blogs and Podcasts

The weblog or **blog** became a popular form of expression for writers in the late 1990s. These posts, which are usually not very long, can take the form of a diary, a journal, or an opinion about a particular event or subject. Sport blogs have become very popular, both as part of the online presence of sports reporters and as a means of expression for players, fans, and owners. Savvy owners such as Mark Cuban of the Dallas Mavericks and Ted Leonsis of the Washington Capitals and Wizards may update their blogs regularly. The popular website Yahoo! employs a large number of sport bloggers on its sport portal, including blogs for the NFL (Shutdown Corner), MLB (Big League Stew), soccer (Dirty Tackle), and the National Hockey League (Puck Daddy). Yahoo! also links to other sport blogs, such as DC Sports Bog, Sports by Brooks, and The Big Lead.

blog—Term (shortened version of "web log") for an online journal or diary focused on the writer's particular interest in an aspect of sport (e.g., the Miami Heat, the English Premier League, professional football) and typically used as an opportunity to offer commentary and provide web links to related content (e.g., other blogs of interest).

Many websites aggregate blogs for sport fans. Soccerlens provides news and views (http://soccerlens.com). SB Nation covers many sports, leagues, teams, and players (www.sbnation.com). Sports Blogs aggregates more than 1,000 blogs that cover sport (www.sportsblogs.org). FanSided (www.fansided.com) and RantSports (www.rantsports.com) also offer a variety of content created by sport bloggers.

Video and audio versions of blogs are called podcasts, and they are used by many members of the sport media, as well as teams, leagues, and athletes. For many, video offers a more entertaining way to interact with fans, and website publishers like video because advertisements can be imbedded at the beginning of the podcast. A variety of websites offer podcasts relating to sport. One of the more interesting cases is that of Bob Ryan, who in many ways fits the old-school definition of a sports reporter but does his own podcast called Globe 10.0. Ryan discusses the hot topic of the day with other reporters from the *Boston Globe*, where he has been covering Boston sports since the days of the legendary Bill Russell and Red Auerbach.

This new media can be put to good use by sport managers who work for professional teams or college athletic departments. For example, blogs can be posted by coaches and players, and the sport communication office can help them craft their message. Blogs can also be posted in response to particular events or to counteract

SUCCESS STORY

Photo courtesy of Reid Cherner.

Reid Cherner, Sports Reporter

Reid Cherner has been a sports reporter for *USA Today* since 1982, during which time he has covered high school athletics, college basketball and football, sports television, horse racing, and 10 Olympic Games. Cherner has also served as a golf editor and tennis editor. He started in the journalism business at the *Alexandria Gazette* and the *Brazil Times* in Indiana before moving to the Gannett-owned *USA Today*, which has a larger circulation (more than 2 million) than any other U.S. daily, including such prominent publications as the *Wall Street Journal*, the *New York Times*, and the *Washington Post*.

Having seen many changes in the newspaper business, Cherner is a big believer in the use of Twitter, which he sees as a way to gather information from a large number of sources and as a great source of story ideas. In every area he covers, athletes and coaches send tweets, and sports reporters post to Twitter and Facebook during games. Cherner also likes being able to embed video in his stories; for example, if he is covering a golf tournament in which the winner makes a big putt at the end, he can send readers right to the network that covered the putt with a video post.

Cherner views today's media technologies as tools for reaching readers. He and his paper can use Twitter, Facebook, the print newspaper, websites, blogs, and streaming video. They can also use one of these components of their operation to promote another part. In addition, a story by Cherner can be picked up by other newspapers, networks, bloggers, and websites. All of this movement promotes Cherner as a sports reporter and his newspaper as a source of great stories.

Cherner also loves smartphone apps, which put a huge library at his fingertips for conducting research even while riding on the bus or subway. He still believes, however, that the foundation for every good reporter is his or her work ethic. Did the reporter make that extra call and do the necessary legwork to get the story correct? The new media will help a reporter only if he or she is committed to doing the job well.

a negative piece written by someone else. In addition, they serve as a great tool for inviting fans to log on to a team or league website to access exclusive content that is not available anywhere else, thus bringing additional traffic to the site, which makes the marketing director very happy.

Ethics and Sport Media

The enormous power and reach of the media make it especially important to consider well the ethical standards to which the profession aspires on a daily basis. To that end, every reporter for a major newspaper, radio station, or television network has studied those standards and been briefed on them in corporate meetings. The ascendance of new media, however, has brought with it substantial concern about media ethics. Specifically, what ethical responsibility do bloggers and other members of the new media bear in the world of 21st-century sport? Do new media operators have an obligation to host commentators who don't hide behind anonymous noms de plume on the web? Do the dynamics of the web encourage irresponsible posting of gossip on some sport sites?

Truth is a major foundation of all responsible media. Readers, listeners, and viewers must be able to rely on what they read and hear from the media. The media must also demonstrate that they are responsible enough to get the story right. Accuracy involves making that extra phone call, checking that final time with a source, and spending that extra time in the library to understand the industry, team, league, or company that the reporter is covering. Most codes of ethics published by newspapers, radio stations, and television networks call for their employees to stay away from reporting on people or issues where they have too much personal interest at stake. They are also urged not to accept lavish gifts from, say, the owner of the local professional sport team, since doing so could compromise (or be seen as compromising) their ability to function as an independent reporter rather than being a booster of a particular athlete, team, or coach.

A reporter who gets too close to a coach or athlete may find his or her independence tested. For example, if an athlete or coach gets into trouble with the law in the United States, he or she has the same presumption of innocence that all American citizens are guaranteed. On the other hand, it is also possible that the accused person is guilty, but what if the sports reporter has grown too close to the player or coach? Members of the public depend on the media to gather information that they themselves don't have the ability to find, and the building blocks for a great story are still the basic questions of journalism: who, what, when, where, why, and how? If members of the public see that these questions are not being asked, they lose trust in the media. They also question the media's credibility if they get a sense of piling on in the reporting of a story. Such perceptions can hinge not only on what is reported but also what is left out, which sometimes serves as a subtle indication of bias.

The new media of bloggers, tweeters, podcasters, and Facebook posters will and should be judged according to the same measuring sticks used for traditional media. A blogger, for instance, must check facts. More broadly, when reporters or sport management professionals tweet, post to Facebook, or otherwise post online, they are publishing information. And when they do so, they have satisfied one of the requirements of a defamation charge. Sport management professionals simply must ensure that the information they post online or produce in print is accurate. Indeed, tweets and Facebook entries are in some ways more permanent than a newspaper story. A newspaper publisher prints only so many newspapers, and they are

MAJOR THEMES IN SPORT COMMUNICATION ETHICS

Truth	Independence
Accuracy	Accountability
Fairness	

Concepts from Schultz et al. 2010.

INTERNATIONAL APPLICATION

Eurosport

Eurosport was launched in 1989 as a European version of ESPN. It is currently available in 59 countries, most of which are on the European continent, but can also be seen in parts of Asia and North Africa. Headquartered in Paris, Eurosport is the largest cable sports network in Europe. The French media company TF1 currently owns 100% of Eurosport. In 1999, this media company also launched a website that is now offered in 11 languages and attracts millions of unique visitors a month.

In 2007, Eurosport partnered with Yahoo! Europe to host its sport website, and it expanded its media business to include an all-news network, an HD channel, and an iPhone app; as of February 2010, the app had been downloaded more than a million times (Cushnan, 2010). Eurosport has also begun to manage and produce international sport events—for example, the FIA World Touring Car Championship.

Eurosport combines studio programming with presentation of live and recorded sporting events. Viewers can watch soccer, tennis, handball, golf, rugby, snooker, biathlon, figure skating, Formula One racing and other motorsports, Australian rules football, cricket, and martial arts. In 2010, the network also presented a full schedule of events from the Vancouver Winter Olympics.

usually available only in a limited geographic area. In contrast, a Facebook post or a tweet can be read anywhere in the world, and that should give the writer pause. Moreover, a blogger's audience is just as human as the readership of the newspaper reporter who writes for the local daily, and words can damage reputations, feelings, and job prospects.

Many resources publish discussions about ethical issues in journalism—for example, *Broadcasting & Cable* and the *Columbia Journalism Review*. Many newspapers and television networks also publish their own code of ethics on their website.

The Short of It

- Despite all the technological changes in sport media, the ability to write well is still an important skill for all sport managers.
- The emergence of new media technology has not changed the ethical obligations of those who communicate with the public through sport media.
- Journalists use Twitter to disseminate information and find out what athletes and coaches are tweeting.
- Internships with media companies and sports information offices on college campuses offer great opportunities for students to build their skills.

CHAPTER 10

Sport Economics

Jim West

In this chapter, you will learn the following:

✓ The difference between micro- and macroeconomics
✓ Unique economic circumstances of professional and collegiate sport
✓ The importance of economic impact studies in sport
✓ The dynamics of demand, supply, and market equilibrium

> The biggest thrill wasn't in winning on Sunday but in meeting the payroll on Monday.
>
> **Art Rooney**, owner of the Pittsburgh Steelers during the early years of the NFL

Kevin Plank, founder and CEO of Under Armour, has seen his company grow by leaps and bounds. The company has had to contend not only with strong competitors (e.g., Adidas, New Balance, Nike, Puma) but also with the less-than-ideal market forces affecting the world economy around the end of the first decade of the 21st century: high unemployment rates, stagnant wages, and sluggish economies. This business climate makes it hard to grow a company. Under Armour has had to find a stable economy in which to manufacture its shoes, which involves finding a labor market where the work will be done for a cost that is comparable to what its competitors pay for the manufacture of their shoes. In making such a decision, any company that chooses to manufacture its products abroad must analyze the government where the factory will be located in order to be certain that its investment will be a sound one. (As discussed later in this chapter, government policies can help promote the formation of businesses and markets.) Indeed, Under Armour's major competitor—Nike—has moved its manufacturing locus several times in order to lower its labor costs. Business decisions can also be affected by many other factors. For example, Under Armour might decide to ramp up production of a new line of shoes or apparel if banks are offering loans with low **interest rates**. It might also decide to ramp up production for cleats in order to meet demand in growing sports such as lacrosse, soccer, and cricket. In fact, analyzing such trends in demand is an important job for sport managers who work for companies, such as Under Armour, that sell in markets around the world. One valuable resource for performing such research is the Sports & Fitness Industry Association (SFIA), formerly the Sporting Goods Manufacturers Association.

interest rates—Cost of borrowing money charged by lending institutions such as banks and credit unions; measured as a percentage of the money borrowed (e.g., 7.6 percent).

Sport economics is the study of how individuals and firms react to incentives, how they handle scarcity, and how particular economies have been structured both by the market and by government. This chapter analyzes factors that affect sport microeconomies, such as the English Premier League (EPL), the National Football League (NFL), the Indian Premier League (IPL), National Collegiate Athletic Association (NCAA) football, sports broadcasting, and the manufacture of basketball or running shoes. The chapter begins by reviewing key economic terms, then examines economies in professional sport leagues and collegiate athletics. It also addresses government regulation, fiscal policy, gambling, and the role of fantasy leagues in the sport economy, as well as the effect that the global economy has had on the sport industry. The success story for this chapter highlights former NFL commissioner Pete Rozelle, and the international application focuses on cricket in India and the fabulously profitable IPL.

Macro- and Microeconomics

Macroeconomics involves big-picture issues, such as employment, money supply, interest rates, economic growth, and **inflation**; microeconomics, on the other hand, looks at individuals, companies, and groups of firms to see how they make decisions affecting household income, industry economies, and corporate balance sheets. Thus the study of professional sport leagues is a microeconomics pursuit, but this does not mean that inflation, interest rates, or an economic downturn will not affect the profitability of, say, the Dallas Cowboys, Manchester United, the Montreal Canadiens, or the Boston Celtics. In the case of baseball, the Major League Baseball Players Association is a microeconomic factor, but a downturn in the overall economy can also affect wages. Similarly, New York Yankees star Alex Rodriguez, despite making a very good living, will be affected by a jump in a macroeconomic measure such as the inflation rate.

Economic factors can also exert effects across sports. For example, a sudden rise in unemployment in Canada will affect professional sport franchises in the National Hockey League (NHL) and the Canadian Football League (CFL)—the fewer employed potential consumers in an area, the fewer potential ticket buyers (Leeds, 2005). In another example, the study of the NHL or the CFL falls within the realm of the microeconomic, but macroeconomic issues come into play when considering how many people are employed in the United States or Canada. All would agree, of course, that a thriving economy employs more workers, which in turn gives those workers discretionary income with which to buy tickets to see their favorite NHL or CFL players and teams.

Gross domestic product (GDP) is a macroeconomic term that refers to the value of the total goods and services produced in a given year by a country's economy. Growth in GDP indicates that the economy is expanding, which usually means more jobs; as discussed later in this chapter, a growth in GDP in India has helped fuel the IPL's growth. When the domestic economy does not grow, it is considered to be in **recession**. A recession can negatively affect the sport industry in two respects. First, if revenue declines, then leagues, teams, athletic departments, marketing and management agencies, and sporting goods manufacturers may have to reduce costs, which may involve firing employees. Second, a recession may force businesses to lower their prices in order to attract customers, which may result in even lower revenue and force further layoffs. As these scenarios illustrate, sport managers must pay attention

inflation—Sustained increase in the price of a good or service, or of many goods and services, in an economy.

gross domestic product (GDP)—Total value of all goods and services produced in a particular economy in a given year.

recession—Period during a business cycle when the production of a particular economy recedes or shrinks in terms of measurable outputs, such as GDP, employment, consumer income, and exports; usually marked by a rise in the unemployment rate and a drop in wages.

to current macroeconomic news. For example, a sudden spike in the unemployment rate might be a good time to run a "buy one get one free" sale at a sporting goods store or a "kids get in free" day at the weekend hockey game in Calgary or Montreal.

Another macroeconomic measure used by economists in the United States to analyze the relative strength or weakness of the economy is the interest rate charged by banks and by the U.S. Federal Reserve System (the central banking system) for the use of their money. A lower interest rate means that money is cheaper, which means that businesses are more likely to borrow in order to expand. When businesses expand, they generally hire more employees to fuel and administer that expansion.

Rapid business expansion can spur a concomitant rise in the cost of hiring new employees; wages increase when the demand for workers is greater than the supply. An increase in wages can cause inflation, which can have a debilitating effect on wide areas of the economy. For example, inflation can increase the cost of transporting tennis shoes from factories to stores; similarly, a rise in food prices can force stadiums and arenas to raise their concession stand prices. Sport teams also have to travel to play away games, and an increase in the cost of air travel could spur teams to raise their ticket prices (Borland & MacDonald, 2003). In an example from the media, a rise in the production costs of sports programming might cause consumers to see an increase in their cable television rates; in fact, in some cases, when cable companies and satellite providers have increased their rates, they have blamed the increase on rights fees charged by sport entities such as the EPL, the NFL, and the National Basketball Association (NBA).

There are exceptions. For example, in some cases, producers may not mind selling less of a product if they can charge more per unit and thus bring in more total revenue than if they had lowered the price and sold more of the product. This approach is used in selling club seats and luxury suites at sport venues. Facility owners charge more

Management Insight

The Federal Reserve System (aka the Fed), which is the central banking system of the United States, is made up of 12 district banks and 25 regional branches. The system is run by a seven-member board of governors, along with a committee that helps make day-to-day monetary decisions. Each governor is appointed by the U.S. president and serves a 14-year term. The chair of the Fed serves a four-year term. Over the years, the Fed chair has often been a focus of media scrutiny; for example, current (as of 2012) chair Ben Bernanke and predecessors Alan Greenspan and Paul Volcker have all been the subject of countless articles about their Fed terms and even their personal lives. The Fed attempts to use sound policy for money supply and interest rates in order to preserve orderly dynamics in financial markets. It also maintains bank accounts for the U.S. Department of the Treasury and many government agencies. When the Fed lowers what is called the discount rate, businesses can borrow money less expensively. If the Fed keeps interest rates down, the cost of borrowing may also drop for consumers, which means they may have more discretionary income to spend on leisure items such as tickets to sport events, tennis lessons, and fishing poles.

for access to these sections; as a result, even though there are relatively few available, the owner makes more money than he or she would if these locations were used to provide more general seating. In another kind of exception, consumers' reaction to a price change is sometimes slow—if, for example, consumers are searching for a suitable substitute but none is readily available at that time. The degree of this responsiveness associated with a product (good or service) is referred to by economists as **elasticity of demand**. The demand for a product can also be affected by a change in the price of another product; for instance, a drastic increase in the price of golf clubs could lower the demand for golf balls. The measure of this type of consumer reaction is called the **cross-price elasticity of demand**. In another example, a large increase in gas prices could reduce sport tourism around the country; if so, fewer sport fans would choose to drive to visit halls of fame, golf resorts, and spectator events. Similarly, if the Los Angeles Lakers and the Los Angeles Clippers both decided to double their ticket prices, it is possible that nearby high school and college basketball teams would see a rise in attendance at their games (Leeds, 2005).

The number of choices available to consumers and suppliers in any given market is a function of that market's structure. Is the market characterized by **perfect competition**—that is, do buyers and sellers have many choices at similar prices and levels of quality? Or are consumers confronted with a market dominated by one supplier, who effectively controls supply, quality, and price? This type of market is called a **monopoly**. If, for example, you live in Chicago and love professional basketball, you have only one local choice, the NBA's Chicago Bulls. If, however, you like college or high school basketball, then the Chicago market does not look so bad for you; in addition, you have options in how you react to price hikes by the Bulls (Masteralexis, Barr, & Hums, 2012).

A market that falls between monopoly and perfect competition for the consumer is called an **oligopoly**. In this type of market, consumers do have a few choices, but suppliers enjoy more security than in a perfectly competitive market. The restaurant business involves a market that could be called perfectly competitive. As a restaurant owner, you must compete in terms of price, service, location, and quality, and consumers can vote with their feet. If you don't please a consumer the first time, you may lose him or her forever. Examples of monopoly, on the other hand, can be found in single-team professional football towns, such as Green Bay, Wisconsin, and in the one-team professional basketball market in San Antonio, Texas. A good example of oligopoly is the market for caffeinated soda, which is ruled by Pepsi, Coca-Cola, and Dr. Pepper.

The sport enterprises found in an economy vary by their respective business objectives. A sport organization can seek to maximize profit, revenue, or winning. Most enterprises focus on profit maximization, which hinges solely on

elasticity of demand—Measure of a market's reaction to a change in a particular product's price.

cross-price elasticity of demand—Effect of a product's change in price on the demand for a second product that can be complementary to or substitute for the first.

perfect competition—Market condition in which there is a large number of buyers and sellers, there are no barriers to entry or exit, no single entity controls the market, and information is readily available regarding price, cost to produce, and quality.

monopoly—Market in which one seller has either no competitors or only competitors with a small fraction of the market.

oligopoly—Market that is controlled by a very small number of sellers and, typically, is very expensive for new sellers to enter.

Management Insight

When prices rise—for example, the cost of sports television programming, basketball game tickets, or golf clubs—consumers look for substitutes for those commodities. On the other hand, if the price of, say, golf clubs drops, then consumers can afford to purchase more of that product (Leeds, 2005). These reactions by consumers to price changes are referred to in economics as the law of demand.

When a company in the sport industry—say, an apparel or shoe company, or a sport team—sees that a product is popular and can be priced higher, the company will attempt to meet market demand (and make more money) by supplying more of that product. For example, the EPL, Real Madrid, and FC Barcelona have each met the increased demand for soccer in the United States by selling more media rights to their games to U.S. media companies (Niemann, Garcia, & Grant, 2011). Similarly, when the Dallas Cowboys organization realized that its brand was popular outside the borders of Texas, it made Cowboys branded gear available all over the United States. These changes in behavior by suppliers are referred to in economics as the law of supply.

The price of a product is determined by both the quantity supplied by producers and the quantity demanded by consumers. The price where demand and supply are equal is known as **market equilibrium**. The intersection of the product supply curve and the consumer demand curve for that product, or market equilibrium, can be seen in figure 10.1.

> **market equilibrium**—Condition in which the price established for a product is such that demand for the product is equal to the amount produced.

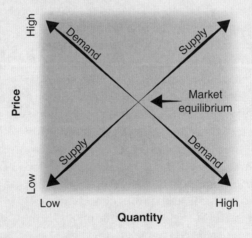

FIGURE 10.1 Demand and market equilibrium.

There is only one boss. The customer. And he can fire everybody in the company from the chairman on down, simply by spending his money somewhere else.

Sam Walton, founder of Walmart

attaining the largest possible net profit margin (after expenses). In contrast, revenue maximization (also known as sales maximization) involves generating the most revenue (sales) possible. This does not always translate into maximized profit, since emphasis is not placed on the expenses incurred in pursuit of revenue. The third approach—win maximization—is favored by many professional sport teams. Sport franchises in a league are interdependent, and while each team emphasizes winning, the teams also share revenue as the league seeks to maximize competitiveness. This approach relates to utility maximization in professional sports where a combination of profits and wins is paramount (Rascher, 1997).

Finally, sports and sport organizations are influenced by sport delivery systems, which reflect each sport's respective cultural, economic, and political foundations. Therefore, a sport organization's location influences how it is organized. The infrastructure of a sport enterprise (whether community, school-based, or business-oriented) is also influenced by its position on several axes: pleasure versus performance orientation, mass participation versus elite competition, not-for-profit versus for-profit organization, and amateur versus professional status. The overall professional sport system in the United States, for example, is an elite, competitive, performance-based, for-profit enterprise—and the pinnacle of sport business.

The Economics of Sport Leagues

A professional sport league is itself a sort of economy formed by a collection of team owners who pay players to perform a certain number of times each season and compete for championships. Each league is governed by a commissioner, who is appointed by the owners and who assembles a league office to administer the rules and the business of the league.

Professional leagues serve as the basis for an exclusive sport labor market. In the United States, owners, player's associations, and managers are governed by the National Labor Relations Act and the corresponding National Labor Relations Board. In addition, each league operates according to a collective bargaining agreement that was hammered out through negotiation with the relevant players association. Players have the right to organize (e.g., form a players union), bargain collectively via player representatives, and strike. In fact, players unions or associations have become quite powerful. They have negotiated very high minimum salaries for their members, lucrative merchandising agreements, and large salary pools; they have also given their members excellent guidance in working with agents and marketing representatives.

Rules of play for each league are established by the league office with input from owners and sometimes from coaches or general managers. Rules have often been changed in an attempt to increase a sport's popularity. Examples abound: Professional basketball added the 24-second clock and the 3-point shot; on the college level, when organizers increased the number of referees from two to three, a study performed by economists found that fewer fouls were called, players adjusted, and the change resulted in a more aesthetically pleasing game (Goff & Tollison, 1990). Instant replay has been added by a number of sports to confirm officiating decisions, and, given the controversy about referee error in recent World Cup's, it merits consideration for use in future editions of that event. Leagues have also added official time-outs to accommodate broadcasters' desire to run more commercials during telecasts. In England, professional soccer uses a white ball to make it easier for spectators to follow the action.

Leagues invariably try to promote competitive balance among their members. Competitive balance preserves the uncertainty of outcome that fans want in sport. Studies of unbalanced leagues have shown that attendance drops when fans already know who will win a particular game, and attendance and television viewership are of course key components of a league's economic health. Other measures used by leagues to preserve balance include the reverse-order player draft, the salary cap, the luxury tax assessed against owners who overspend, trade deadlines to prevent the dumping of players near the end of the season, and revenue sharing. It is no coincidence that of the big four professional sport leagues in the United States (MLB, the NBA, the NFL, and the NHL), the one with the most revenue sharing—the NFL—is the healthiest (for more information, see the profile of former NFL commissioner Pete Rozelle in this chapter).

Teams in these leagues compete not only in games but also for players in the free agent market; however, they function as a single entity in terms of marketing, scheduling, negotiation of national television deals, and many sponsorship opportunities. Owners also control the entry of new franchises and the movement of current franchises to different cities. Each league is vigilant to avoid diluting the market with its product, and owners tend to seek to preserve monopoly positions in large population centers. Owners of professional franchises also like options. They want an exclusive market for their team and plenty of choices if they decide that their current location has not sufficiently enhanced the value of their franchise. Macroeconomic factors such as full employment and low interest rates create an environment that produces many entrepreneurs who want to join the exclusive club of professional sport team owners.

 Pro football was nothing until he became commissioner.

Red Auerbach, Hall of Fame Boston Celtics coach, talking about Pete Rozelle

SUCCESS STORY

Pete Rozelle, Former NFL Commissioner

Pete Rozelle grew up in the United States as a "depression baby." His youth was marked by a combination of tremendous economic hardship and having to serve his country in World War II. When Rozelle returned from Naval service on an oil tanker in the Pacific theater, he completed his college education at the University of San Francisco (USF). By the time he graduated, Rozelle had played baseball and basketball and dabbled as a sports information assistant, both at USF and at Compton Community College. He then entered the world of public relations, working first for an independent firm, then with the NFL's Los Angeles Rams, and also as a public relations assistant during the 1956 Olympic Games in Melbourne, Australia. Soon after returning from the Olympics, he was hired as general manager for the Rams, and he remained in that position until he was named as the surprise choice for NFL commissioner in 1960. Rozelle served as NFL commissioner until 1989, and many people both in and out of football think he was the best professional sport leader of his era. Rozelle was rewarded for his accomplishments by being elected into the Pro Football Hall of Fame in 1985.

When Rozelle became NFL commissioner, the league had only 12 teams, NFL games were rarely seen on television, individual teams negotiated their own TV packages, and the league did not bring in much revenue from marketing and merchandising. By the time Rozelle retired, the league had 28 teams, NFL Properties had been created to consolidate marketing and merchandising in the league office, the *Monday Night Football* television franchise had been created, and the overall financial health of each football team was greatly improved. How did he do it? For one thing, he moved the league offices to New York and began to court the major TV networks, which were also headquartered there. He was also instrumental in the passage of the Sports Broadcasting Act of 1961, which permitted the NFL to aggregate its negotiations with the networks for TV contracts; his savvy lobbying, of course, also benefited the NBA, MLB, the NHL, and the NCAA.

Rozelle's tenure also saw the merger of the NFL with the American Football League and the creation of the Super Bowl. But perhaps his biggest effect on the overall health of the NFL economy came through his work to convince the owners to share gate and television revenue. This profit sharing permitted smaller-market teams to stay competitive with franchises located in larger population centers, thus maintaining the league's competitive balance. As a result, for example, the city of Pittsburgh—home of the Steelers—does not suffer for being a smaller-market team in the NFL.

The Economics of College Athletics

The market created by the formation of the NCAA most closely resembles a cartel. However, the NCAA is different from other cartels in that (as discussed in more detail in chapter 5) it was created not for economic reasons but to address safety-related concerns about college football. From these humble beginnings in 1906, the NCAA has grown to preside over the athletic economy, as it were, of more than a thousand schools and hundreds of thousands of athletes who participate in athletics at those schools. Some of these athletes pay full tuition, others enjoy partial scholarships that cover a portion of tuition, and still others—those who are the most athletically accomplished and heavily recruited—receive full scholarships. The expenses covered by full scholarships are detailed in the voluminous book of rules that the NCAA publishes every year. Current guidelines allow athletic scholarships to cover the cost of room, board, books, tuition, and fees. Non-athletes on full *academic* scholarship are often also granted the cost of attendance, which includes flights to and from home at the beginning and end of each semester, as well as additional stipends for meal money. This difference has prompted much discussion by schools, conferences, and the NCAA and has resulted in proposed legislation allowing conferences to grant a US$2,000 stipend to students on full athletic scholarship.

Athletes who receive a full scholarship agree to limits on how they associate with player agents, when they declare for a professional league's entry draft, and how much income they can earn during their time on scholarship. The value of a full scholarship is the same for the worst player and for the best player on the team. Thus, a potential first-round draft choice in the NBA receives no more in benefits than a scholarship teammate who never plays in a game.

The type of labor market power held by a cartel is called monopsony power. The NCAA uses this type of power to control compensation and sets limits on the number of games each team can play, how many days and hours players are permitted to practice, and what type of gifts each player can receive for winning a league title or national championship. As a nonprofit organization, the NCAA also enjoys tax-exempt status, as do the athletic departments at NCAA schools—even those that gross more than US$100 million annually and pay some of their coaches millions of dollars a year (Mahony & DeSchriver, 2008).

The NCAA pools television income from championship broadcasts and returns a large percentage of this money to the individual schools that make up the organization. Conferences and leagues within the NCAA do the same thing with the television money earned from their regular season games and conference tournaments. Indeed, leagues have been formed around the popularity of their teams among television audiences, and some leagues have become quite attractive to networks such as ESPN, Fox, and CBS. Nonetheless, the value of a scholarship has remained fairly stable (taking inflation into account) over the last 30 years; that is to say, the overall value of scholarships has paralleled the overall cost of a college education, meaning that it has risen but not nearly at the rate of increase for television contracts, sponsorships, and attendance revenues received by the NCAA and its member conferences and institutions. The argument for this lack of correlation between the income generated and the value of a scholarship hinges on the notion that athletes are attending college in order to pursue their education, that their compensation is a free education, and that anything more than this would distract them from their studies.

Outside Influences That Affect Sport Economies

The entities that most dramatically affect sport economies around the world are the governments—national, state, and local—that wield power where businesses are located. Certain kinds of tax policy, for instance, can absolutely hamstring a business; conversely, lower property tax rates for a new stadium can encourage a team to renovate or relocate in order to receive such breaks. Similarly, tax policy in Canada might encourage free agents in MLB, the NBA, or the NHL to leave that country and sign with a team in the United States. The effect of a government action may also be selective. For example, a luxury tax will not greatly affect the sale of baseball gloves but could drive potential customers out of the yacht and sailboat markets.

In the last two decades, some cities have offered sweetheart deals to encourage professional teams to move to their area (Weiner, 2000). In doing so, supporters may paint a rosy picture of the benefits for local taxpayers by citing **economic impact studies**, which estimate changes in factors such as employment, revenue generation, and taxation derived from sporting events or facilities (DeSchriver & Mahony, 2011). Other studies, however, have shown that taxpayers do not receive much benefit at all (Matheson, 2008; Baade & Matheson, 2011). In fact, experts disagree sharply about the effect of sporting facilities and events, and estimates can be manipulated by biased researchers (DeSchriver & Mahony). For the sake of all parties, impact studies should be accurate, and sport managers must take care to use accurate studies in seeking or justifying subsidies (e.g., tax breaks, facility construction) from local communities (Fort, 2010). Such research often addresses spending patterns and hiring impacts; for example, both mega events (e.g., the Olympic Games, the World Cup, the Super Bowl) and local events can foster considerable economic activity. Intangible effects (e.g., civic pride in hosting a successful Special Olympics competition) are typically not addressed in an economic impact study (Styles, Baker, & Hurley, 2004).

> **economic impact study**—A study performed in order to estimate the effect a team, sports league, sports facility, or sporting event has on a particular economy.

Teams pay close attention to changes in tax law. For example, a change in tax law governing the expense of entertaining lobbyists might negatively affect the purchase of tickets to games played by professional teams in Washington, DC. On the other hand, a local government's decision to build a subway stop near a stadium or arena owned by an MLB or NHL franchise will add value to that facility and increase the foot traffic to events at that location.

The first lesson of economics is scarcity; there is never enough of anything to fully satisfy all those who want it. The first lesson of politics is to disregard the first lesson of economics.

Thomas Sowell, economist, professor, and author

Another area of the law—intellectual property protection—has had a positive effect on the sport economies of the world. For example, trademark enforcement reduces the sale of knockoff Air Jordans and unlicensed New York Knicks jerseys. Patent protection enhances the market for new inventions in the world of sporting goods. New technology has also been a big driver of revenue in the world of sport media, which has added new revenue streams thanks to smartphones, advances in television (3-D, high-definition, and satellite), and the expansion of Internet media. Google, YouTube, Facebook, and Twitter have all been used as additional platforms for marketing professional teams and leagues, college teams and conferences, and individual athletes themselves.

Any nation's sport industry is greatly affected by that country's type of government. Generally speaking, the sport industry favors open markets. China and India, for example, have seen tremendous growth in their sport industries since their economies moved toward open market structures (Gupta, 2010; Antoniewicz, 2008). Another area of concern is security. If a government has problems in this area, the trouble not only affects the nation's general economy but also makes it more difficult for team owners and sport entrepreneurs to develop sport properties in that country. One example is Pakistan, whose neighbor India has developed a wildly successful cricket league (the IPL), even as Pakistan's internal issues with bombings, government corruption, and allegations of match fixing have prevented it from duplicating India's success. Cricket is just as popular in Pakistan, but that country has not yet provided fertile ground for business. Sport economies flourish in places with a stable democratic government that respects property rights and maintains an effective legal system for enforcing contracts; nations that provide such conditions also encourage sporting goods companies to build factories there.

More broadly, a government that implements policies encouraging open markets can spur the development of an entire economy, which can end up benefiting a sport entrepreneur such as the NFL's Pete Rozelle or the IPL's Lalit Modi. Would Yao Ming have played basketball in the United States if China had not opened its markets to U.S. companies? Chinese government policies have helped grow the NBA in China and spurred the growth of basketball leagues indigenous to China; specifically, the Chinese government consciously decided to introduce commercial principles to its management of the sport of basketball (Tan & Bairner, 2011). Similarly, when India moved to a market-based economy in the 1990s, that country saw a huge growth in GDP, standard of living, and the size of the middle class, all of which helped create the IPL (featured at the end of this chapter).

Discrimination, on the other hand, has been a market force that has limited economic growth in the sport industry, and government intervention in this area has helped open markets to large groups of people who previously did not have access to the sport economy. Three key examples of such intervention in the United States are Title IX (Education Amendments, 1972), the Americans With Disabilities Act of 1990 (ADA), and the Supreme Court decision in *Brown v. Board of Education* (1954).

Title IX of the Education Amendments of 1972 opened up athletic opportunities for women at the high school and college levels; indeed, since the act's passage, the United States has seen an explosion of female participation in athletics. This increase has also benefited sporting goods manufacturers by helping to create a huge market for women's running shoes, sports apparel, golf clubs, and other sport-related items. Similarly, the ADA (1990) has opened up athletic participation and competition to individuals with disabilities. The Special Olympics movement is one example of the far-reaching effect of the ADA and similar legislation around the world (see chapter 4 for more about the Special Olympics). The Paralympic Games have been aligned with the Olympic Games, and new technologies make it easier for persons with a disability to participate in a variety of sports, including basketball, skiing, and hockey. Beyond these changes at the elite level, inclusive sport at all levels of competition, as reflected by accommodations made for athletes, has not only made it commonplace for individuals with disabilities to spectate or compete alongside their able-bodied peers but also opened a new market within the sport economy. The Supreme Court's decision in *Brown v. Board of Education* (1954), which declared racial segregation in the nation's public schools to be unconstitutional, opened the schools to a large segment of the U.S. population, thus also opening school athletic teams to a group of athletes who had been previously excluded based on their race. These three governmental actions (Title IX, the ADA, and the *Brown* decision)—combined with the courage of athletes such as Jackie Robinson, Sweetwater Clifton, Billie Jean King, Casey Martin, and Sam Cunningham—have helped expand the sport economy in the United States and create a sport marketplace that comes closer to fair and open competition for all.

Another market force that influences the sport economy is fan interest in gambling. Legal and illegal gambling are very large industries, both in the United States and wherever one finds professional sport around the world. In the United States, fans bet on contests in all of the major professional sport leagues, as well as college football and basketball games. This betting is legal in Nevada, and many countries other than the United States permit gambling on athletic contests in, for example, the EPL, the J. League (Japan's soccer league), professional golf, auto racing, and tennis. Places where betting is quite popular include Hong Kong (China), Japan, the United Kingdom, France, Australia, and Italy (Beech & Chadwick, 2004).

In the United States, fantasy leagues have become popular, and many media companies have taken advantage of this development with advertising campaigns to promote their sponsorship of these leagues (Swangard, 2008). From an economic standpoint, football is probably the major beneficiary of the near-obsession with gambling in the United States. Of the reported 32 million people who participated in fantasy leagues in 2011, more than 24 million were members of an NFL league (Fantasy Sports Trade Association, 2012). Indeed, Sunday has become a day of activity for many football fans, as they keep close track of game results and update the statistics of their chosen fantasy team for the week. Fantasy leagues provide a good example of innovation in the sport industry by a few perceptive sport managers. This relatively recent phenomenon, enabled by the Internet, has created a new revenue source for sport leagues and sport media companies (Swangard). Similarly, sport-related video games have contributed to a new area of the sport economy, and product placement within those games has become a new avenue for sponsorship revenue. Such changes illustrate the fact that sport management students who monitor industry developments and understand sport history and sport sociology can position themselves to be ahead of new trends and thus make themselves valuable to a sport industry employer.

INTERNATIONAL APPLICATION

Indian Premier League

India's professional cricket league, the Indian Premier League (IPL), has become one of the most successful and profitable sport leagues in the world. In 2010, for example, a new franchise in the city of Pune was auctioned off for more than US$300 million. To put this in perspective, Michael Jordan bought the NBA franchise in Charlotte, the Bobcats, in the same year for just over US$200 million. The IPL was the brainchild of Lalit Modi, an Indian businessman, and Andrew Wildblood, an IMG executive based in England. The first match was played in April 2008, and the league has grown quickly ever since. The games, played in large stadiums around India, draw huge crowds and impressive television ratings (Gupta, 2010).

In just a few years, the IPL has created a brand in India that leagues around the world are going to study and emulate. The league started out with eight teams from major population centers: the Delhi Daredevils, the Rajasthan Royals, the Kolkata Knight Riders, the Royal Challengers Bangalore, the Chennai Super Kings, the Mumbai Indians, the Kings XI Punjab, and the Deccan Chargers (now folded into another Hyderabad franchise). Games are played over a span of 45 days, during which one or two games per night are televised all over India. At the end of the season, the top two teams compete for the championship.

The IPL has signed deals to televise its games across Asia and into Europe and Oceania. Broadcasting rights were sold to Sony for US$1.94 billion over a period of 10 years (Gupta, 2010). Google and YouTube have also signed with the IPL, and the first year of the deal did much better than expected. Google signed major advertisers (e.g., HSBC, Hewlett-Packard, Samsung, Airtel), and more than 50 million views were recorded during the 2010 season on the IPL's YouTube channel.

In fact, the IPL has become so popular and lucrative for cricketers that its teams attract some of the best athletes from around the world (Gupta, 2010). As a result, the league has helped an already popular sport become even more popular in India. Cricket is by far the most watched spectator sport in India, and, with the country's population over a billion people, advertisers have flocked to the broadcasts to sell their products. The Pune franchise was added for the 2011 season, and the league's revenue is projected to continue its rise (Gupta).

One foundation of the IPL's tremendous growth has been the overall strength of the Indian economy. The middle class in India has seen staggering growth in overall discretionary income, which fuels spending on leisure activities. Couple this with the growth of the GDP in India, and more and more people can afford to buy products advertised on IPL telecasts.

Teams and the league as a whole take advantage of every opportunity for signage; even players' helmets and referees' uniforms are used for product placement. Kingfisher Airlines has a multiyear deal to outfit the referees. Attending games has become the thing to do among wealthy people, Indian government officials, and the Bollywood set. Like professional athletes in the United States, IPL stars have signed big endorsement deals, both with Indian companies and with multinational companies doing business in India. In addition, all IPL teams have merchandising agreements with manufacturers that produce branded products, such as key chains, hats, polo shirts, coffee cups, and water bottles. The league has also signed a multimillion dollar deal for its website rights.

The IPL has proposed adding games and raising the per-team salary cap to permit teams to be more competitive in their bidding for the best bowlers, batsmen, and all-rounders from the cricket-playing countries of the world. In the future, the IPL's growth could be hampered by two main areas of concern: security issues amid the specter of the 2011 Mumbai bombings and allegations of corruption (Gupta, 2010). For example, the recently formed anticorruption arm of the Board of Control for Cricket in India (BCCI), spurred by an investigative report by India TV, alleged that both players and IPL executives were involved in such acts as match-fixing and illegal payments (Gallapudi, 2012). As sport and society often reflect each other, the microcosm of cricket could have a positive influence on society if the IPL cleans up its act.

The Short of It

- Governmental policies such as federal legislation, the income tax rate, and interest rates affect sport businesses.
- A unique aspect of sport leagues is that they are permitted by current common law to act in an anticompetitive manner in relation to business practices, in order to preserve competitive balance on the playing field.
- A recession in the world economy has an impact on the sports industry.
- When analyzing the economies of college and professional sports, the impact of television money cannot be underestimated.

Sport Finance

In this chapter, you will learn the following:

✓ What a balance sheet and income statement include
✓ Major revenue sources and expenses in the sport industry
✓ The importance of television revenue in college and professional sport
✓ Major differences between the finances of a professional team and those of a college team

> Beware of little expenses. A small leak will sink a great ship.
>
> **Benjamin Franklin**

Sandy Barbour, the athletic director at the University of California, Berkeley, and Robert Birgeneau, the university's president, were faced with a tough decision. The U.S. economy and, to a greater extent, the California economy were experiencing a downturn that was reducing the state's contributions to all of its academic institutions. Meanwhile, the costs of operating 29 athletic programs in the Pac-10 (now Pac-12) Conference were moving in the opposite direction. In response, with Birgeneau's approval, Barbour took the drastic step of eliminating five intercollegiate athletic programs: baseball, men's and women's gymnastics, women's lacrosse, and rugby, even though the rugby team had recently won a national championship and the baseball team had been in existence for 119 years; in fact, several Cal grads were playing for teams in Major League Baseball (MLB).

When Barbour and Birgeneau announced their decision in the middle of 2010, they became two of the most unpopular people on campus. At the same time, a number of alumni, former players, and other donors went to work (Berenson, 2011) and ended up raising enough money (almost US$10 million) to satisfy the administration that the eliminated teams would be on solid footing for years to come. As a result, Barbour made the dramatic announcement that they had been reinstated right in the middle of the Bears' run to the College World Series in 2011 (Berenson).

Every enterprise, from a mom-and-pop startup to a municipal T-ball association, must pay attention to the money leaving its business in the form of expenses and to the money it generates in the form of revenue. As the Cal story illustrates, universities and their athletic departments—even though they are in the education business—must also obey this rule of finance. So, how does sport finance work? The answer to that question is the focus of this chapter, which addresses a number of more specific questions, such as the following: How does one account for revenue and expenses? What is an income statement? What is a balance sheet? What is the typical financial structure of a high school athletics department? How does a college athletics department make money? The chapter also explains how the major U.S. professional sport leagues operate. It will come as no surprise that salaries account for a large part of the expenses incurred by a typical professional franchise in MLB, the National Hockey League (NHL), the National Basketball Association (NBA), and the National Football League (NFL). It might surprise you, however, to learn just how important television revenue has become to both professional and intercollegiate sport business.

Quick Facts

- In 1919, Boston Red Sox owner Harry Frazee sold Babe Ruth to the New York Yankees for US$125,000.

- In 2001, baseball star Alex Rodriguez signed a 10-year contract with the Texas Rangers worth US$252 million.

- In 2009, soccer star Cristiano Ronaldo was sold to Real Madrid by Manchester United for £80 million (more than US$120 million at the time).

- Chicago's iconic baseball park, Wrigley Field, was built in 1914 for US$250,000 with a seating capacity of 14,000.

- The new Yankee Stadium, which opened in 2009, cost US$1.2 billion to build.

- If you had bought a 30-second television commercial during the broadcast of Super Bowl XLIII in 2009, it would have cost you about US$2.6 million. The ad rate for 30 seconds during Super Bowl I in 1967 was US$37,500.

- Total revenue from the University of Texas athletic program during the 2007–2008 fiscal year was US$120,288,370. In 2011, Texas announced a partnership with ESPN to start the Longhorn Network.

Accounting 101

In evaluating a company, an investor or potential buyer typically asks to see its balance sheet and its latest income statements. If the organization is a nonprofit or municipal sports department, the financial manager may have to report to a board of directors or city manager on a regular basis in order to determine the organization's financial health or reassure taxpayers' representatives that their money is being spent wisely. A **balance sheet** is a snapshot of the organization's business taken at a certain point in time (Fried, Shapiro, & DeSchriver, 2008). A sport manager can use it to determine the organization's assets and the extent of its liabilities.

balance sheet—Statement of assets and liabilities at a certain point in time; a measure of the owner's equity in the business.

assets—Ownership interest in property, equipment, cash, and buildings that have accumulated in the conduct of an organization's business activity.

Assets are property owned by the organization that have commercial or monetary value. A professional sport team's largest asset is often its home stadium, and the second-largest would be the collective value of its player contracts. Teams that are members of a league, such as the NFL or the English Premier League (EPL), also have an asset in their league membership itself, since leagues permit only a select number of teams to join their exclusive club (Masteralexis, Barr, & Hums, 2012). Assets can look very different in other segments of the sport industry. For example, a company that manufactures basketball shoes and sports apparel owns a factory and equipment, raw or semifinished materials needed

cash—Asset, usually held in a bank account or money market fund, that an organization has accumulated over the course of its business operations.

accounts receivable—Revenue owed from customers and vendors.

liabilities—Debts, both long- and short-term, that a business accumulates during its operation.

owner's equity—Measure of an organization's ownership interest in that entity; the result of subtracting total liabilities from total assets.

for making shoes, **cash** that it has accumulated in bank accounts, product inventory, and obligations from business partners to pay money for products already sold—that is, **accounts receivable**. In yet another segment of the industry, a balance sheet for a college or university might include the fields where its teams play games or practice, athletic equipment used by its student-athletes, cash on hand in university bank accounts from the sale of merchandise, and accounts receivable from alumni season ticket holders.

Liabilities are the financial obligations that an organization owes to another organization for goods or services already delivered or soon to be delivered. These obligations can take the form of short-term or long-term debt and can include money borrowed from a bank (Ham, 2005). Short-term debt is usually owed within a year of the date on which the loan, the good, or the service was delivered. Long-term liabilities can take the form of a one-year promissory note or a ten-year municipal or corporate bond. These options for borrowing must be evaluated wisely by an organization; indeed, the way in which a financial manager structures borrowing can separate a profitable organization from one that loses money. A manager who borrows only when necessary or when interest rates are low will outperform one who burdens the organization with too many liabilities for its asset base or revenue stream.

The difference between assets and liabilities is the **owner's equity**. If the organization is "in the black," its assets are greater than its liabilities; if, on the other hand, it is "in the red," its liabilities are greater than its total assets. To put it another way, the owner's equity is the value of the business if all assets were sold and all liabilities were paid off (Robinson, 2010). If the amount of the liabilities is greater than that of the total assets, then the owner has no equity in the business.

OWNER'S EQUITY = ASSETS – LIABILITIES

Balance Sheet for Baker Esherick Sport Enterprises, Inc.

Cash	US$150,000	
Credit card receivables	75,000	
Other accounts receivable	56,000	
Total value of inventory	700,000	
Land, plant, equipment	1,500,000	
Accounts payable		US$250,000
Long-term obligations		873,000

What is the owner's equity in this firm?

The second stage of analyzing an organization's financial health involves examining its **income statement**, which has two major components: revenue and expenses. Income statements provide a good indication of a sport organization's financial health over a period of time (Ham, 2005).

Revenue is defined as the monetary or commercial value of normal business operations, as well as the money brought into the business by one-time financial transactions. For example, revenue for a typical professional sport franchise's home games would come from ticket sales, merchandise sales, and concession sales (Ham, 2005). For shoe manufacturers such as Nike and New Balance, revenue comes from the sale of shoes to sporting goods wholesalers or retailers. High school and college athletic departments take in revenue when they sell tickets to home games and signage for sponsorships.

Expenses are the costs that the organization incurs in order to produce revenue or to conduct other necessary mission-driven actions. One large source of on-going expense for many organizations is employee compensation; in fact, for professional sport teams, players' salaries are the single biggest annual expense (Masteralexis et al., 2012). For-profit businesses usually have to pay taxes, and some organizations also incur marketing and advertising expenses in order to generate sales. Other possible expenses include rent and maintenance paid for office and operations space, gyms, or playing fields. If, instead, a team (high school, college, or professional) builds a new stadium, then the construction costs constitute a very large expense; in addition, if the organization borrows money to pay for the facility, then the cost of that borrowing (i.e., the interest) is another expense.

Most businesses compile income statements over three-month periods, which are often referred to as quarters (each being one-fourth of a year). The statement thus provides a snapshot four times a year of how profitable or unprofitable the

income statement—Statement, compiled over a set period of time (e.g., quarterly, semiannually, or annually), summarizing the revenue earned by an economic entity and the expenses incurred in order to operate its business.

revenue—Income earned in the operation of an organization's business.

expenses—Cost of business operations.

REVENUE – EXPENSES = NET PROFIT (LOSS)

Baker Esherick Sport Enterprises, Inc.

Sales	US$123,000	
Interest earned on cash	4,000	
Salary expense		US$40,000
Interest expense		50,000
Rental expense		12,500
Taxes		8,700

What was the firm's net profit or loss?

organization is. Some sport organizations tend to generate most of their revenue in certain quarters, whereas in other quarters their revenue is almost nonexistent. In North America, for example, a professional football team does not play games in the spring and summer months but enjoys large revenue streams between September 1 and January 1. With such variations in mind, managers look at their income statements annually, semiannually, and quarterly in order to consider possible moves designed to raise revenue or lower expenses.

Good managers always look at both sides of the ledger when analyzing a financial statement. Improvements can be made in how the organization spends money in order to produce revenue. For example, it might behoove an organization to look for a different supplier who can provide less expensive raw materials or to raise ticket prices in order to cover an increase in expenses. Similarly, a college or high school athletic director might examine a breakdown of revenue and expenses for each sport and conclude that a few sports need to be eliminated if the department is to survive. Or a marketing director might look at advertising expenses for the past year and decide that it would be cheaper to move all advertising away from television and radio media and onto less expensive sport-related websites.

Sport managers must familiarize themselves with balance sheets and income statements, as well as the components of their organization that make up these financial statements (Ham, 2005). Sport management students who understand the flow of money in the sport industry—both in the form of revenue produced and in the form of expenses incurred—are better prepared to suggest effective decisions for a potential employer in the sport industry. Implementing what seems like a great idea with no understanding of its effect on the organization's bottom line does *not* garner respect in the workplace.

Interscholastic Sport Finance

At the level of individual schools, athletic department finances in the United States are managed by the athletic director with assistance from the school's business manager and principal. At the macro level, public high school athletic departments are financed by local school districts (Humphrey, 2002; Jensen & Overman, 2003). As a budget item, athletics can fluctuate with tax collections and the local economy; in other words, funding for athletic buildings and grounds depends in large part on the local tax base. A well-funded local government can build top-quality gymnasiums and football fields, provide the best in team uniforms, and fund more teams (and teams with more members) than a less wealthy community with a small tax base. Local taxpayers will also be asked to provide money to maintain athletic fields and improve outdated fields (Masteralexis et al., 2012; Humphrey).

Some high schools have sufficient budget and athletic interest to field a ninth-grade team in many sports, as well as a junior varsity and a varsity team. Other schools may be represented by only one team in many sports. In some districts facing severe budgetary pressure, high school athletics has been canceled completely (Masteralexis et al., 2012). Each district in the United States is different, and the intensity of interest in sport varies from region to region. Within this landscape, a school's overall and athletics budgets are decided by taxpayers, the local school board, and the superintendent of schools; in addition, coaches and athletic directors usually have some input in the process.

Salaries for coaches at the high school level usually come in the form of stipends that often bear no relation to the amount of time and effort that many coaches invest in their teams. High school coaches are, for example, salaried math teachers, science teachers, assistant principals, art teachers, physical education teachers, and special education instructors. In other words, teaching is their primary job, and coaching one, two, or three teams during the academic year is a way to earn extra money or do something they love (Krotee & Bucher, 2007). In lieu of a stipend, some teachers are granted a reduced course load to free up time to plan for their coaching duties, and some districts combine a lighter teaching load with a stipend (Jensen & Overman, 2003).

Public high schools usually charge a nominal admission fee to their varsity games; they may waive admission for nonvarsity contests or charge only for varsity football games. Depending on the jurisdiction, a school system may aggressively sell signage space for local companies to advertise in its gymnasiums and stadiums (Krotee & Bucher, 2007; Stotlar, 2005; Jensen & Overman, 2003; Humphrey, 2002), and some schools have sold stadium naming rights (Stotlar). Schools can also bring in revenue by selling advertising space in game programs and selling season passes to all student activities (e.g., football games, field hockey games, music recitals, and theatre performances). Many schools also charge a nominal fee for parking at athletic events. Schools can reduce costs by staffing events with parents who volunteer their time; some schools pay a minimum hourly wage or a per-game fee to student attendants.

Another popular way to bring in money is through direct fundraising efforts, such as booster clubs, private donations, and team fundraising events. Some schools set up a separate group for each team, administered by a senior team member's parent, to raise money for equipment that is not covered by the school district—for example, warm-up jerseys for the basketball team, travel bags for the baseball team, summer camp fees for the softball team, or travel money for an out-of-town rowing regatta (Whisenant & Forsyth, 2011; Krotee & Bucher, 2007; Jensen & Overman, 2003). Despite the usefulness of such endeavors, the athletic director and coaches must maintain a healthy skepticism about activities undertaken by parents; the athletic program must stay under the control of the principal, the athletic director, and the coaches (Krotee & Bucher).

Parents and booster club members also are asked to volunteer at concession stands during home games, and schools can bring in substantial income from concession sales (Jensen & Overman, 2003). The athletic director must maintain control of the revenue and ensure careful accounting of all revenue and expenses (Krotee & Bucher, 2007). As with event parking, students can help with concessions, which gives sport management students a great way to learn about high school sport administration.

School districts have also used activity fees as a source of revenue to support both athletics and other extracurricular activities (Jensen & Overman, 2003; Krotee & Bucher, 2007; Humphrey, 2002). Fee-based financing has migrated to high school athletics from county and municipal sport programs, where it has been used to pay for the operation of public parks, recreation facilities, and tourist attractions built with taxpayer money. When this approach is used by schools, parents are charged a fee for each activity in which their child participates. This "pay-to-play" strategy has not been well received in many jurisdictions, but with the tightening of budgets around the country school board members have tried to devise ways to preserve programs that are popular within the school and in the community at large (Masteralexis et al., 2012).

Many high school athletic contests are now televised—far more than even 10 years ago (Schultz, Caskey, & Esherick, 2010). Interscholastic games, especially football and basketball, have been aired by ESPN, CBS Sports, Comcast SportsNet, and Fox Sports. Local groups also broadcast games on public access cable channels. As with college and professional sport, the home team owns the rights to the telecast. A nationally televised game by ESPN nets revenue for the home team, and the away team may receive a travel fee. However, since the audience for most high school athletic contests is relatively small, the revenue that individual schools receive for these games is minimal. For example, when two of the top basketball teams in Illinois played on ESPN, each school pocketed a check for US$1,000 (Keilman, 2011). The local cable channel may broadcast the game as an attempt to secure more local subscribers and protect itself against competition from national satellite television companies. It may receive permission to televise with no money changing hands, and the schools recognize the value of exposure for their teams.

Websites covering high school sport have also sprung up all over the country. Some are produced by companies that cover high school sport nationally, whereas other companies focus on local teams (e.g., Rivals, DCSportsFan, iHigh, and MaxPreps). These sites give fans information and sometimes video, but, as with television rights, they do not provide a reliable revenue stream for any high school athletic budget. Many state activity associations also provide online access to radio or video feeds produced by local media outlets.

Intercollegiate Sport Finance

College athletic finances vary with the size of the college, the college's interest in athletics, and the size of the program's fan base. The University of Michigan, which enrolls 40,000 students and plays football in a stadium seating more than 100,000, has a completely different athletic department balance sheet than Kalamazoo College, which enrolls 1,400 students and fields no football team. Furthermore, four-year schools are different in financial makeup than two-year junior colleges and community colleges. In addition, schools that belong to the NCAA pursue a different athletic mission than those that belong to the National Association of Intercollegiate Athletics (NAIA). Even within the NCAA itself, schools in the Football Bowl Subdivision (FBS) of Division I devote more resources to their athletic departments than do NCAA Division III schools (Masteralexis et al., 2012). At every level of intercollegiate athletics, however, fiscal responsibility rests in the hands of the athletic director.

Another common denominator at all of these schools is the presence of some measure of athletic interest among students, faculty, staff, and alumni. The expression of that athletic interest can be examined by looking at a school's balance sheets and income statements. Salaries paid to coaches, income generated from ticket sales, revenue from the sale of T-shirts and other merchandise, television revenue, and the cost of the school's athletic facilities all point to the relative importance of intercollegiate athletics on that campus. Some college teams play before very few fans, never appear on television, receive no athletic scholarships, and play for a coach who is a full-time faculty member and part-time coach. At the other end of the spectrum, the Southeastern Conference (SEC), for example, includes universities (e.g., Alabama, Florida, Louisiana State, Auburn) that have more football fans than many NFL franchises. Their football coaches are paid more than many coaches in the NFL, and their merchandise sales from football jerseys and related items dwarf some athletic budgets at smaller colleges around the country. A Saturday football game is *the* place to be in the fall in the college towns of Baton Rouge, Gainesville, Auburn, and Tuscaloosa. This type of scene also plays out in other parts of the country; for example, Michigan, Nebraska, Texas, Notre Dame, and Southern California have fielded football teams for more than 110 years and are still going strong. Nor is fervor confined to football. Kentucky, Kansas, and Duke have been playing intercollegiate basketball for more than 100 years and still attract strong fan bases. Clearly, the sport history of such schools affects their resource allocation.

Revenue Sources

Ticket sales to games constitute a major source of revenue for most college athletic department budgets (Duderstadt, 2000). Of course, selling more tickets means bringing in more revenue for athletic programs, which has led some schools to build very large venues. See table 11.1 for a list of the five largest college football stadiums and the five largest college basketball arenas in the United States.

Game tickets can be purchased by students, local fans, alumni, or school employees. Season ticket packages are sold at many schools, and the sale of prime seating packages can raise substantial revenue at major Division I schools. For teams in great demand, schools often require that a potential ticket buyer first make a donation to the school in order to secure a highly desirable seat location (Grant, Leadley, & Zygmont, 2008). Others sell personal seat licenses that give purchasers the right to buy season tickets at a certain spot in the venue. Colleges have also begun offering club and luxury box seating at arenas and stadiums equipped with such options. This part of an athletic department offers many employment opportunities for sport management graduates who possess sales skills.

Several schools have introduced a new concept in revenue referred to as a "seat mortgage," which permits fans to secure seats, and even sell them, for a specified term of years (Clark, 2009). The University of California, Berkeley, has used this concept to raise funds to renovate its football stadium; specifically, Cal has put three thousand seats on the market in this fashion, the best of which cost between US$175,000 and US$220,000 and are paid for over a term of 50 years. The less expensive mortgages

TABLE 11.1 Five Largest College Football and Basketball Venues in the United States

Venue	Location	Capacity	Institution
FOOTBALL			
Michigan Stadium	Ann Arbor	109,901	University of Michigan
Beaver Stadium	University Park	107,282	Penn State University
Neyland Stadium	Knoxville	104,079	University of Tennessee
Ohio Stadium	Columbus	102,329	Ohio State University
Los Angeles Memorial Coliseum	Los Angeles	93,607	University of Southern California
BASKETBALL			
Carrier Dome	Syracuse	33,000	Syracuse University
Rupp Arena	Lexington	23,500	University of Kentucky
Marriott Center	Provo	22,700	Brigham Young University
KFC Yum! Center	Louisville	22,600	University of Louisville
Dean E. Smith Student Activities Center	Chapel Hill	21,750	University of North Carolina at Chapel Hill

From Brown and Morrison 2008.

go for US$40,000 over a 40-year term. Cal hopes to raise US$270 million and is partnering with Stadium Capital Financing Group, a Morgan Stanley entity, to finance the mortgages. The University of Kansas is using a similar approach to fund a luxury club addition; its mortgage seats cost US$105,000 over 30 years.

Another common source of revenue for college athletic departments is the corporate partnership, which can take various forms, including signage in stadiums and arenas, advertising on tickets stubs, game program advertisements, prominent placement of logos during media conferences, provision of team uniforms or footwear, provision of concession products for resale, and naming rights at prominent athletic venues on campus (Grant et al., 2008). In fact, corporate partnerships have become such big business that marketing companies (e.g., Learfield and IMG College) package these opportunities and offer guarantees to universities in exchange for the outsourcing of this activity.

Sponsorship is important to athletic budgets at every level of intercollegiate athletics. For example, multinational pizza companies may advertise with large schools (e.g., Michigan, Tennessee), but they also want to affiliate with smaller athletic programs because—well, it goes without saying that college students like pizza! In fact, affiliating with a university athletic program is good business for many companies. Both financial institutions and cable television companies, for example, have put their names on college arenas (Madkour, 2009). College campuses need what cable companies provide: television, broadband, and telephone service. Similarly, competition to provide for the insurance needs of college students has led to partnerships with insurance companies, and team shoe and apparel deals are a natural form of partnership with sports apparel companies. Sport drink and soda companies can also be found partnering with college athletic programs all over the country (Grant et al., 2008). Corporate sponsorships are usually handled by the marketing director for the athletic department. This unit can be quite large at schools with major basketball and football programs, thus providing another place where sport management students can serve as interns in order to improve their skills and enhance their resumes.

Another dependable kind of revenue stream involves licensing the name of the university, the image of the team mascot, or the team logo or nickname for use on items such as hats, T-shirts, water bottles, seat cushions, pens and pencils, and coffee cups (Regan & Bernthal, 2005; Masteralexis et al., 2012). In such deals, the school grants a manufacturer the right to use its trademarks in exchange for a fee. For some major basketball and football programs, the resulting revenue can reach into the millions of dollars (Duderstadt, 2000), and that amount can be pushed even higher by a national championship, a bowl victory, or a conference championship. The major player in this market is Collegiate Licensing Company (CLC), which began doing licensing deals in 1981 with the University of Alabama and its football coach, Bear Bryant (Duderstadt). The company is now owned by IMG and manages licensing for more than 200 schools, many conferences, a number of college football bowls, the NCAA, and the Heisman Trophy. Overall, the collegiate licensing market had grown into a US$4.3 billion industry by the 2008–2009 collegiate sport year, during which CLC's largest producer of licensing revenue was the University of Texas, which made US$8.8 million in royalty revenue (Klayman, 2009).

For NCAA Division I basketball programs and NCAA Football Bowl Subdivision (FBS) programs, television deals can provide many of these schools with a potent revenue stream (Duderstadt, 2000). A significant number of teams that played in FBS programs received millions of dollars in television revenue each year from their conference-wide television contracts (Grant et al., 2008). The four schools that participate in the new semifinal championship format in college football will each receive substantial revenue from their participation in this event. Schools also receive a big part of the revenue from the television contract for the NCAA Men's Division I Basketball Championship tournament in the form of checks from their leagues at the end of every fiscal year. The history of these contracts is summarized in table 11.2.

The NCAA's current contract with CBS Sports and Turner Sports to air the tournament covers a 14-year period; if the contract is not renegotiated along the way, its value to the NCAA and its member schools will be US$10.86 billion. In football, ABC has an eight-year contract, during which it will televise eight Rose Bowls and two other BCS bowls; the contract is worth US$300 million. Fox Sports signed a deal with the BCS for US$320 million to televise the Fiesta, Orange, and Sugar Bowls for six years, as well as the BCS National Championship Game (until 2013–2014). And ESPN, CBS, NBC, FOX, and ABC all have regular-season deals with major conferences around the country. This revenue is divided among each conference's schools, usually based on some formula giving more revenue to teams that make

TABLE 11.2   History of Television Contracts for the NCAA Men's Division I Basketball Championship Tournament

Term	Years	Amount (US$)
2010–2024*	14	10.86 billion
2004–2013	11	6 billion
1996–2003	8	1.73 billion
1991–1995	5	715 million
1988–1990	3	165 million
1985–1987	3	96 million
1982–1984	3	48 million

*Extension/renegotiation of previous contract

Data from O'Toole 2010; NCAA March Madness History 2008.

more television appearances (Grant et al., 2008). As an example, in 2011, it was reported that each school in the SEC made US$19.5 million from their television contracts (Durando, 2012). A concluding note to readers on this subject: The television contract details, the revenue distribution, and the team selection methodology for the new semifinal and championship games in college football (2014–2015 season) were not final when this book was published.

Many college and university athletic departments hire development and alumni relations staff members to build relationships with potential donors from the alumni rolls and with local business executives. Because an athletic event is a major entertainment vehicle in many university towns, the games provide a natural venue for developing relationships with fans who can help with major fundraising efforts. Alumni donations constitute a major revenue stream for most schools (Duderstadt, 2000; Grant et al., 2008), and many schools use their high-profile basketball or football coaches to meet and greet potential donors. When billionaire T. Boone Pickens donated US$165 million to the athletic department at his alma mater, Oklahoma State University (Associated Press, 2006), he earmarked his gift for the upgrading and maintenance of OSU's athletic facilities. The Pickens donation surpassed the previous largest single athletic donation, which was bequeathed by Las Vegas casino owner Ralph Englestad to the University of North Dakota for construction of a new hockey arena. Carmelo Anthony, NBA all-star and member of Syracuse University's 2003 national championship basketball team, pledged US$3 million to help his former school fund a basketball practice facility. Indiana University (IU) also received a major gift to upgrade its men's and women's basketball facilities when the Cook Group pledged US$15 million for new locker rooms, offices, meeting rooms, and a new basketball court; it is the single largest gift ever given to IU athletics. With such possibilities on the table, many U.S. universities have hired development officers, or even a staff of sport managers, to handle relationships between the athletic department and alumni.

Other revenue sources for athletic departments include concession sales at athletic events, student fees designated for the athletic department, subsidies or draws from schoolwide budgets for use by the athletic department, and per-game guarantee fees for some away game contracts. Schools that are lucky and good enough to participate in football bowl games (i.e., NCAA Division I, FBS) also receive sizable checks for these appearances (Grant et al., 2008). Colleges also present their own games, particularly basketball and football, through radio broadcasts that are also commonly streamed via the Internet. The resulting revenue stream is dwarfed by television revenue in the case of all FBS schools but provides a much higher percentage of media revenue at the smaller schools in all three divisions of the NCAA and at NAIA schools.

Expenses

For most schools, the largest budget item in the expenditure column is made up of salaries paid to head coaches, assistant coaches, the athletic department's managerial staff, facilities staff, and training staff (Grant et al., 2008). In the major conferences in NCAA Division I, particularly at schools in conferences like the SEC and the Big Ten, coaching salaries constitute a genuinely big ticket item that may easily reach several million dollars annually (Krotee & Bucher, 2007; Berkowitz & Upton, 2012).

Along with the rapid rise in coaches' salaries, the NCAA and many athletic directors have expressed concern about the expansion of this "arms race," as it were, to include new athletic facilities that help schools recruit the best athletes (Duderstadt, 2000). If one conference member renovates its stadium, the next school wants to build a completely new facility (Duderstadt). If one football program updates its weight room, 10 other schools soon follow suit (Grant et al., 2008). In college basketball, many big-time programs have decided that they need fancy practice facilities that can carry quite a price tag; see table 11.3 for a list of some of the costliest venues.

These expenses can be used as a great way to bring focus to alumni giving campaigns: "Let's help Coach build a new weight room" (or world-class locker room, or whatever the perceived need may be). Once the money is spent, of course, the question will soon follow: Did this new facility help generate more revenue? More wins?

TABLE 11.3 Cost of Basketball Practice Facilities

Institution	Cost (US$)
University of Kentucky	30 million
West Virginia University	23.6 million
University of Michigan	23.2 million
Virginia Tech	21 million
Indiana University	16.5 million

Data from Yost 2009; Muret 2011.

The only thing worse than being in the arms race is not being in the arms race, because then you won't have the best people coaching for you.

Bob Bowlsby, former Stanford athletic director

To round out the major expense items for an athletic department budget, we certainly must add the cost of athletic scholarships (Duderstadt, 2000). NCAA Division I and Division II schools and NAIA schools all grant athletics-based financial aid, which adds up to a major expense at many schools (Grant et al., 2008). Other costs include facility maintenance expenses, travel expenses for away games, travel expenses for recruiting trips, sports equipment, and uniforms for each team (Krotee & Bucher, 2007). An athletic department also incurs promotional expenses, legal expenses, and insurance costs (Duderstadt).

Finance in Professional Sport

Fiscal health in professional sport relates to the entertainment value of the enterprise; for teams, of course, it hinges in no small part on the ratio of wins to losses. But the successful management of any professional sport business also depends on the skill of the sport managers who oversee season ticket sales, marketing, broadcasting, and sponsorship sales and those who manage the organization's relationship with the local government, local schools, and the surrounding community.

The financial model in professional team sport bears some resemblance to that of NCAA Division I athletics, but there are a few major exceptions. For one thing, college athletes are either paying tuition or receiving financial aid, whereas professional athletes in leagues such as the NFL, NHL, EPL, NBA, and MLB are all paid a handsome salary for their services. As a result, player salaries account for a large portion of each professional team's operating costs and may in fact be an owner's largest continuing expense. A second major expense for professional teams involves facilities—whether in the form of maintenance costs for a team-owned facility or rental expense for a facility that is leased from, say, a local stadium authority.

Given that salaries form a major expense for professional sport team owners, they generally try to keep these costs down as much as possible. However, despite the best collective efforts of owners in all of these leagues, salary expenses never seem to go down. At the end of the 2000s, for example, the highest payroll in MLB was that of the New York Yankees at US$209.1 million. The New York Knicks occupied the top salary position in the NBA at US$95.3 million, and in the NHL the prize went to the Colorado Avalanche at US$61.3 million. The NFL team that spent the most on player salaries was the Washington Redskins at US$123.4 million (Brown & Morrison, 2008). These numbers help explain why ticket prices are so high and why you might suffer sticker shock if you go to buy a soda or hot dog at a game.

The maintenance costs and interest associated with owning a sport venue used to be major expenses for many sport team owners. Today, however, many franchises

⭐ SUCCESS STORY

Alex Martins, CEO and President of the Orlando Magic

Alex Martins, CEO and president of the NBA's Orlando Magic, has been involved in sport management for more than 20 years. Martins had humble beginnings in the sports information office as a student at Villanova University in Philadelphia, where he earned a B.S. in business. He also holds a master's degree in business administration from the University of Central Florida. Martins is intimately involved in all business operations of the Magic, including revenue-generating departments such as season ticket promotions, sales, marketing, corporate partnerships, and broadcasting, as well as community relations and government relations. Many members of Martins' executive team hold a degree in sport management or sport business.

Photo courtesy of Fernando Medina, Orlando Magic.

Martins prepared for his current position with the Magic through a wide array of sport-related experiences. He worked in sports information on two college campuses, in public relations for two professional basketball franchises (the Hornets and 76ers) and USA Basketball, and in sport communication for the NFL's Cleveland Browns and of course for the Orlando Magic. He even did a stint in golf with a PGA Tour event called the Tavistock Cup.

Martins' most recent pet project was helping to oversee the design, construction, and opening of a new home for the Orlando Magic. The Amway Center opened in October 2010 to rave reviews around the NBA. Martins also serves on several charitable boards and on other Orlando community committees. He is the chair of the Metro Orlando Economic Development Commission. Martins' alma mater, the University of Central Florida, selected him as its commencement speaker in August 2008. The Rotary Club of Orlando named him Outstanding Business Professional of the Year in 2011.

have convinced the local community to bear the cost of a new arena or major stadium renovation (Masteralexis et al., 2012). As discussed in chapter 10, this practice has generated some controversy.

As with some high school and many college athletic departments, professional sport teams attempt to establish partnerships or sponsorships with local or national businesses (Fried et al., 2008). In addition, the league office markets and arranges sponsorships for the league as a whole (Horrow & Swatek, 2011; Conrad, 2006). In all major leagues, every team sells space for stadium signage in order to bring in revenue. Teams in some leagues (e.g., the English Premier League) also sell advertising space on players' uniforms, and the Indian Premier League (IPL) even sells space on umpires' jerseys! Because most games are televised, such signage is viewed both by fans present at the venue and by those watching via broadcast. The NBA Board of Governors recently approved the placement of an advertiser's patch on team uniforms, beginning in the 2013–2014 season.

Many owners also sell naming rights for their facilities. FedEx, for example, paid the Washington Redskins US$205 million over 27 years for the right to name the Redskins home stadium FedEx Field. Thus FedEx receives exposure to fans every time a Washington game is shown on television and to thousands of drivers who see FedEx Field every day while commuting to work on the Washington area beltway; the company even receives exposure by appearing as part of the stadium name printed on each game ticket. In similar football-related deals, the Philadelphia Eagles play at Lincoln Financial Field, which costs the Lincoln Financial Group about US$7 million a year to name, and Lucas Oil agreed with the Indianapolis Colts and the local stadium authority there to pay US$122 million over the course of 20 years for the right to name the football stadium Lucas Oil Stadium. In soccer, the EPL team Arsenal plays in Emirates (the name of an airline) Stadium, and Manchester City plays in Etihad (Airways) Stadium. In the NBA, the Cleveland Cavaliers play in the Quicken Loans Arena, and the Denver Nuggets play in the Pepsi Center. MLB's San Francisco Giants play in AT&T Park, and the St. Louis Cardinals play in Busch Stadium III. And in multisport deals, the Boston Celtics and Boston Bruins both play in TD Garden, previously known as the Boston Garden (US$120 million), and the Los Angeles Lakers and Clippers of the NBA and the Kings of the NHL all play in the Staples Center (US$116 million).

Though these deals are all lucrative, it is television revenue that has become *the* major source of a professional sport league's health in the United States and in some other places, including the English Premier League and the IPL (Fried et al., 2008; Garland, Malcolm, & Rowe, 2000). The healthiest leagues and most profitable teams have the largest television contracts. One variation involves the Spanish football league, in which individual teams control their own rights (Garcia, Olmeda, & Gonzalez, 2011); currently, this gives a huge advantage to Real Madrid and FC Barcelona. Because of the popularity of these teams worldwide, the TV revenue generated from this popularity provides them with an ample revenue stream to pay the best players in the world to play for their franchises.

The NFL, on the other hand, has multiyear deals with multiple networks (NBC, FOX, ESPN, CBS, and DirecTV), and, as if that were not enough, it has also launched its own television network (the NFL Network). All of these deals provide each NFL team owner with a very large annual paycheck. The right to broadcast the Super Bowl rotates between the networks. The NBA has major television contracts with TBS and ESPN (including ESPN on ABC), and NBA teams also have smaller packages with their local television networks. MLB franchises all have local television deals, some of which are quite lucrative, particularly for large-market teams in cities such as New York, Chicago, and Los Angeles. The New York Yankees organization has its own network, known as the YES (Yankees Entertainment and Sports) Network. The owner of the Baltimore Orioles, Peter Angelos, has a majority ownership of Mid-Atlantic Sports Network, which broadcasts Orioles games, as well as games played by the Washington Nationals. MLB also has national television deals with Fox, ESPN, and TBS. The National Hockey League has not been as successful with

English Premier League

The English Premier League (also referred to simply as the Premier League) was established in 1992 by a group of soccer clubs in England. The league is composed of 20 clubs based in cities around England and is the most profitable soccer association in the world. The league negotiates its own television and sponsorship contracts with some of the largest multinational companies in the world.

The Premier League has a title sponsor in Barclays bank (and thus is officially known as the Barclays Premier League), as well as official sponsors, broadcast partners, website partners, and radio broadcast partners. The league currently has television contracts with ESPN and Fox Sports. Each team negotiates its own deals for beer sponsorships, official car supplier sponsorships, official timekeepers, and other categories of sponsorship that can change from season to season. Each team also maintains a website where fans can buy merchandise, such as team watches, official team kits, team shin guards, team logo football tables, water bottles, flags, pennants, goalie gloves, and mobile phone accessories and services (e.g., text alerts, wallpaper, games, and animation).

EPL teams have become so popular and profitable that they attract the most talented soccer players from around the world. Some teams have also attracted ownership from outside the United Kingdom. For example, Russian billionaire Roman Abramovich owns Chelsea, and American businessman Malcolm Glazer owns Manchester United. The Fenway Sports Group, which owns MLB's Boston Red Sox, recently purchased the Liverpool soccer team; one of the group's partners is NBA star LeBron James.

The revenue-producing components of these club teams are very similar to the revenue sources of teams in the four major professional leagues in the United States (i.e., MLB, NBA, NFL, and NHL). Teams sell individual game and season tickets for home games, and special seating is offered in the form of club-level seating and luxury boxes, for which the buyer must pay a large premium. The teams and the league bring in substantial revenue from their worldwide television contracts, and merchandising and concessions are also major revenue producers.

Three Premier League revenue sources are not found on the balance sheet of a U.S. professional team: gambling, ads on uniforms, and transfer fees. Gambling on soccer games is legal in the United Kingdom and is a revenue producer for the league and its teams. Each team can also sell sponsorship space on players' uniforms; this practice has thus far been resisted by the NFL, NHL, and MLB. A transfer fee, received when a Premier League player is purchased by another team, brings another major expense for a Premier League team that adds a player to its roster in this manner. Each franchise operates an academy that trains younger players to join its team at the Premier League level, but teams can also earn transfer fees when other teams want to acquire the rights to these young players. Some clubs also field a women's team. The influx of television revenue has enabled teams in the Premier League to be major players in the transfer market over the years; the sharing of this revenue, similar to the NFL, has provided all teams with a large and dependable source of income. This has not insured that teams have spent this transfer money wisely, however (Garganese, 2012)!

For more information on European football, see these websites:

www.fifa.com	International Federation of Association Football
www.premierleague.com	English Premier League
www.uefa.com	Union of European Football Associations

the sale of its national TV package. The current deal with Comcast-NBC Sports is an improvement over past deals but is not at the level of the other three leagues (Fried et al., 2008; Hughes, 2011; Swangard, 2008). Like the NFL, the NHL and the other members of the Big Four have started their own television networks.

Even with this intense media exposure, ticket sales still form a major pillar of the revenue foundation for professional sport franchises. Game and season tickets for professional sporting events are much more expensive than tickets for high school or college events; indeed, at some professional sport venues, anything but the cheapest tickets are too expensive for the regular entertainment budget of a middle-income family of four (Horrow & Swatek, 2011). Concession prices at professional games have risen with ticket prices, and the high prices of food and beverages at a sport venue typically do not reflect the items' actual cost; rather, they are a function of the fact that fans cannot leave the venue to find a cheaper alternative during the game.

Owners of today's stadiums and arenas also sell access to club seats and luxury boxes, which come at a high cost (Horrow & Swatek, 2011). Some of these seats provide food and beverages with the price of the ticket, and many premium seats are used for business entertaining. In times of economic downturn, these revenue streams do not perform as well.

The Short of It

- Player salaries are a major source of expense for professional sport teams.
- Alumni giving in intercollegiate athletics is a revenue source not available to professional sport teams and their owners.
- Sport facilities are a major source of expense for teams at every level—professional, college, and high school.
- Sponsorships are a major source of revenue at all levels of team sport.

CHAPTER 12

Ethics in Sport Management

PA Photos

In this chapter, you will learn the following:

✓ The difference between ethics and morals
✓ The nature of codes of ethics found in the world of sport
✓ Questions to ask yourself when facing an ethical challenge as a sport manager
✓ An effective process for making ethical decisions

> We do not act rightly because we have virtue or excellence, but we rather have those because we have acted rightly.
>
> **Aristotle**

The National Football League's (NFL's) Rooney Rule turned 10 years old in 2012. Many articles have been written to consider how effective this rule has been in improving the hiring of minority candidates for NFL head coaching and upper management positions. The Rooney Rule initially required that any team with a head coaching vacancy interview at least one minority candidate; since 2009, it has also been applied to general manager openings. The purpose of the rule is to open up the hiring process to a wider group of candidates than had typically been considered by NFL owners in the past.

The Rooney Rule highlights an age-old ethical dilemma that many sport managers face when making decisions within their sphere of influence. Specifically, a team owner can comply with the letter of the rule by interviewing one minority candidate, but isn't it important for truly ethical sport managers to comply with both the letter and the spirit of the law (or, in this case, the rule)? An owner who grooms minority candidates for upper management positions, who encourages head coaches to hire and teach and nurture minority assistant coaches for head coaching positions—that is an owner who truly believes in the rule and lives in genuine compliance with it.

In the course of studying this book, you have been exposed to a breadth of information about sport management, and it is now time to consider how to effectively apply it in complex situations. For example, although processes and actions that are legal often parallel those that are ethical, the fact remains that legality and ethics are not the same thing. Sport managers must, of course, know their legal responsibilities and abide by the law, but they should also be guided by ethical principles. In today's sport industry, the pressure to produce wins and revenue can test even the most ethical leader's ability to do the right thing. Your own course of action as a sport manager or leader in a given situation will be influenced by the prevailing ethos of your organization and by your personal philosophy regarding ethical considerations. Therefore, it is important for you to develop a personal philosophy based on fundamental knowledge of ethics in order to enhance your ability to make ethical decisions (Baker, 1999).

The first step in developing your personal philosophy is to do some soul searching and self-reflection. Begin by identifying what is important to you, both personally and professionally. Write it down. The most important step in ethical decision making is to know what is important—that is, what you will base your decisions on. Next, prioritize all relevant interests that are important; identify which are more important and which are less important. Then articulate your priorities very clearly. Identify what you can compromise and what you cannot. The following step is very clear, but not always easy: Act on your priorities. If you enact your philosophy by staying true to your priorities, then you are acting with integrity (Baker, 1999).

Sport managers who do not purposefully consider their personal philosophy of ethics may find themselves hiring the wrong person for the wrong job. For example, an athletic director who firmly believes in the value of education *and* winning games needs to hire coaches who share this view. Many athletic directors have found out the hard way what happens when they hire a coach who is concerned only with winning; typically, an investigation by the National Collegiate Athletic Association (NCAA) follows soon thereafter. Similarly, the director of a national sport federation who is committed to pursuing excellence without performance-enhancing drugs needs to inculcate the entire organization with this ethic; indeed, all personnel—coaches, athletes, athletic trainers, and other medical personnel—need clear guidance. In the absence of strong and ethical leadership, competitive and economic pressure to win can blur the judgment of athletes and accommodating personnel, sometimes resulting in embarrassment for an entire nation's sport community. The intense media scrutiny applied to athletes these days via such media as Facebook, Twitter, smartphones with cameras, sports talk radio, and blogging makes it easier than ever to expose cheaters; as a result, it is more important—and in some ways easier—than ever to bring a strong and uncompromising philosophy to competing, coaching, and practicing sport management.

What is ethics? The terms *ethics* and *morals* are often used interchangeably, but they are in fact distinct from each other. **Ethics** is concerned with how people determine right and wrong and how they should live; **morals**, on the other hand, are concerned with fundamental cultural **values** that influence individual behavior. Ethics, though distinct from morals, also addresses people's preferred values and their behavior. Thus, it is easy to understand why the terms are sometimes used interchangeably. Both are rooted in values and expressed in behaviors. For example, sport entities, including businesses and professional associations, often articulate a code of ethics to guide the norms and expected behaviors of personnel within the organization. Such entities do not, however, produce a code of morals. Morals are much more personal, although like ethics they are often derived from religious or cultural standards.

ethics—How people determine right, wrong, and how they should live.

morals—Fundamental cultural values that influence individual behavior.

values—Deeply rooted beliefs and perceptions that guide behavior and that influence (and are influenced by) norms or societal standards for acceptable behavior.

Values can have either a terminal (end goal) focus or an instrumental (behavioral) focus (Rokeach, 1973). The relationship of individual values, behavioral norms, and ethics provides insights into the concept and utility of ethics itself (Malloy, Ross, & Zakus, 2003). Values are deeply rooted beliefs and perceptions that guide behavior and are influenced by norms, or societal standards for acceptable behavior. In combination, values and behavioral norms inform ethics, which can be used in the decision-making process.

"Ethics" are the notions, ideas, and feelings that control a person's words, actions, decisions, and conduct.

Steve Starrett, professor and expert on engineering ethics

Theoretical Foundations

Ethics provides insight into the actions chosen by individuals and why they choose them. Ethical decision making can be grounded in various theoretical foundations. Prominent ethical ideologies include teleology, deontology, and existentialism. **Teleology** is basically a cost-benefit ethical approach in which one weighs the consequence of conduct. Thus it can be viewed as akin to Machiavelli's notion that "the ends justify the means;" in other words, actions can be justified if they produce desired outcomes. **Utilitarianism**, which is a teleological approach, promotes the notion of the "common good," or societal benefit, wherein outcomes that provide the most benefit to the greatest number of people are favored over those that provide benefit to a comparative few or a single individual (Mill, 1861). **Consequentialism**, another teleological concept, calls for behavior to be based on what is good, as judged by its result (Malloy et al., 2003).

For example, the pricing of food and beverages at a sport venue presents an ethical dilemma for team owners and concession managers. Do they pursue their interest in bringing in as much revenue as possible from paying customers by doubling or tripling the price of hot dogs, soda, and beer simply because they have a captive audience? Player salaries are high, and owners do have to operate their businesses in a manner that ensures profit. From a Machiavellian perspective, then, the *end* is profit, and the *means* is the charging of unconscionably high food prices at the concession stand. Of course, Machiavellians might approve of this approach, but will customers agree? Consequentialists and utilitarians might argue that if vendors and teams don't make a profit and can't pay the ever-escalating salaries of players, they will go out of business and leave fans with no team to root for at all. It is more likely, however, that a consequentialist will view the "good" action here as providing fair product pricing for customers that still yields appropriate profits. From a utilitarian perspective, the *common* good would prevail, meaning that fair pricing would ensure the greatest benefit to the most customers and still result in a profitable business, albeit substantially less profitable than Machiavelli would want.

On the other hand, **deontology**—as a nonconsequentialist approach—calls for behavior to be based on what is right (Malloy et al., 2003). Deontology promotes the concept that there are universal truths and laws of behavior, according to

teleology—Cost-benefit ethical approach that weighs the consequence of conduct.

utilitarianism—Teleological ethical approach promoting the common good, or societal benefit, and favoring outcomes that provide the most benefit to the greatest number of people.

consequentialism—Teleological ethical approach calling for behavior to be based on good results.

deontology—Nonconsequentialist ethical approach calling for behavior to be based on what is right, on universal truths, and on laws of behavior on the basis of which people possess a duty to others in society as a categorical imperative regardless of situational outcome.

In law a man is guilty when he violates the rights of others. In ethics he is guilty if he only thinks of doing so.

Immanuel Kant, 18th-century German philosopher

which people possess a duty to others in society as a categorical imperative (Kant, 1785/1993). For example, if murder is always bad, then no circumstances would justify it, because a universal law of behavior says that committing murder is unacceptable. Or, returning to the sport venue concessions example, a soda should not cost double at the stadium what it costs at the restaurant across the street. Deontologically, it is simply not right to double the price of an item just because the consumer has no alternative inside the stadium.

A third approach in normative ethics is called virtue ethics, which is concerned with moral character rather than with moral duty (as in deontology) or with consequences (as in teleology). For example, imagine that it is evident that a need exists. A utilitarian approach would maximize overall well-being, and a deontologist might focus on the golden rule ("do unto others as you would have them do unto you"), whereas a virtue ethicist might focus on more personal charitable or benevolent motives (Hursthouse, 1999). This approach aligns with the influence of existentialism on ethics, which yields a focus on the individual, on what is authentic and true for the individual in a given circumstance (Malloy et al., 2003). For example, the owner of a sporting goods manufacturing company could be acting on this virtue ethic motive if, though facing economic pressure, he or she decides against moving operations to a cheaper labor market overseas in order to preserve jobs in his or her home country. Indeed, athletic shoe manufacturer New Balance uses the fact that its products are manufactured in the United States as a differentiator in its advertising campaigns. It wants to be perceived as more virtuous because it does not use cheaper labor in China or Vietnam in order to make more money.

Ethical Decision Making

Applying theoretical foundations contributes to consistency in ethical decision making. For example, the ethics of justice, grounded in Kohlberg's (1981) stages of moral development, focuses on individual rights and ensuring minimum damage. It reflects a deontological ethical perspective, in that decisions are made on the basis of universal principles and rules that are considered to be impartial, fair, and equitable in the treatment of individuals. Though Kohlberg categorized responses to ethical dilemmas in alignment with the six underlying stages of moral development, Haidt (2001) argued that such rationalization reflects an after-the-fact justification of intuitive decisions made without ethical considerations. In contrast, the ethics of care is a normative ethical theory focused on the interdependent relationships of all individuals and the situational contexts in which they occur (Gilligan, 1982). Decisions grounded in the ethics of care give a central position to the attachment to others, positive relations, and needs of others in a given situation.

Integrity is doing the right thing, even if nobody is watching.

Anonymous

Though these two approaches offer different foundations for ethical decision making, both the ethics of justice's fair and equitable treatment of all people and the ethics of care's holistic, contextual, need-based nature can be justified in decision-making applications. For example, if a professional sport team's owner were constructing a stadium in a downtown neighborhood, an ethics of care would focus on concern for those who live and work in that neighborhood. Thus an ethical owner would construct a stadium that added value to the neighborhood, and neighbors would also be consulted and brought into the planning process for the stadium.

Starratt (1991) adds the ethics of critique to the individual's ethics toolbox in the decision-making process. The ethics of critique focuses on the moral issues and structural properties associated with relevant individuals, groups, circumstances, and environments. Starratt argues that we can fully inform ethical decision making by merging a deontological ethics of justice (attempting to answer the query, "How can we fairly govern ourselves?") with an ethics of care ("What do our relationships call for?") *and* an ethics of critique ("Where do we fail in our own ideals?"). It is a common belief among leaders in sports and business and among accreditation bodies and the academic community that it is essential for sport managers to apply the aforementioned foundations for ethical decision making in managing sport enterprises.

The Process of Ethical Decision Making

How do sport managers use ethics in their decision making? They can turn to several common approaches that align with the ethics ideologies presented in the preceding section. For example, the utilitarian approach of supporting the common good might result in some limited infringement on individual liberties, such as searching handbags, in order to enhance the safety of the overall group of attendees at a sporting event. Sport managers might also apply the golden rule; for instance, if you are leading a sales team, your decisions might be guided by how you yourself would want to be treated as a staff member. Sport managers using a deontological approach guided by universal rules of behavior might commit themselves to social justice and to including all participants, regardless of special circumstances, as in the Sport for All movement. A sport manager might also guide a decision by considering how it would be assessed by his or her professional colleagues, what a valued mentor would do in the same situation, or even how the decision would be viewed by members of the public. One thing, however, is certain: It is important for sport managers to use a consistent ethical foundation for decision making.

Knowledge of ethical ideologies does not in itself ensure that a person consistently makes ethical decisions. So, how does ethical decision making work in sport management? It all begins with the individual. Each person must have an ideologically grounded philosophy based on his or her personal and professional values and informed by the person's rights and responsibilities both in his or her sport organization and in the larger society. Each person's decisions can also be affected by alignment with the mission and values of the sport organization in which he or she is employed.

For example, is the organization engaged in commercialized, performance-oriented sport (as in a professional sport franchise) or is it a participation-based sport organization (e.g., a community youth league)? It is not uncommon for people to leave or to be fired from their positions when their ethics do not align with those of the organization. Most youth leagues require that all participants play a certain minimum portion of each contest, and coaches in these leagues are encouraged to provide an educational and enjoyable atmosphere for all participants, regardless of their ability. On the other hand, if you coach the NFL's Dallas Cowboys, it might be nice to play everyone on your roster, but your goal is to win games. There is no ethical pressure to ensure that the Cowboys' third-string quarterback gets in the game in the fourth quarter! Pro football is a business in which owners set out to make money and provide entertainment for the fans. In contrast, in an educational environment such as a youth football team, an ethical sport manager ensures that all kids play in every game, and the goal of the competition is to exercise, have fun, and grow as a person. The different goals of these organizations guide the decisions made by their respective sport managers. Still, each person must know the difference between right and wrong and then act on the basis of his or her established personal and professional philosophy.

Quick Facts

- Experts say that athletes will soon be able to genetically enhance their muscles through gene doping, making them faster, stronger, and better able to recover.

- The National Association of Sports Officials receives a report of physical violence against a coach, fan, or official approximately once every three days; the group believes that this is just the "tip of the iceberg."

- Eighteen U.S. states have laws regarding assault on a sport official.

- Between 2001 and 2011, 53 of 120 large Division I universities were found to have committed major violations of NCAA rules.

- Despite an average of about six major violations each year at the Division I level, the NCAA has enacted the "death penalty," which essentially puts a sport team out of business for a period of two years, only once, when it punished Southern Methodist University's football program in 1987.

Jim Larranaga, College Basketball Coach

Photo courtesy of George Mason Athletics.

In 2006, basketball coach Jim Larranaga (now at the University of Miami) led the George Mason University Patriots to a surprising appearance in the NCAA Final Four, claiming a first-round victory over Michigan State University without his starting point guard, Tony Skinn. But the stage had been set for that story more than a week earlier, when the Patriots, enjoying a successful season, played a Colonial Athletic Association semifinal tournament game, which would turn out to be their last of the regular season. The team lost to Hofstra, 58-49, but what happened during the closing minutes of the game, and in the hours that followed, involved an unpredicted challenge that required ethical decision making on Larranaga's part.

With about a minute to go in the game, and facing a four-point deficit, Mason's senior point guard, Skinn, hit a Hofstra player with a below-the-belt punch. The blow was unseen by the referees, but play stopped as the Hofstra player fell to the ground. Larranaga hadn't seen the incident either, but he later said, "I knew something bad had just taken place. I could tell by his reaction when I asked him what happened that he had done something he had regretted. We all have moments in life where we do something or say something we wish we could take back an instant later. I think this was one of those times. Tony Skinn is a very, very good kid. He made a mistake. I didn't think there was any choice at all but to take him out of the game immediately, regardless of the score" (Feinstein, 2006). Skinn went to the bench, and Hofstra edged out the Patriots for the win. Immediately after the game, Coach Larranaga watched the tape to see for himself what had happened. What he witnessed led him to a decision. With the support of athletic director Tom O'Connor, George Mason announced that Skinn would be suspended for the next game, which jeopardized the team's chances of getting into the NCAA tournament, because an invitation to the tournament hinges in part on the availability or absence of key players.

"When we recruit a player, we tell him that there are three things that are absolutes if they are going to be a part of our program," Larranaga said. "The first is that they always have a positive attitude. The second is an unconditional commitment to what they're doing on the court and in the classroom, and the third is that they act in a first-class manner at all times. I know some people will find that corny, but that's been the way I've coached for 22 years. If any of our kids fails to meet one of those principles, I'm going to respond. Unfortunately, Tony failed to meet one of those on Sunday night. I'm not going to tell you I did it without any hesitation. . . . But there's no question in my mind that it was the right thing to do" (Feinstein, 2006).

"It sends chills through my entire body to hear what Jim did," said Duke coach Mike Krzyzewski of Larranaga's decision. "Honestly, if he was here right now, I'd give him a big hug. We need more coaches to have the courage to step up in situations like this and say to our kids, 'That's wrong; I'm not making excuses for you.' If I were in the same situation, I hope I'd be gutsy enough and strong enough to do the same thing, but I can't swear to you that I would" (Feinstein, 2006).

After an anxious wait to hear their fate, the Patriots received an at-large bid to the NCAA tournament—their first appearance in five years. A relieved Skinn said, "It's all everybody has been talking about, so definitely, in the back of my mind, I was hoping and praying that incident wouldn't cost the team. . . . I was nervous. I'm just glad we made it" (Goff, 2006). Coach Larranaga said, "Tony has experienced something that is so difficult, that kind of adversity, it's hard to even imagine what's going through his mind. . . . I know Tony regretted it and was sorry the moment he did it, but the healing process takes longer than just that moment. For George Mason University, our men's basketball program, and especially for Tony, by being invited to the tournament, it helps put that behind us" (Goff, 2006). And they did just that.

Larranaga's team prevailed even in the midst of Skinn's suspension. Despite having never won an NCAA tournament game, the Patriots upset Michigan State in the first round without their starting point guard. Skinn then rejoined his teammates and played throughout Mason's storied march through North Carolina, Wichita State, and Connecticut to reach the national semifinal game against Florida. The Patriots' tournament run proved memorable, but the lessons learned from Coach Larranaga and his team extend beyond the court. In the pressure-packed, publicly scrutinized world of modern college sport, it provides an example of ethical decision making.

Personal and Professional Philosophy

Your professional actions should be guided by your professional philosophy. Ultimately, that philosophy is driven by your personal and professional values. It begins with your answers to what is important to you in the following areas:

- In your personal life?
- In sport?
- In your work?

These questions help you identify your principles and the foundations of your professional values. List everything of importance, then establish your priorities by rank-ordering the values you have identified. If they come into conflict, identify which values supersede others. What is most important? What is least important? What falls in between?

This seemingly simple exercise will yield insights that can guide your professional decision making. Remember that it does no good to articulate a philosophy and then put it on the shelf. A philosophy becomes useful when you employ it to guide your decisions. Even so, articulating a philosophy does not necessarily make difficult decisions easier; it does, however, make your decisions much clearer. Identifying a professional philosophy, then using it to make decisions, can be the most useful activity that you perform as an aspiring sport manager. Acting in accordance with your established professional philosophy puts you on the path to professional integrity (Baker, 1999). You may also find that your philosophy helps you in your search for meaningful employment after graduating from college; an understanding of your own values can eliminate potential jobs that are in conflict with those values.

What you decide is important, but why and how you make the decision is critical. When you base your decisions on an established philosophy, your decision making is more consistent. No one can predict every possible situation, and sport managers may face a wide array of ethical questions related to, for example, the use of their time, the organization's money, the use of facilities, what is said to the media, and relationships with clients and vendors. But everyone can articulate an explicit philosophical foundation upon which to base their decisions.

Here is a real-life example that most people would not anticipate facing. In 1998, Nykesha Sales, the University of Connecticut Huskies' senior basketball star and a future WNBA star, was only one point shy of Kerry Bascom's school scoring record when she suffered a season-ending Achilles tendon injury. With the regular season nearing an end, the top-ranked Huskies were about to play fellow national title contender and league rival Villanova University. Prior to the game, Villanova coach Harry Perretta received a call from Huskies' coach Geno Auriemma. The two arranged to allow Sales, who was using crutches, to score a basket in order to obtain the scoring record. Villanova was also allowed to score a basket so that the game would effectively start evenly at 2 to 2. Coach Auriemma and Coach Perretta then found their teams at the center of a national debate. Many people discussed the decision on a local level, and the national media also gave it considerable attention and editorial coverage. Auriemma, who was both criticized and praised, defended the decision and noted that Bascom had given it her blessing. Sales recently said, "I wasn't sure about it, I had to ask my mom about it. It happened, and then I was in the hospital [for surgery] after that and it was all over ESPN, everywhere . . . I just wanted to take it back. Just erase it, but they said I couldn't do that. It was a big deal then" (Held, 2011).

The decision and the way in which it was carried out brought into play many values associated with sport, and with life, including compassion, competition, and good sporting behavior. However, the point of considering this situation here is not to evaluate the decision but to emphasize that sport can be unpredictable. Injuries, for example, are certainly a part of sport, but they are not predictable. Sport outcomes, such as wins and record-breaking performances, are also unpredictable. And, in this particular case, could either coach expect to be making or receiving a phone call that culminated in such an unusual beginning of a game? In an unprecedented situation like this, each participant—whether requesting the unusual action or receiving that request—must have a clear set of priorities. Given the time pressure, the scrutiny of public attention, and the high stakes, this situation could never have been predicted, so those involved had to respond on the basis of an established professional philosophy grounded in their values. How would you handle such a situation? Your decision should be determined by your professional philosophy, which should reflect what is important to you and clarify your priorities.

Identifying and using a professional philosophy is not a one-time action. Sport managers can use this invaluable tool any time they are faced with a circumstance that requires a decision. In fact, as individuals grow and evolve, it is important that they reexamine their guiding philosophy, which is likely to evolve despite retaining its essential ethical ideological foundations.

Codes of Ethical Conduct

Many sport organizations have established a code of ethics in order to foster integrity and ethical behavior within the organization. A code of ethics must articulate the values upon which the organization is grounded. It can be targeted for specific purposes. For example, the National Association of Basketball Coaches (NABC) Code of Ethics (1987) includes a preliminary statement that outlines the rationale and enumerates five targeted functions of the code (see figure 12.1). The NABC code goes on to include a preamble and twelve principles or standards of ethical behavior, then concludes with implementation and enforcement procedures. The International Olympic Committee (IOC) Code of Ethics (2009), though structured differently, accomplishes its own ethical ends (see figure 12.2). It also begins with a preamble to establish context, then proceeds to introduce foundational principles of dignity, integrity, resources, candidatures (candidacies), relations with states, and confidentiality. It concludes with a section on implementation.

Any code of ethics should encourage ethical behavior within the context of the sport organization, thus serving as a guide for stakeholders' actions. In order to be effective, a code must be appropriately specific. If it is too vague, it offers no guidance; if it is too specific, it offers only limited applicable direction. Therefore, a code of ethics should be based on values-guided themes that reveal the organization's ethical philosophy. The code must state explicitly to whom it applies, and it must be relevant to the actualities of the organization and its stakeholders (Mahony, Geist, Jordan, Greenwell, & Pastore, 1999). In the end, a sport organization's code of ethics serves as an important articulation of its values and an important guide for constituents' behavior. Ultimately, however, the application of ethical standards within any sport organization depends on the actions of its stakeholders, including the sport managers who make key decisions.

National Association of Basketball Coaches Code of Ethics

Adopted 1987, New Orleans, Louisiana

PRELIMINARY STATEMENT

The National Association of Basketball Coaches (NABC), the professional organization for coaches of men's basketball teams in the United States, is taking a strong leadership position at this time to develop a code of ethical conduct. This is especially appropriate as the sport of basketball nears its 100th anniversary. Moreover, the immense popularity of basketball, advanced levels of competition and the public pressure on both coaches and athletes suggest quite clearly the need and importance of an ethical code. A Code of Ethics can act as a professional guideline in gaining and maintaining the respect and confidence of athletes, other coaches and the public, as well as providing each basketball coach with the incentive to conduct himself in a highly ethical manner. A Code of Ethics has the potential to serve the following functions:

1. Allow basketball coaches to maintain autonomy and establish guidelines for the protection of coaching.
2. Further the development of basketball coaching as a profession.
3. Insure that coaching will be carried out with the highest possible standards.
4. Inform member coaches of acceptable behavior in order to provide self-regulation of conduct.
5. Reassure the public that basketball coaches are deserving of public trust, confidence and support.

PREAMBLE

The Code of Ethics of the basketball coaching profession sets forth the principles and standards of basketball coaching and represents the aspirations of all members of the NABC. Ethics are defined as principles for right action. These principles are not laws but standards and are intended to guide basketball coaches individually and collectively in maintaining the highest professional level of ethical conduct.

PRINCIPLES

1. Coaches are accountable to the highest standard of honesty and integrity. All practices should be consistent with the rules of the game and the educational purposes of the institution.
2. Coaches are responsible for assisting athletes in acquiring the necessary knowledge and skills of basketball as well as promoting desirable personal and social traits in athletes under their direction.
3. Coaches treat all persons with dignity and respect providing a model of fair play and sportsmanship.
4. Coaches observe the letter and intent of the rules of the sport and insist that athletes and teams under their direction do the same.
5. Coaches clarify in advance and act in full accordance with institutional, conference and national governing body rules while avoiding actions that may violate the legal and/or civil rights of others.

6. Coaches have a primary concern for the health, safety and personal welfare of each athlete. The athlete's education is also held foremost.

7. Coaches perform their duties on the basis of careful preparation, ensuring that their instruction is current and accurate. They use practices for which they are qualified and continually acquire new knowledge and skills.

8. Coaches accurately represent the competence, training and experience of themselves and their colleagues.

9. Coaches honor all professional relationships with athletes, colleagues, officials, media and the public. They avoid conflicts of interest and exploitation of those relationships, especially by outside parties.

10. Coaches have an obligation to respect the confidentiality of information obtained from persons in the course of their work.

11. Coaches take an active role in the prevention and treatment of drug, alcohol and tobacco abuse.

12. Coaches carry out all obligations of employment contracts, unless released from those obligations by mutual agreement. When considering interruption or termination of service, appropriate notice is given.

IMPLEMENTATION

The Code of Ethics will be used as a condition of membership in the National Association of Basketball Coaches. All members will be provided a copy of the Code as a part of the membership application. To qualify for membership, an applicant must sign a statement acknowledging having read the Code and subscribing to the principles of the Code.

ENFORCEMENT

The coaches of the colleges, universities and institutions that are members of the NABC are also members of governing organizations for those schools (NJCAA, NAIA and NCAA). The enforcement of a violation of the Code of Ethics will be executed by the rules, regulations and procedures of the governing organization.

FIGURE 12.1 The NABC code of ethics lists 12 principles of right action for coaches of men's basketball teams in the United States.

Reprinted, by permission, from National Association of Basketball Coaches, 1987, *NABC basketball code of ethics* (Kansas City, KS: NABC). Available: http://www.nabc.org/NABC_Releases/ethics/index

Ethical Challenges in Sport Management

In the face of ethical challenges, sport managers must apply their knowledge and skills to meet each demand by making ethically grounded decisions based on foundational values. What types of ethical challenge exist in sport? As discussed earlier, some challenges cannot be predicted, but we can nonetheless gain some sense of the types of ethical dilemma that can arise in sport management and in sport itself. For example, when the United States Anti-Doping Agency (2010) surveyed adults involved in sport, more than 75 percent of them identified the use of performance-enhancing drugs as the most serious concern facing sport. Moreover, in certain managerial positions, one can anticipate dealing with doping

International Olympic Committee Code of Ethics

PREAMBLE

The International Olympic Committee and each of its members, the cities wishing to organise the Olympic Games, the Organising Committees of the Olympic Games and the National Olympic Committees (hereinafter "the Olympic parties") restate their commitment to the Olympic Charter and in particular its Fundamental Principles. The Olympic parties affirm their loyalty to the Olympic ideal inspired by Pierre de Coubertin. Consequently, at all times the Olympic parties and, in the framework of the Olympic Games, the participants, undertake to respect and ensure respect of the present Code and the following principles:

A. DIGNITY

1. Safeguarding the dignity of the individual is a fundamental requirement of Olympism.
2. There shall be no discrimination between the participants on the basis of race, gender, ethnic origin, religion, philosophical or political opinion, marital status or other grounds.
3. All doping practices at all levels are strictly prohibited. The provisions against doping in the World Anti-Doping Code shall be scrupulously observed.
4. All forms of harassment of participants, be it physical, professional or sexual, and any physical or mental injuries to participants, are prohibited.
5. All forms of participation in, or support for betting related to the Olympic Games, and all forms of promotion of betting related to the Olympic Games are prohibited.
6. Also, in the context of betting, participants in the Olympic Games must not, by any manner whatsoever, infringe the principle of fair play, show non-sporting conduct, or attempt to influence the result of a competition in a manner contrary to sporting ethics.
7. The Olympic parties shall guarantee the athletes conditions of safety, well-being and medical care favourable to their physical and mental equilibrium.

B. INTEGRITY

1. The Olympic parties or their representatives shall not, directly or indirectly, solicit, accept or offer any form of remuneration or commission, nor any concealed benefit or service of any nature, connected with the organisation of the Olympic Games.
2. Only gifts of nominal value, in accordance with prevailing local customs, may be given or accepted by the Olympic parties, as a mark of respect or friendship. Any other gift must be passed on to the organisation of which the beneficiary is a member.

FIGURE 12.2 The IOC Code of Ethics is intended for not only Olympic organizing bodies but also for host cities and participants.

Reprinted, by permission, from IOC, 2012, *International Olympic Committee code of ethics* (Lausanne, Switzerland: IOC). Available: http://www.olympic.org/Documents/Commissions_PDFfiles/Ethics/Code-Ethics-2012.pdf

3. The hospitality shown to the members and staff of the Olympic parties, and the persons accompanying them, shall not exceed the standards prevailing in the host country.

4. The Olympic Parties shall respect the Rules Concerning Conflicts of Interests Affecting the Behaviour of Olympic Parties.

5. The Olympic parties shall use due care and diligence in fulfilling their mission. They must not act in a manner likely to tarnish the reputation of the Olympic Movement.

6. The Olympic parties, their agents or their representatives must not be involved with firms or persons whose activity or reputation is inconsistent with the principles set out in the Olympic Charter and the present Code.

7. The Olympic parties shall neither give nor accept instructions to vote or intervene in a given manner within the organs of the IOC.

C. RESOURCES

1. The Olympic resources of the Olympic parties may be used only for Olympic purposes.

2.

   2.1 The income and expenditure of the Olympic parties shall be recorded in their accounts, which must be maintained in accordance with generally accepted accounting principles. An independent auditor will check these accounts.

   2.2 In cases where the IOC gives financial support to Olympic parties:

      a. the use of these Olympic resources for Olympic purposes must be clearly demonstrated in the accounts;

      b. the accounts of the Olympic parties may be subjected to auditing by an expert designated by the IOC Executive Board.

3. The Olympic parties recognise the significant contribution that broadcasters, sponsors, partners and other supporters of sports events make to the development and prestige of the Olympic Games throughout the world. However, such support must be in a form consistent with the rules of sport and the principles defined in the Olympic Charter and the present Code. They must not interfere in the running of sports institutions. The organisation and staging of sports competitions are the exclusive responsibility of the independent sports organisations recognised by the IOC.

D. CANDIDATURES

The Olympic parties shall in all points respect the various manuals published by the IOC linked to the selection of host cities of the Olympic Games, in particular the Rules of Conduct Applicable to All Cities Wishing to Organise the Olympic Games.

The cities wishing to organise the Olympic Games shall, inter alia, refrain from approaching another party, or a third authority, with a view to obtaining any financial or political support inconsistent with the provisions of such manuals and the Rules of Conduct.

(continued)

E. RELATIONS WITH STATES

1. The Olympic parties shall work to maintain harmonious relations with state authorities, in accordance with the principle of universality and political neutrality of the Olympic Movement.

2. The Olympic parties are free to play a role in the public life of the states to which they belong. They may not, however, engage in any activity or follow any ideology inconsistent with the principles and rules defined in the Olympic Charter and set out in the present Code.

The Olympic parties shall endeavour to protect the environment on the occasion of any events they organise. In the context of the Olympic Games, they undertake to uphold generally accepted standards for environmental protection.

F. CONFIDENTIALITY

The Olympic parties shall not disclose information entrusted to them in confidence. The principle of confidentiality shall be strictly respected by the IOC Ethics Commission in all its activities. Disclosure of other information shall not be for personal gain or benefit, nor be undertaken maliciously to damage the reputation of any person or organisation.

G. IMPLEMENTATION

1. The Olympic parties shall see to it that the principles and rules of the Olympic Charter and the present Code are applied.

2. The Olympic parties shall inform the IOC President of any breach of the present Code, with a view to possible referral to the IOC Ethics Commission.

3. The IOC Ethics Commission may set out the provisions for the implementation of the present Code in a set of Implementing Provisions.

FIGURE 12.2 *(continued)*

issues that would require ethical decision making. Also of concern was the criminal behavior of some well-known athletes and the focus on money; for example, commercialization in education-based sport raises issues such as the prospect of paying collegiate athletes.

Broader societal issues also manifest in sport and may present ethical challenges in the decisions that sport managers must make in order to address a wide variety of specific circumstances. For example, social justice issues involving race, ethnicity, gender, and the inclusion of special populations provide the foundation for many ethical challenges requiring decisions in sport employment, eligibility, and financial support. One example in which sport managers have attempted to meet such a challenge head on is the NFL's Rooney Rule, discussed at the start of this chapter. Social responsibility, for individuals and organizations, involves ethical underpinnings and implications (Ridinger & Greenwell, 2005). For example, ethical decisions abound

Doping and the Tour de France

The Tour de France, which is the most prestigious cycling race in the world, lasts three weeks, covers 3,400 to 3,600 kilometers (2,112 to 2,236 miles), and ranges through the Pyrenees and the Alps to the race's finale in Paris. Allegations of drug use date back to the race's inception in 1903, when the purpose of taking drugs such as ether was to numb the pain, but today there has seemingly emerged a substance-based competition—a race within the race—to increase performance capacity. Though the issue was originally ignored, testing was begun in the late 1960s, and since then the International Cycling Union (UCI, after its French name, Union Cycliste Internationale) and the Tour have prohibited the practice of using performance enhancers. Also known as doping, the practice has evolved, as ether and alcohol gave way to amphetamines and steroids. More recently, as testing experts struggle to catch up with doping techniques, the favored performance-enhancement choices for riders have included erythropoietin (EPO), human growth hormone (HGH), blood doping transfusions, and testosterone variations. However, each year, even as doping substances and strategies are evolved in an ongoing attempt to stay ahead of detection capabilities, cyclists are disqualified as a result of testing positive for performance enhancers.

In 1998, the World Anti-Doping Agency (WADA) was established to assist in global efforts to curtail doping. Even so, Tour de France winners such as Alberto Contador and Floyd Landis have tested positive for doping, and suspicion surrounds many riders. In 2012, Lance Armstrong was stripped of his Tour de France victories due to overwhelming evidence of doping. Allegations leveled against other riders and teams have persisted. Since 2008, the use of what is called a biological passport has made it more difficult for cyclists to use many doping techniques. As a result, fewer positive tests are confirmed. Cyclists may still be doping, but methods and dosages have definitely changed. Have the changes affected performance? Perhaps. Whether due to fewer instances of doping, reduced doping, or altered doping strategies, race stage times have increased in recent years (Tucker & Dugas, 2011). Whichever is the case at the moment, doping is likely to exist as long as competitive pressure remains intense in high-stakes sporting events such as the Tour de France. Still, aside from the many identified and yet-to-be-determined health risks, doping raises ethical issues. For example, Niiler (2011) asks whether, given the history of doping in the Tour, it should be legalized in the sport. After all, isn't doping like any new technology used to enhance performance? The Tour de France has maintained its firm answer: no.

Given the context of the policies and enforcement strategies used by the Tour, the UCI, and WADA—and given the general consensus among leading sport scientists, managers, and organizers—it seems evident that doping should and will remain banned. In the face of a century of tradition, the Tour de France has confronted the issue of doping. The Tour has engaged key partners and actively managed the execution of its policies. Enforcement through testing has increased, penalties are substantial, and, though doping cyclists are still getting caught, the reduced number of failed doping tests, combined with the slower times in race stages, all suggest that the Tour's anti-doping efforts are succeeding.

about fair play and good sporting behavior. Whether the issue involves violence and aggression, rule violations in recruiting, the participation of ineligible athletes, or unethical business practices, sport managers must rely on their ability to be consistent in making ethical decisions. They must know what is important, identify their values-based priorities, apply appropriate ideological frames, and make ethical decisions. This is required by the many unpredictable challenges they will face.

As you read the International Application about doping in the Tour de France, recognize that such rule violations involve actions and decisions by individuals. What tour manager, sponsor, or support staff member knew of such doping but turned a blind eye? Which coaches encouraged it? Which ones discouraged doping and thus willingly faced slower times by their athletes and teams? Did members of the medical profession help disguise the use of doping practices? Did a doctor administer a performance-enhancing drug and attend to the athlete to monitor the intake of the drug? Did sport journalists publish speculative articles, or did they research the facts and verify them with credible sources? As you enter the world of sport management, it is important to have identified your personal philosophy so that when you face unexpected situations you have a compass by which to make decisions.

The Short of It

- Sport managers who are well grounded in ethics will be better prepared for the challenges awaiting them in the sport industry.
- When confronted with challenging decisions, sport managers can find useful resources in the many codes of ethics available in sport.
- A great way to understand your own values is to list the things that are important to you in your personal and professional life. This list may also help you pick the job that best fits your own code of ethics.

Epilogue

The Future of Sport Management

How do you go from where you are to where you want to be? I think you have to have an enthusiasm for life. You have to have a dream, a goal. And you have to be willing to work for it.

Jim Valvano,
college basketball coach

During the global financial crisis that began in 2007, sport management graduates have had to ride out sluggish economies just like everyone else. Jobs have been scarce for recent graduates not only in the sport industry but in every industry. The sport industry's prospects for growth, however, are good. Sport operates at the intersection of the manufacturing, media, tourism, and entertainment industries. In each of these industries, one key to growth is to take advantage of trends toward globalization. This of course requires hard work, and the message that sport management students should take from Jim Valvano's statement quoted here is that they must be willing to *work* at their craft while establishing professional goals to accomplish early in their career. This epilogue sets the context for that effort by surveying several trends in sport management: the growth of sport management as an academic discipline, the effect of continuing technological advances, the development of new sports, the effect of globalization and emerging markets, and the importance of social responsibility and inclusion in sport.

The Academic Discipline of Sport Management

As you learned in chapter 1, sport management as an academic discipline has made huge strides around the globe. From humble beginnings on the campus of Ohio University in 1966, the field has grown to see the formation of the World Association for Sport Management (WASM), which was created through cooperation by six continental associations: the European Association for Sport Management (EASM), the Asian Association for Sport Management (AASM), the African Sport Management Association (ASMA), the Latin American Association for Sport Management (Asociación Latinoamericana de Gerencia Deportiva, or ALGEDE), the Sport Management Association of Australia and New Zealand (SMAANZ), and the

North American Society for Sport Management (NASSM). Each of these groups brings together scholars and students from its continental area who are hungry to learn about the latest research in the field; each also interacts with sport industry professionals and their representative organizations.

Future meetings of these groups will bring about increasing collaboration, more sport management research projects, and joint presentations covering the international landscape of sport. This growth in intercontinental academic cooperation will benefit not only students in academic sport management programs but also the sport industry as a whole. Students who are interested in research and in teaching sport management should attend these organizations' conferences, which include opportunities for students to present research projects. In fact, teaching and research in sport management are growth areas, and jobs are available for sport management graduates who want to enter the world of higher education (Mahoney, 2008). Students who choose a different path in the sport industry can still be helpful to the programs from which they graduated, and to the discipline as a whole, by staying connected with their faculty and programs after graduation. Academic programs and faculty members need constant feedback from recent graduates about the relevance of academic programs and the current state of the sport industry. Recent graduates can also serve as excellent mentors for current sport management students.

Advances in Technology

The sport industry continues to be affected by ongoing technological advances, and both students and faculty must monitor these advances and study the ways in which new innovations affect the sport landscape. Similarly, schools must prepare their graduates to take advantage of new concepts, inventions, and opportunities. For example, technology has already reshaped the newspaper industry; as a result, students who foresee a career in sport journalism must learn new skills and adjust their expectations. Jobs are drying up in the old media, but many new opportunities are developing online. Can 21st-century sport managers use these changes to create more jobs in sport journalism?

Indeed, academic programs should not only prepare students to work in the sport industry but also nurture those who have the entrepreneurial spirit to shape and expand the industry. Sport management graduates should be looking, for example, to develop the next service that will, like Google or Facebook, drive advertising dollars in the direction of sportswriting. Content writers are already needed for sport blogs, Twitter feeds, sport-related websites, and Facebook pages covering teams, leagues, and sports. E-readers (e.g., Nook, Kindle) and tablets (e.g., the iPad) are helping create a new generation of readers hungry for content from sportswriters in the form of online newspaper articles, magazine pieces, and sport biographies. In fact, Amazon has reported that e-books are already selling faster than paper books (Wollman, 2011). Sport management students must recognize such trends and develop the skills needed in order to make the most of them. There is no more important skill than being able to write, and you can develop your writing ability and other key skills both in the classroom and by taking advantage of internship and practicum experiences. Students who are curious about the sport industry will be able to ride the waves of change—and those with an entrepreneurial spirit will be able to make some waves of their own!

Even as new technology has negatively affected job opportunities on the print side of sport media, it has exerted a very different effect on the video side. New technology has enabled the creation of more sports networks as cable companies have moved from analog to digital broadcasts and deployed better satellite technology. The presence of more sports networks, of course, means more need for talented professionals, both in front of and behind the camera. As a result, sport management opportunities abound in this area at all levels of the employment scale. Networks need employees with the skills to manage day-to-day operations, produce shows, operate cameras, sell advertising, and program the network, and these positions call for knowledge and experience in sport management, sport communication, sport journalism, and sport marketing. By showing that you have developed such skills, you can differentiate yourself in the job marketplace. Do an internship with a local, regional, or national sports network. Learn how to operate a digital camera, how to edit what you have filmed, and how to produce a program—all while continuing to develop your skills in written communication. These days, if you are interested in working in sport journalism, you should know how to post your stories to a website and how to post video (Schultz, Caskey, & Esherick, 2010). In addition, continuing technological development may enable the growth not only of giant sports networks but also of smaller sports broadcasting opportunities. We cannot know the details of the future, but without question technology will continue to affect how we watch and manage sport.

Technology will also affect the ways in which sport is officiated and played. After the 2010 World Cup, for example, debate arose among media, fans, and participants about whether soccer should join ice hockey in using electronic "eyes" at the mouth of the goal. Indeed, instant replay and other uses of new camera technology are constant subjects at meetings in the National Hockey League, the National Football League (NFL), the National Basketball Association (NBA), and Major League Baseball. Technological improvements can also directly affect athletes' performances—for example, enabling long-drive golfers to hit their drives more than 400 yards (i.e., well over 350 meters) and pole-vaulters to clear heights once never imagined. Technology also plays a role in safety concerns. For example, the growing concern regarding concussions in contact sports will surely lead helmet manufacturers to apply every available technology to reducing the incidence of such injuries. Doctors have also employed technology to radically improve the treatment of sport-related injuries and will surely find new ways to apply technology in caring for athletes. Surgeons already use revolutionary innovations in performing knee and hip replacements, and arthroscopic surgery has greatly reduced recovery time and enhanced the prospects for returning to competition after an injury. Technology may even prolong an athlete's career; examples of this are the recent surgeries to baseball pitchers, aptly named 'Tommy John' surgery. These innovations can be applied to help both elite athletes and Saturday morning amateur participants. Sport managers will be instrumental in managing all of these changes and ensuring the availability of the most current performance and safety technologies.

Technological change continues to produce governance challenges for executives in sport leagues and in high school and college athletic departments. In managing technological change, athletic directors and community sport leaders must address multiple factors: athletes' safety, competitive fairness, and cost savings. For example, the use of performance-enhancing drugs is not going away; in fact, advances in the practice are making performance enhancement more difficult to detect. Such challenges are part of what sport management programs must prepare their students to face. Professionals who can make policy in a manner that is well informed, democratic, ethical, and effective will help improve the playing of sport, enhance player safety, and provide fans with an experience they can countenance. This area of sport management will require today's sport management graduates—including you—to make many decisions about the application of technology. As time goes on, technological advances yet unforeseen will surely arise, and sport managers will envision new ways to use advancing technology in the realm of sport. For example, just 20 years ago, the streaming of games to smartphones had not even been conceptualized, much less achieved, yet today it is commonplace. This sequence illustrates how an enterprising sport leader must envision what can be made possible by technological advances. Sport entrepreneurship will undoubtedly continue to offer numerous opportunities for sport managers and visionaries. It is simply a matter of dreaming what could be, pursuing that dream, and overcoming obstacles that arise. Sport management programs need to prepare those students who are so inclined to pursue entrepreneurial endeavors now and in the future.

Technology affects how fans experience sport, both as in-person spectators and as broadcast viewers. With this in mind, the fan experience at ball games and other athletic events has been studied by marketing companies and by the innovators who have developed, among other things, larger television screens for use at games and Wi-Fi access for mobile devices in stadiums and arenas. Why? Because the future of spectator sport hinges on making fans comfortable and grabbing their interest. In 2010, three new major stadiums, each costing more than US$1 billion to build, opened in the United States: Cowboys Stadium, the New Meadowlands Stadium (now MetLife Stadium), and the new Yankee stadium. These projects, of course, provided great opportunities for the professionals who were hired to design, build, and operate the facilities. They have also provided fans with state-of-the-art venues in which to watch football and baseball games. What further developments await? Will sport managers enhance the fan experience through, for example, moving sidewalks that take them to and from their cars in the stadium parking lot?

Technology can also be used to engage fans' interest in the competitive action, and who knows what the future holds in this area? It would now be possible, for example, for coaches on the bench or sideline to send in-game text messages to fans.

 Business, more than any other occupation, is a continual dealing with the future; it is a continual calculation, an instinctive exercise in foresight.

Henry R. Luce, magazine publisher

Sport managers could even facilitate interaction between fans and coaches, or even players, during time-outs. Indeed, every NBA coach is already miked during national television broadcasts. These possibilities, or others, will be made into realities by sport managers, and organizations will reward not only the sport managers who come up with such ideas but also those who use the resulting innovations to design creative marketing plans and ticket sales campaigns. What is the next step for access for fans? Sport managers could decide, for example, that cameras in the huddle will broadcast images only to fans who carry approved mobile devices in the arena or stadium. Such a move could be used to enhance value for sponsoring partners and create sponsorship opportunities for an exclusive carrier or phone manufacturer. Sports broadcasts are also going to be affected considerably as consumers continue to adopt 3-D television. All of these examples focus on professional sport, but surely new technology will be applied in all segments of the sport industry.

Such developments in technology provide opportunities for sport managers to do creative work in a variety of areas. Sport management graduates who possess marketing skills will be poised to promote exciting new ways of enhancing the fan experience. Graduates who understand the sales process—or, even better, possess sales experience—will be prepared to drive revenue associated with these new developments. And sport management graduates who bring academic preparation and internship experience in managing and operating sport facilities can put themselves at the forefront of coming innovations. Some sport management students might even be involved in developing the new technology itself. What might be invented next by a sport management graduate, engineer, or designer who has just been hired by a golf club manufacturer such as Callaway? Or by a sport management graduate recently hired on at, say, Under Armour to come up with a cutting-edge running shoe? *Someone* will design the next groundbreaking piece of sports equipment or apparel. Whoever the designer turns out to be, it is likely that a sport management graduate will be placed in charge of marketing it.

Those who coach and care for athletes will also be affected by technology-driven changes. Professionally prepared coaches and general managers will be able to take advantage of new technology to win games and fill stadiums. What advances in medical care, nutrition, or weightlifting will give the next athlete an edge? In addition, advances in performance-enhancing drugs and masking agents will continue to make drug testing difficult, and sport managers will need to meet that challenge. In fact, many challenges to sport governance will stem from technological innovation, and those challenges will have to be met by the sport managers who are responsible for rules of competition, codes of conduct, equipment guidelines, and management and operating procedures.

Development of New Sports

The sport industry has always seen growth and change driven by the invention and adoption of new sports, as well as the emergence of less popular sports into new prominence, and these dynamics will continue to play out in the 21st century. For example, can an *old* sport, soccer, finally become as popular in the United States as it is in the rest of the world? If so, watch out baseball! In fact, if one recent poll gives any indication, soccer is already finding a new home in the United States (Black, 2012), where it ranked just below American football in popularity among those in the 12-to-24-year-old age group. Fans and participants in the United States can also choose from a wide variety of additional sports—some new, others older—beyond the country's big four leagues (baseball, basketball, football, and hockey)—among them skiing, motocross, NASCAR (which has been gaining more mainstream interest in its own right), and both traditional and beach volleyball. Boxing has seen better days, but mixed martial arts (MMA) has attracted many former boxing fans as well as new converts to combat sport. The Ultimate Fighting Championship (UFC), the world's largest MMA promotion company, has captured fans around the globe, and the relatively new market for MMA has shown steady growth (Schorn, 2009; Wertheim, 2007). As part of this growth, MMA instructors, coaches, and training facilities have emerged. New developments such as the emergence of MMA provide new business opportunities for sport management graduates who are well grounded in finance and economics and possess the needed leadership skills.

Other emerging sports—including snowboarding, skateboarding, and wakeboarding—have been a great boon to manufacturers of sports equipment. In addition, new facilities have been built to cater to the interest in these sports, and skateboarding parks and snowboarding trails can now be found around the world. As these sports have gained in popularity, the International Olympic Committee (IOC) has created space in the Olympic program for some of them. Their growth has also been aided by television networks that have created new programming to capitalize on viewers' interest. The ESPN-owned event known as the X Games is now a TV staple, the Dew Tour has become popular for fans of skateboarding and BMX, and the CBS Sports Network has created its own event, called the Alt Games, which includes the college championship in paintballing. Sport management students must be able to take advantage of the new markets and the related job opportunities created by these sports. For example, skateboard parks and snowboarding trails need managers. More broadly, the sport management student who understands the value of paying constant attention to current events, diligently tracking trends in the sport industry, and gaining an academic grounding in sport history will be able to spot trends that employers can use in developing marketing plans, business plans, and new sport-related products. The challenge to the sport management graduate is to possess a solid complement of sport management skills and spot meaningful trends in the marketplace.

Globalization and Emerging Markets

The rapidly growing sport of basketball is crossing borders via many avenues, not the least of which is the NBA's global interest in market expansion. Just as new sports can rise to popularity, so new markets can emerge for existing sports. In fact, the internationalization of sport in general is well under way. Though the popularity of a given sport varies from country to country, existing sports do cross borders and gain new audiences and participants. Sometimes the rise of a new sport depends on local appeal (e.g., surfing requires waves), but it is clear that, overall, sport is truly a *glocal* (i.e., both global and local) phenomenon.

China, which has become an economic juggernaut and even passed Japan as the world's second-largest economy, has used sport as one entry point into the global economy. At the same time, China's economic growth has contributed to the ongoing development of the sport industry. The NBA, for example, now employs more than 100 people in China, and this development is not due merely to the popularity of recently retired NBA star Yao Ming. The 300 million English speakers—and even more basketball fans—in China have been the target of NBA marketing efforts. The potential new customers are also attractive to the NBA's broadcast partners, groups who advertise during NBA games, and U.S. manufacturers of sports apparel and equipment (as you might expect, many sporting goods manufacturers already house factories in China). Beyond the NBA, sport managers worldwide have tapped into the international market to create new revenue streams for their companies, leagues, and teams; on the academic side, sport management programs around the world have recognized the importance of China as a sport marketplace and a producer and have encouraged their students to think globally. Chinese companies also recognize the importance of world markets. For example, Haier, a Chinese manufacturer of home electronics and appliances, acquired the designation of official television for the NBA in 2011 and 2012, through its paid sponsorship of the league. Sport management students who are interested in the global aspects of the sport industry should consider doing a summer abroad to work for, say, a sport team in Europe, a sport league in China, or a sport governing body in Australia. Such experiences can help the student develop a more global consciousness even as they add value to their resume, by helping acquire new skills that can be brought to the global sport marketplace.

India, home to more than a billion people, is another country with a sport market that offers opportunities for sport management students who are ambitious and adventurous. India has already created a world-class professional cricket league through slick marketing and wall-to-wall television coverage, and it now attracts the world's best cricketers. The Indian Premier League (IPL) has franchises in many of India's major cities, and its growth is managed, of course, by sport leaders in India. An enterprising sport management graduate might just be able to help the IPL grow even more. Each of its franchises needs employees who bring ticket-selling skills, marketing skills, and management skills. In addition, Indian companies that sponsor the league need savvy marketing managers to recognize IPL sponsorship opportunities that will drive sales while enhancing the sponsor's image. Cricket is not the only sport that is growing in India. IMG and the Indian conglomerate Reliance have formed a partnership to promote basketball. With the help of the NBA, this business arrangement could prove lucrative to all concerned—and a great opportunity for entrepreneurial sport management graduates who don't mind traveling or relocating. In support of these ventures, and others like them, the Basketball Federation of India, the NBA, and Reliance could all use young, savvy sport management graduates who are familiar with basketball and possess well-developed skills learned through four years of academic and professional preparation in the discipline.

Brazil is another emerging market that has captured the attention of the world sport industry and sport management students. Indeed, Brazil will soon be at the center of attention in the sporting world as it hosts the World Cup in 2014 and the Summer Olympics in 2016. Administering these huge world sporting events clearly creates a need for competent sport managers. More specifically, sport management graduates with appropriate experience and expertise will be needed to help with the work of building and managing sport venues, marketing the World Cup and the Olympic Games, managing event operations, overseeing sport tourism, organizing and implementing communication plans, and managing both ticketing and fans (Danylchuk, 2012).

As the sport industry continues to globalize, sport managers will be increasingly able to enhance their employment opportunities by developing their ability to use multiple languages. Do you speak Portuguese, Chinese, Spanish, or French? Whether you are meeting the needs of sport management students in Latin America or corporations doing business around the globe, the ability to use multiple languages will create job opportunities for you; knowing two languages gives you the skill set of two people, which might just lead to a job offer. The NBA, for example, needs multilingual employees for its push into India. American sport leagues seek multilingual employees to carry out recruiting, marketing, sales, and other efforts. It is true that English has traditionally been a language of business worldwide, but multilingualism is quickly becoming the norm. Are you willing to learn a language? Can you move to a foreign country? It is essential for aspiring sport managers to prepare for the new global village. Along with studying abroad, consider doing an internship with an international or multinational sport organization to gain a window into the world of international sport.

Sport management students can also gain international experience through organizations devoted to using sport for development and peace (SDP). Though SDP is a somewhat recent development, it is already a pervasive global phenomenon. In fact, since sport diplomacy came to prominence in the "ping pong diplomacy" between China and the United States in the 1970s, it has become a regular tool used by nations and nongovernmental organizations around the world. Here are a few of the many examples: the United Nations Office on Sport for Development and Peace, NBA Cares, the Sport Diplomacy Initiative, PeacePlayers International, Magic Bus, the U.S. Department of State, Sport and Peace, the Real Madrid Foundation. Through these and any number of other international and "glocal" organizations, sport has become a player in movements for peace, human rights, conflict resolution, and personal and community development. Sport managers in these areas develop and implement programs in relationship building aimed at solving problems through sport.

Social Responsibility and Inclusion in Sport

Adapted sport applies inclusionary beliefs and practices in societies around the world by enabling persons with a disability to engage in sport. It also engages a market that was once ignored by sport, as women largely were several decades ago. At this point, of course, the female demographic has long been a major force in sport marketing, and adapted sport has now come into its own as a unique market as well. In response, sporting goods and services that were previously not produced have been developed to meet the growing demand from this emergent market. Furthermore, the many new opportunities now made available through the Paralympics, the Special

All I know surely about the obligations of man, I owe to football.

Albert Camus, 20th-century French philosopher

Olympics, and many other sport organizations—both adaptive and otherwise—mean that access to sport for persons at all ability levels is quickly being internationalized.

As these developments illustrate, sport management graduates can do more than be part of the growth engine for the sport industry; though that may be exciting in itself, sport managers can also help extol and enact virtues such as corporate social responsibility, community building, personal development, ethical behavior, and genuine concern for the environment. We can, for example, value competition without the use of performance-enhancing drugs. Indeed, sport managers can positively affect issues involving gender, race, ethnicity, disability, and various socioeconomic factors. The sport industry needs people who will fight battles that advance both the industry and society as a whole—people like Billie Jean King, Jackie Robinson, Casey Martin, Oscar Pistorius, and Marvin Miller. They all broke new ground, not in wins and losses, but in the opening up of sport opportunities to a larger population.

In this spirit, it is incumbent upon sport managers to embody and act on the spirit of Title IX at the college and high school levels. Sport managers can also promote the Paralympic Games and the value of enabling and encouraging sport participation for individuals with disabilities. Similarly, architects and builders can use green technology in designing and constructing new stadiums and arenas. NASCAR, for example, has built the first "green" racetrack, the Pocono Raceway, which is powered by renewable energy. Taiwan has built a sport facility in Kaohsiung that is the first fully solar powered stadium. Lincoln Financial Field, the home of the NFL's Philadelphia Eagles, is equipped with solar panels and wind turbines, along with a generator that runs on biodiesel fuel. In addition, numerous sport organizations—including the International Basketball Federation (FIBA), the International Federation of Association Football (FIFA), the IOC, the English Premier League, and the NFL—have invested heavily in programs to give back to their respective communities.

Clearly, then, sport managers can be at the forefront of promoting wellness, conflict resolution, and development (personal, social, and economic) through sport. There is more work to be done in all of these areas by all of us in the industry. As Hums (2010) has noted, future sport management graduates will face competing pressures in the form of social conscience and the need for profit in the sport industry. Fortunately, sport can be very profitable *and* be managed in an ethical manner; or, as Joy DeSensi (2012) put it in an essay titled "The Power of One for the Good of Many," "sport can be a mutual quest for physical as well as moral excellence" (p. 128). Provided that sport is properly managed, it can indeed help make the world a better place. As if that weren't enough, the sport industry can provide many amazing and exciting employment opportunities for students of sport. Follow Jim Valvano's advice to work enthusiastically in pursuit of your dreams, improving the sporting world one workplace at a time. We hope you are prepared to begin the adventure!

Appendix A

Learn More About Sport Management

Books

▶ Beech, J., & Chadwick, S. (2004). *The business of sport management*. Essex, England: Pearson Education.

▶ Chelladurai, P. (2006). *Human resource management in sport and recreation* (2nd ed.). Champaign, IL: Human Kinetics.

▶ Chelladurai, P. (2009). *Managing organizations for sport and physical activity*. Scottsdale, AZ: Holcomb Hathaway.

▶ Gillentine, A., Baker, R., & Cuneen, J. (2012). *Critical essays in sport management*. Scottsdale, AZ: Holcomb Hathaway.

▶ Gillentine, A., & Crow, R.B. (2009). *Foundations of sport management* (2nd ed.). Morgantown, WV: Fitness Information Technology.

▶ Hoye, R., Nicholson, M., Smith, A., Stewart, B., & Westerbeek, H. (2012). *Sport management: Principles and applications* (3rd ed.). New York: Routledge.

▶ Lussier, R.N., & Kimball, D.C. (2009). *Applied sport management skills*. Champaign, IL: Human Kinetics.

▶ Masteralexis, L.P., Barr, C.A., & Hums, M.A. (2012). *Principles and practice of sport management* (4th ed.). Sudbury, MA: Jones & Bartlett.

▶ Parkhouse, B.L. (2001). *The management of sport: Its foundation and application* (3rd ed.). Boston: McGraw-Hill.

▶ Pedersen, P.M., Parks, J.B., Quarterman, J., & Thibault, L. (Eds.). (2011). *Contemporary sport management* (4th ed.). Champaign, IL: Human Kinetics.

▶ Robinson, L., Chelladurai, P., Bodet, G., & Downward, P. (2011). *Handbook of sport management*. New York: Routledge.

▶ Rosner, S., & Shropshire, K.L. (2010). *The business of sports* (2nd ed.). Sudbury, MA: Jones & Bartlett.

▶ Stier, W.F., Jr. (2008). *Sport management: The business of sport*. Boston: American Press.

▶ Trenberth, L., & Hassan, D. (2011). *Managing sport business*. New York: Routledge.

▶ Wong, G.M. (2013). *Careers in sports* (2nd ed.). Sudbury, MA: Jones & Bartlett.

Resource Guides

▶ Plunkett, J. W. (2011). *Plunkett's Sport Industry Almanac*. Houston, TX: Plunkett Research, Ltd.

▶ *Sports Business Resource Guide and Fact Book*. (Published annually). Charlotte, NC: Street and Smith's Sports Business Journal/Sports Business Daily.

Journal Articles

▶ Boucher, R.L. (1998). Toward achieving a focal point for sport management: A binocular perspective. *Journal of Sport Management, 12,* 76–85.

▶ Costa, C. (2005). The status and future of sport management: A Delphi study. *Journal of Sport Management, 19,* 117–142.

▶ Doherty, A. (January 2013). "It Takes a Village:" Interdisciplinary Research for Sport Management (The 2012 Earle F. Zeigler Award Lecture presented at the NASSM 2012 Conference, Seattle, WA). *Journal of Sport Management, 27*(1), n.a.

▶ Zeigler, E.F. (1987). Sport management: Past, present, future. *Journal of Sport Management, 1*(1), 4–24.

Journals in Sport Management

▶ *Applied Research in Coaching & Athletics Annual.* Boston, MA: American Press.

▶ *Case Studies in Sport Management.* Champaign, IL: Human Kinetics.

▶ *European Sport Management Quarterly.* Oxford, UK: Taylor & Francis.

▶ *International Journal of Sport Communication.* Champaign, IL: Human Kinetics.

▶ *International Journal of Sport Finance.* Morgantown, WV: Fitness Information Technologies.

▶ *International Journal of Sport Management.* Boston, MA: American Press.

▶ *International Journal of Sport Management & Marketing.* Geneva: Inderscience.

▶ *International Journal of Sport Policy and Politics.* Oxford, UK: Taylor & Francis.

▶ *International Journal of Sports Marketing & Sponsorship.* Buckfastleigh, UK: IMR.

▶ *Journal of Coaching Education.* Reston, VA: NASPE.

▶ *Journal of Contemporary Athletics.* Hauppauge, NY: NOVA Science.

▶ *Journal of Intercollegiate Sport.* Champaign, IL: Human Kinetics.

▶ *Journal of Issues in Intercollegiate Athletics.* Chapel Hill, NC: CSRI.

▶ *Journal of Legal Aspects of Sport.* Wichita, KS: SRLA.

▶ *Journal of Sport Administration & Supervision.* Online.

▶ *Journal of Sport Management.* Champaign, IL: Human Kinetics.

▶ *Journal of Sports Economics.* Thousand Oaks, CA: SAGE.

▶ *Journal of Sports Media.* Lincoln, NE: University of Nebraska Press.

▶ *Journal of the Study of Sports and Athletes in Education.* Walnut Creek, CA: Left Coast Press.

▶ *Journal of Venue & Event Management.* Online.

► *QUEST*. Champaign, IL: Human Kinetics.

► *Sport Management and Related Topics*. Online.

► *Sport Management Education Journal*. Champaign, IL: Human Kinetics.

► *Sport Management Review*. Amsterdam: Elsevier.

► *Sport Marketing Quarterly*. Morgantown, WV: Fitness Information Technologies.

Websites

www.asma-online.org	African Sport Management Association
www.aasmasia.com	Asian Association for Sport Management
www.cosmaweb.org	Commission on Sport Management Accreditation
www.easm.net	European Association of Sport Management
www.algede.com	Latin American Association for Sport Management
www.aahperd.org/naspe	National Association for Sport and Physical Education
www.nassm.org	North American Society for Sport Management
www.smaanz.org	Sport Management Association of Australia and New Zealand

Electronic Forums

www.nassm.com/InfoAbout/Other/ListServ	Sport Management Listserv/E-Forum

Sample International Sport Organizations

www.fiba.com	International Basketball Federation
www.fifa.com	International Federation of Association Football
www.olympic.org	International Olympic Committee
www.paralympics.org	International Paralympic Committee
www.specialolympics.org	Special Olympics

Sample United States Governing Bodies

www.ncaa.org	National Collegiate Athletic Association
www.nfhs.org	National Federation of State High School Associations
www.teamusa.org	United States Olympic Committee
www.usabasketball.com	USA Basketball
www.usavolleyball.org	USA Volleyball
www.ussoccer.com	U.S. Soccer

Sample Professional Leagues

www.basketball-bundesliga.de	Basketball Bundesliga (German league)
www.premierleague.com	English Premier League (soccer)
www.iplt20.com	Indian Premier League (cricket)
www.lfp.es	La Liga (Spanish soccer league)
www.mlb.com	Major League Baseball
www.nba.com	National Basketball Association
www.nfl.com	National Football League
www.nhl.com	National Hockey League
www.lega-calcio.it	Serie A (Italian soccer league)

Sample Sporting Goods Manufacturers

www.adidas.com	Adidas
www.championsports.com	Champion Sports
www.converse.com	Converse
www.cybexintl.com	Cybex
www.head.com	Head
www.newbalance.com	New Balance
www.nike.com	Nike
www.proform.com	ProForm
www.rawlings.com	Rawlings
www.rossignol.com	Rossignol
www.spalding.com	Spalding
www.speedousa.com	Speedo
www.sfia.org	Sports & Fitness Industry Association
www.umbro.com	Umbro
www.underarmour.com	Under Armour
www.upperdeck.com	Upper Deck
www.wilsonsports.com	Wilson

Appendix B

Implementing Sport Management in the Real World

Coach

☐ You are a leader and are responsible not only for the competitive performance of athletes but also for the operation of the sport (whether team or individual). By managing athletes and operations in an ethical fashion, you set a tone that your athletes can emulate.

☐ In your position as a coach, you interact with many stakeholders (e.g., athletes, administrative managers, donors, and fans). You need good communication skills, which will help you not only develop good personal relationships with athletes and coworkers but also interact effectively with members of the media, and make successful promotional appearances on behalf of the team.

☐ Understand the fundamentals of promotion in order to market your program both in recruiting players and in raising money. Develop a solid grasp of new media for use in promoting athletes, marketing the team, and providing information to parents and fans.

☐ As the leader of a team or sport, you must compete for resources for the athletes under your tutelage. By understanding major expenses and revenue sources, you will be better able to argue intelligently for more resources.

Athletic Director

☐ In collegiate and scholastic settings, you are the CEO of the sport program. An understanding of balance sheets and income statements will provide a measure of the position; the financial information in these instruments gives you a starting point to develop short-term and long-term strategic plans for your program.

☐ Hire coaches who bring a solid ethical approach to the game and to their relationships with athletes in order to prevent trouble down the road.

☐ You can benefit from working with student interns from the sport management discipline; this helps you pursue the long-term goal of building an athletic department while also grooming potential future employees and members of the sport industry's professional community.

☐ Make a point to engage in professional networking; a solid network of contacts can be a great resource when looking to hire new coaches and other employees.

☐ Be aware of the economic environment in which you operate your department. Awareness of macroeconomic indicators such as inflation, interest rates, and unemployment rates helps you make good decisions regarding contract negotiations with coaches, the building of new facilities, and the hiring of departmental personnel. For example, a sudden drop in interest rates could signal an opportunity to renovate a facility or build a new one.

☐ Be aware of your regulatory environment, including rules and regulations from groups such as conferences, state associations, and national bodies such as the National Collegiate Athletic Association regarding recruitment, eligibility, and academic progress. You must also be aware of applicable legislation. For example, understanding Title IX both prevents problems and provides direction in terms of funding and staffing female sport programs.

☐ Read not only trade journals but also academic journals that provide research-based strategies for use at the high school and college levels.

Golf Course Manager

☐ You are responsible for the overall operation of your sport business. As a result, you must use effective communication skills to interact with a variety of stakeholders, such as customers, sponsors, members, employees, and vendors.

☐ Market the golf course to both businesses and consumers. Understand the potential of social media in creating marketing opportunities that can increase the course's potential for bringing in revenue.

☐ Use the course's income statement to inform your marketing plan by identifying not only expenses that might be reduced but also revenue streams that might be enhanced. For example, golf clubs can provide a source of retail sales both at the course site and online. You can also enhance revenue with creative use of e-commerce opportunities for items such as apparel sales and green fees.

☐ Attract, hire, and effectively manage the best possible employees for each position. Your hiring decisions regarding, for example, greenskeeper and other maintenance staff will affect everyone at the club.

Marketing Director

☐ Your role can include all aspects of marketing. You might need to arrange for advertising agreements, both with advertising agencies to whom you outsource campaigns and to distribution networks such as media outlets. You might meet with prospective sponsors and negotiate sponsorships. You will likely arrange promotions and develop supporting materials to attract customers and subsequently enhance their experience.

☐ Understanding consumer preferences is essential for success in this role. You will need to oversee market research to better understand your target market segments. You will then need to use that information to inform your marketing decisions.

☐ You must align your marketing interests with the mission of the sport organization for which you work. You cannot be haphazard about your marketing strategies. Instead, you will need to develop and execute a comprehensive marketing plan.

☐ You will promote the organization's product, whether it is a team or a line of sports apparel. To do so, you must develop and implement a mix of marketing strategies that include, for example, public relations, promotions, and sponsorship sales.

☐ You will work with people in a variety of capacities. You will work with other personnel in the organization to oversee activities such as sponsorships and to coordinate public relations campaigns.

You must also interact with employees in many other units whose work is affected by marketing efforts—for example, ticket sales staff, media relations staff, and even employees who work in manufacturing or game operations.

☐ When you work for an athletic department or professional team, you do not need to know the sport or team in the same way that a coach does. You do, however, need to acquire some fundamental knowledge of the product; for example, effective marketing of a football program requires some basic knowledge of the game.

General Manager for a Professional Sport Team

☐ You are the leader of all operations related to staffing and preparing the team for competitive performance. Hire the best coaches, player personnel staff, and scouts to ensure that the team can acquire the best players and develop and use them effectively.

☐ Understand two factors that may be out of your control but will affect the way in which the job needs to be done. First, develop an excellent understanding of the collective bargaining agreement struck between the players union and league owners in order to use the agreement to best position the team competitively. Second, seek clear direction from the franchise owner about the organization's goals. For example, how does the owner think about wins and profit? Some owners favor one over the other.

☐ Have good communication skills both within and beyond the organization. Within the organization, effective communication can project a sense of competence throughout the management suite. Outside the organization, local and national media can influence the franchise's public image, and communicating effectively with media members will make you better able to position the franchise favorably.

☐ New technology can help you acquire an edge over your competition. Keep track of advances in areas of technology that can improve scouting and the statistical analysis of team and player performance.

Sport Director for a Nonprofit Organization

☐ As sport director for a nonprofit organization (e.g., Catholic Youth Organization, Jewish Community Center, Boys & Girls Club), you must be able to work effectively with both finances and people. Closely monitor spending and revenue sources with the help of well-prepared income statements.

☐ Hire, lead, and manage the staff who deliver the organization's sport programming.

☐ Develop a solid understanding of the ethical and legal responsibilities entailed in managing programs for young people. Provide effective and principled leadership in these areas to position the organization to deliver programming that helps young people develop in engaging and healthy ways.

☐ Managing a nonprofit will involve marketing and fundraising. Develop a coherent mission statement that can be the centerpiece for a marketing strategy that will enhance fundraising for your organization.

Public Relations Director

☐ Your primary role is to inform the public about the organization. You must know the product (e.g., a sport league or conference) very well and have excellent communication skills.

☐ Be versatile enough to use both traditional and new media. For example, understand how to compose a media release and manage a media conference. Also understand (along with sport managers in similar fields, such as sports information and community relations) how to get the word out via new media and social media such as websites and Twitter. The array of communication tools now available requires that you have the judgment to decide effectively when to use which form of communication.

☐ Interact closely with marketing managers and with personnel in community relations and media relations. The position serves as a point of contact for many external constituencies.

☐ Understand who has the authority in your league or conference or athletic association. Use creative communication strategies to position your organization ahead of your competition. For example, if your marketing director has a creative idea that no other team has used in your league or conference, get the word out to the league office.

Sport Journalist

☐ You must thoroughly know the sport, team, or league you cover. You do so in part by learning what you can about the subject through conversations with those involved, including players, coaches, and managers. As a savvy sport journalist, you also bring a solid grounding in the history, economics, and sociology of the sport or league in question. This awareness allows you to provide readers, viewers, and listeners with valuable context.

☐ Have excellent written and oral communication skills. Depending on the medium—broadcast (radio or television), print (newspaper or magazine), or online (blog, social media, or the web)—you may also need a variety of technical skills.

☐ Understanding the relationship with governing bodies in sport is important to the sport journalist; the reader needs context when a player's union goes on strike or when the NCAA declares a player ineligible.

Director of Ticket Sales

☐ Bring a variety of skills to the job. You need the personnel skills to recognize, hire, and train good people who engage effectively with consumers in order to sell tickets to sporting events. In the course of this work, you will need to model a strong customer service orientation for ticketing personnel, which of course requires excellent communication skills. The director also needs good interpersonal skills to work effectively with consumers and with colleagues in other departments, including finance, marketing, fundraising, and event operations.

☐ Understand and monitor various aspects of the operating environment, including economics, market conditions, and tax policy. Effective pricing of a sport product depends on multiple factors, and you must be aware of economic influences such as supply and demand. Keep an eye on the current state of the local and national economies, since consumers' purchasing power can affect the demand for tickets to entertainment events, including sport events.

☐ Understand the type of market in which you are operating when you price and market either single-game or season-ticket packages. For example, your approach in selling tickets would be greatly affected if the team wields monopoly power in its market—or if, on the other hand, consumers have many options for spending their money on tickets to sport events.

☐ Tax policy can affect your decision making. For example, you must know whether current tax policy treats entertainment expenses as tax deductible. The answer can make a difference in the market for sport ticket sales and influence your sales strategy, particularly for high-end entertainment options such as club seats and luxury suites.

Facilities and Events Manager

☐ Your role is to manage two interrelated aspects of sport operations: facilities and events. Often, each of these areas will have a coordinator who reports to the manager.

☐ Sport facilities managers must consider all aspects of facility operations, including maintenance, security, and safety responsibilities. Events managers must consider all aspects of the conduct of the event.

☐ Developing and implementing a risk management plan, which minimizes risks in the operation of the facility, is a necessary responsibility of this facility management position.

☐ The ability to work with many other divisions is essential in both facilities management and event management. For example, an event manager may need to coordinate with the ticketing office, the marketing department, sponsors, coaches, and, of course, facilities and operations personnel. The facilities manager will need to coordinate with campus security, maintenance staff, ticketing, media relations, and, of course, the event staff.

References

Chapter 1

Coakley, J. (2009). *Sports in society: Issues and controversies* (10th ed.). Boston: McGraw-Hill.

Commission on Sport Management Accreditation (COSMA). (2012). Welcome to COSMA. www.cosmaweb.org.

Fink, J., & Barr, C. (2012). Where is the best home for sport management? In A. Gillentine, R.E. Baker, & J. Cuneen (Eds.), *Critical essays in sport management: Exploring and achieving a paradigm shift* (pp. 17–26). Scottsdale, AZ: Holcomb Hathaway.

Gillentine, A., & Crow, R.B. (Eds.). (2005). *Foundations of sport management*. Morgantown, WV: Fitness Information Technology.

Helyar, J. (2000, September 16–17). Failing effort: Are universities' sports-management programs a ticket to a great job? Not likely. *The Wall Street Journal*, p. R5.

Isaacs, S. (1964). *Careers and opportunities in sports*. New York: Dutton.

Lambrecht, K.W., & Kraft, P. M. (2009, May 27–30). *Opportunities and Challenges in Offering a Sport Management Program in the B-School*. Presented at the North American Society for Sport Management Conference, Columbia, South Carolina, p. 341.

Masteralexis, L.P., Barr, C.A., & Hums, M.A. (Eds.). (2012). *Principles and practice of sport management* (4th ed.). Sudbury, MA: Jones & Bartlett.

North American Society for Sport Management (NASSM). (2012). NASSM home. www.nassm.com.

Parkhouse, B., & Pitts, B. (1996). History of Sport Management. In B. Parkhouse (Ed.), *The management of sport: Its foundation and application* (pp. 2–14). Boston: McGraw-Hill.

Plunkett, J.W. (2011). *Plunkett's sports industry almanac 2012*. Houston, TX: Plunkett Research.

Stier, W. (2001). The current status of sport management and athletic (sport) administration programs in the 21st century. *International Journal of Sport Management, 2*(1), 66–79.

Thompson, A. (2007, October 4). Grease monks: Racing has a haven in Belmont Abbey. *The Wall Street Journal*. http://online.wsj.com/article/SB119144501521848082.html.

Wysong, S. (2006, May 8). Business emphasis keeps programs relevant. *Sports Business Journal* www.sportsbusinessdaily.com/Journal/Issues/2006/05/20060508/From-The-Field-Of/Business-Emphasis-Keeps-Programs-Relevant.aspx?hl=Sports%20Event%20Marketing%20Firm%20Of%20The%20Year&sc=0.

Chapter 2

Adams, J. S. (1977). Inequity in social exchange. In B.M. Staw (Ed.), *It's a pleasure to have you as a colleague and friend*. Santa Monica: Goodyear.

Bishop, G. (2008, April 13). Professor Casserly's lessons outline a course for living. *The New York Times*. www.nytimes.com/2008/04/13/sports/football/13casserly.html?_r=0.

Caroselli, M. (1998). *Great session openers, closers, and energizers*. New York: McGraw-Hill.

Coakley, J. (2009). *Sports in society: Issues and controversies* (10th ed.). Boston: McGraw-Hill.

Commission on Sport Management Accreditation (COSMA). (2010, June). COSMA accreditation principles and self-study preparation. http://cosmaweb.org/node/50

Davis, K. (1991). *Human behavior at work*. New York: McGraw–Hill.

Gillentine, J.A., & Crow, R.B. (Eds.). (2005). *Foundations of sport management*. Morgantown, WV: Fitness Information Technology.

Maslow, A. (1943). A theory of human motivation. *Psychological Review, 50*, 370–396.

Masteralexis, L.P., Barr, C. & Hums, M.A. (Eds.). (2012). *Principles and practice of sport management* (4th ed.). Sudbury, MA: Jones & Bartlett.

McClelland, D.C. (1975). *Power: The inner experience*. New York: Irvington.

Pedersen, P.M., Parks, J.B., Quarterman, J., & Thibault, L. (Eds.). (2011). *Contemporary sport management* (4th ed.). Champaign, IL: Human Kinetics.

Plunkett, J.W. (2011). *Plunkett's sports industry almanac*. Houston, TX: Plunkett Research.

Robinson, M., Hums, M., Crow, B., & Philips, D. (2000). *Making the games happen: Profiles of sport management professionals*. Gaithersburg, MD: Aspen.

U.S. Bureau of Labor Statistics. (2011). Databases, tables & calculators by subject. http://www.bls.gov/data/#employment.

Wolf, E.R. (1990). Facing power—Old insights, new questions. *American Anthropologist, 92*(3), 586–596.

Wysong, S. (2006, May 8). Business emphasis keeps programs relevant. *Sports Business Journal*. www.sportsbusinessdaily.com/Journal/Issues/2006/05/20060508/From-The-Field-Of/Business-Emphasis-Keeps-Programs-Relevant.aspx?hl=Sports%20Event%20Marketing%20Firm%20Of%20The%20Year&sc=0.

Young, D., & Baker, R.E. (2004). Linking classroom theory to professional practice: The internship as a practical learning experience worthy of legitimate academic credit. *Journal of Physical Education, Recreation and Dance, 75*(1), 22–25.

Chapter 3

Berryman-Fink, C., & Fink, C.B. (1996). *Manager's desk reference*. New York: ANACOM.

Blau, P.M., & Scott, W.R. (1960). *Formal organizations: A comparative study*. San Francisco: Chandler.

Chelladurai, P. (2009). *Managing organizations for sport and physical activity: A systems approach*. Scottsdale, AZ: Holcomb Hathaway.

Clothier, J. (2010, July 10). World Cup to the Olympics: Eight sports volunteering opportunities CNN. www.cnn.com/2010/TRAVEL/06/10/sport.volunteers/index.html.

Coward, C. (2011, July 23). East takes All-Star game, festivities a success under the reign of Laurel Richie. Hoopfeed.com. www.hoopfeed.com/content/2011/07/23/east-takes-all-star-game-festivities-a-success-under-the-reign-of-laurel-richie/.

Deming, W.E. (2000). *The new economics* (2nd ed.). Cambridge, MA: MIT Press.

Freelantz Sports Media. (2011, July 7). Laurel Richie leading "amazing women doing amazing things on and off the court." http://freelantzsports.com/2011/07/24/laurel-ritchie-leading-amazing-women-doing-amazing-things-on-and-off-the-court/.

Hersey, P., Blanchard, K.H., & Johnson, D.E. (2001). *Management of organizational behavior: Leading human resources*. Upper Saddle River, NJ: Pearson.

Hersey, P., Blanchard, K.H., & Johnson, D.E. (2008). *Management of organizational behavior: Leading human resources* (9th ed.). Upper Saddle River, NJ: Pearson Prentice Hall.

Horrow, E.J. (2011, October 4). WNBA President Laurel Richie makes marketing the focus. *USA Today*. www.usatoday.com/sports/basketball/wnba/story/2011-10-04/wnba-president-laurel-richie/50661062/1.

Hoy, W.K., & Miskel, C.G. (1982). *Educational administration: Theory, research, and practice*. New York: Random House.

International Federation of Association Football. (2012). *Associations*. www.fifa.com/aboutfifa/organisation/associations.html.

Jordan, J.S., & Kent, A. (2005). *Management and leadership in the sport industry*. In A. Gillentine & R. B. Crow (Eds), *Foundations of Sport Management* (pp. 35–54). Morgantown, WV: Fitness Information Technology.

Lombardo, J. (2011, September 12). WNBA metrics "pointing in the right direction." *SportsBusiness Journal*. http://m.sportsbusinessdaily.com/Journal/Issues/2011/09/12/Leagues-and-Governing-Bodies/WNBA.aspx.

Mintzberg, H. (1975). The manager's job: Folklore and fact. *Harvard Business Review, 53*, 49–61.

Network Journal. (2011). 25 Influential black women class of 2011: Laurel J. Richie. www.tnj.com/2011/laurel-j-richie.

Quarterman, J., Li, M., & Parks, J.B. (2011). Managerial leadership in sport organizations. In P.M. Pedersen, J.B. Parks, J. Quarterman, and L. Thibault (Eds.), *Contemporary sport management* (4th ed., pp. 95–116). Champaign. IL: Human Kinetics.

Smith, M. (2011, April 21). WNBA names Laurel Richie president. ESPNW. http://espn.go.com/espnw/news-opinion/6403641/wnba-names-laurel-richie-president.

Special Olympics. (2012). What we do: Special Olympics mission. www.specialolympics.org/mission.aspx.

Weber, M. (1947). *The theory of social and economic organization*, translated by A. Henderson & T. Parsons. NY: Oxford Univ. Press.

WNBA. (2011, April 21). Laurel J. Richie named WNBA President. WNBA.com. www.wnba.com/news/wnba_president_richie_110421.html.

Wyatt, B. (2010, July 11). Could 2010 World Cup final be the most watched event in history? CNN. www.cnn.com/2010/SPORT/football/07/11/world.cup.final.television/index.html.

Chapter 4

Adams, J.S. (1965). Inequity in social exchange. In L. Berkowitz (Ed.), *Advances in experimental social psychology* (Vol. 2). (pp. 267–299). New York: Academic Press.

Argyris, C. (1964). *Integrating the individual and the organization*. New York: Wiley.

Argyris, C., & Schön, D.A. (1978). *Organizational learning: A theory of action perspective*. Reading, MA: Addison-Wesley.

Argyris, C., & Schön, D.A. (1995). *Organizational learning II: Theory, method, and practice* (2nd ed.). Reading, MA: Addison-Wesley.

Baker, R.E. (2003). *Effective strategies for sport leaders*. Philadelphia: American Alliance for Health, Physical Education, Recreation and Dance.

Baker, R.E., & Baker, P.H. (1999a, November). *Professional dominance or personal autonomy: Achieving the Win-Zone in the decision-making process for athletic inclusion*. Paper presented at the meeting of the North American Society for the Sociology of Sport (NASSS), Cleveland, OH.

Baker, R.E., & Baker, P.H. (1999b, April). *Athletic inclusion: Accommodating athletes with special needs*. International Conference on Sport and Society, Marquette, MI.

Baker, R.E., & Nunes, C. (2003). Coaches as leaders: Strategies for effectiveness. *Strategies: A Journal for Physical and Sport Educators, 16*(3), 36–38.

Bandura, A. (1986). *Social foundations of thought and action: A social cognitive theory*. Englewood Cliffs, NJ: Prentice Hall.

Bass, B.M. (1985). *Leadership and performance beyond expectations*. New York: Free Press.

Bennis, W., & Nanus, B. (2003). *Leaders: Strategies for taking charge* (2nd ed.). New York: Collins.

Blake, R., & Mouton, J. (1964). *The managerial grid*. Houston: Gulf.

Blake, R.R., & McCanse, A.A. (1991). *Leadership dilemmas: Grid solutions*. Houston: Gulf.

Bolman, T.E., & Deal, L.G. (2008). *Reframing organizations* (4th ed.). San Francisco: Jossey-Bass.

Bradley, B. (1978). *Life on the run*. New York: Quadrangle.

Bradley, B. (1998). *Values of the game*. New York: Workman.

Bradley, B. (2008). *The new American story*. New York: Random House.

Bradley, B. (2011). *American voices*. Sirius Radio. www.billbradley.com/american-voices

Bradley, B. (2012). Biography. www.billbradley.com.

Burbules, N.C. (1986). A theory of power in education. *Educational Theory*, (*36*)2, 95–114.

Burns, J.M. (1982). *Leadership*. New York: Harper Perennial.

Carron, A.V. (1982). Cohesiveness in sport groups: Interpretations and considerations. *Journal of Sport Psychology, 4*, 123–138.

Carron, A.V., & Chelladurai, P. (1981). Cohesiveness as a factor in sport performance. *International Review of Sport Sociology, 2*(16), 21–41.

Carron, A.V., Colman, M.M., Wheeler, J., & Stevens, D. (2002). Cohesion and performance in sport: A meta analysis. *Journal of Sport & Exercise Psychology, 24*(2), 168–188.

Certo, S.C. (1992). *Modern management: Quality, ethics, and the global environment* (5th ed.). Needham Heights, MA: Allyn & Bacon.

Chelladurai, P. (1993). Leadership. In R.N. Singer, M. Murphy, & L.K. Tennant (Eds.), *Handbook of research on sport psychology* (pp. 647–671). New York: Macmillan.

Chelladurai, P. (2006). *Human resource management in sport and recreation* (2nd ed.). Champaign, IL: Human Kinetics.

Chelladurai, P. (2009). *Managing organizations for sport and physical activity: A systems approach.* Scottsdale, AZ: Holcomb Hathaway.

Collins, J., & Porras, J. (2004). *Built to last.* New York: Harper Business.

Covey, S. (1989). *The 7 habits of highly effective people.* New York: Free Press.

Davis, K. (1991). *Human behavior at work.* New York: McGraw-Hill.

Davis, S., & Meyer, C. (1998). *Blur: The speed of change in the connected economy.* Cambridge, MA: Perseus.

Deming, W.E. (1986). *Out of the crisis.* Cambridge, MA: MIT Press.

Deming, W.E. (1993). *The new economics.* Cambridge, MA: MIT Press.

Deming, W.E. (2000a). *The new economics* (2nd ed.). Cambridge, MA: MIT Press.

Deming, W.E. (2000b). *Out of the crisis* (2nd ed.). Cambridge, MA: MIT Press.

Etzioni, A. (1961). *A comparative analysis of complex organizations: On power, involvement, and their correlates.* New York: Free Press.

Fiedler, F.E. (1967). *A theory of leadership effectiveness.* New York: McGraw-Hill.

Fullan, M. (2001). *Leading in a culture of change.* San Francisco: Jossey-Bass.

Fullan, M. (2008). *The six secrets of change.* San Francisco: Jossey-Bass.

Gardner, H. (1983). *Frames of mind: The theory of multiple intelligences.* New York: Basic Books

Gardner, H. (1999). *Intelligence reframed: Multiple intelligences for the 21st century.* New York: Basic Books.

Goleman, D. (1995). *Emotional Intelligence: Why it can matter more than IQ.* New York: Bantam Books.

Goleman, D., Boyatzis, R., & McKee, A. (2002). *Primal leadership.* Boston: Harvard Business School Press.

Hersey, P., Blanchard, K.H., & Johnson, D.E. (2008). *Management of organizational behavior: Leading human resources* (9th ed.). Upper Saddle River, NJ: Pearson Prentice Hall.

Herzberg, F. (1968). One more time: How do you motivate people? *Harvard Business Review, 46,* 53–62.

House, R.J. (1971). A path-goal theory of leader effectiveness. *Administrative Science Quarterly, 16,* 321–338.

International Olympic Committee. (2012). The IOC: Count Jacques Rogge. www.olympic.org/count-jacques-rogge.

Kanter, R.M. (1983). *The change masters.* New York: Simon & Schuster.

Kottner, J.P. (1990). What leaders really do. *Harvard Business Review, 68*(3), 103–111.

Krentzman, J. (1997, January/February). The force behind the Nike empire. *Stanford Magazine.* www.stanfordalumni.org/news/magazine/1997/janfeb/articles/knight.html.

Likert, R. (1967) *The human organization: Its management and value.* New York: McGraw-Hill.

Maslow, A. (1943). A theory of human motivation. *Psychological Review, 50,* 370–396.

Maxwell, J.C. (2001). *Developing the leader within you.* Nashville: Nelson Impact.

McClelland, D.C. (1961). *The achieving society.* Princeton, NJ: D. Van Nostrand.

McClelland, D.C. (1975). *Power: The inner experience.* New York: Irvington.

McClelland, D.C., Atkinson, J.W., Clark, R.W., & Lowell, E.L. (1953). *The achievement motive.* New York: Appleton-Century-Crofts.

McClelland, D.C., & Burnham, D.H. (1976). Power is the great motivator. *Harvard Business Review, 54*(2), 100–110.

McGregor, D.M. (1960). *The human side of enterprise.* New York: McGraw-Hill.

McGregor, D.M. (1966). *Leadership and motivation.* Boston: MIT Press.

McGregor, D.M. (2005). *The human side of enterprise* (Annotated edition). New York: McGraw-Hill.

Ouchi, W.G. (1981). *Theory Z: How American business can meet the Japanese challenge.* Reading, MA: Addison-Wesley.

Pink, D.H. (2011). *Drive.* New York: Riverhead Press.

Pyzdek, T., & Keller, P.A. (2009). *The Six Sigma handbook: A complete guide for green belts, black belts, and managers at all levels* (3rd ed.). New York: McGraw-Hill.

Quarterman, J., Li, M., & Parks, J.B. (2007). Managerial leadership in sport organizations. In J.B. Parks, J. Quarterman, & L. Thibault (Eds.), *Contemporary sport management* (3rd ed., pp 335–355). Champaign, IL: Human Kinetics.

Quarterman, J., Li, M., & Parks, J.B. (2011). Managerial leadership in sport organizations. In P.M. Pederson, J.B. Parks, J. Quarterman, & L. Thibault (Eds.), *Contemporary sport management* (4th ed., pp 95–116). Champaign, IL: Human Kinetics.

Schein, E.H. (2004). *Organizational culture and leadership* (3rd ed.). San Francisco: Jossey-Bass.

Senge, P. (1990). *The fifth discipline:* New York: Doubleday.

Vernacchia, R., McGuire, D., & Cook, R. (1996). *Coaching mental excellence.* Palo Alto: Warde.

Vroom, V. (1964). *Work and motivation.* New York: Wiley.

Weese, W.J. (1996). Do leadership and organizational culture really matter? *Journal of Sport Management, 19*, 197–206.

Wolf, E.R. (1990). Facing power—Old insights, new questions. *American Anthropologist, 92(3),* 586–596.

Yukl, G.A. (2006). *Leadership in organizations* (6th ed.). Upper Saddle River, NJ: Pearson Prentice Hall

Yukl, G.A., & Van Fleet, D.D. (1992). Theory and research on leadership in organizations. In M.D. Dunnette and L.M. Hough (Eds.), *Handbook of industrial and organizational psychology* (2nd ed., pp. 147–197). Chicago: Rand McNally.

Chapter 5

Aumann, M. (2010, March 8). The commission: Inside NASCAR's appeals system. NASCAR.COM. www.nascar.com/2008/news/features/03/21/maumann.national.stock.car.racing.commission/index.html.

Big Ten Conference. (2012). www.bigten.org.

Doh, J.P., & Stumpf, S.A. (2005). *Handbook on responsible leadership and governance in global business.* Northampton, MA: Elgar.

Duderstadt, J.J. (2000). *Intercollegiate athletics and the American University.* Ann Arbor: University of Michigan Press.

Hums, M.A., & MacLean, J.C. (2009). *Governance and policy in sport organizations* (2nd ed.). Scottsdale, AZ: Holcomb Hathaway.

International Olympic Committee. (2009). XIII Olympic Congress. www.olympic.org/Documents/Congress 2009/XIII-Olympic-Congress Follow-up EN.pdf.

International Olympic Committee. (2010, October 26). Code of ethics. www.olympic.org/Documents/Reports/EN/IOC%20Code%20of%20Ethics%20_Eng_.pdf.

International Olympic Committee. (2012). Basic universal principles of good governance. www.olympic.org/Documents/Conferences_Forums_and_Events/2008_seminar_autonomy/Basic_Universal_Principles_of_Good_Governance.pdg.

National Collegiate Athletic Association (NCAA). (2012a). Championships. www.ncaa.org/wps/wcm/connect/public/ncaa/championships.

National Collegiate Athletic Association (NCAA). (2012b). Committees. www.ncaa.org/wps/wcm/connect/public/NCAA/About+the+NCAA/Who+We+Are/Committees.

National Collegiate Athletic Association (NCAA). (2012c). Resources. www.ncaa.org/wps/wcm/connect/public/ncaa/resources.

National Federation of State High School Associations (NFHS). (2012). NFHS home page. www.nfhs.org/uploadedfiles/3dissue/AboutUs/NFHSCompanyBrochure/pageflip.html.

Organisation for Economic Co-operation and Development (OECD). (2012). Glossary of statistical terms: Good governance. http://stats.oecd.org/glossary/detail.asp?ID=7237.

Parigi, V.K., Geeta, P., & Kailasam, R. (2004). *Ushering in transparency for good governance*. Hyderabad, India: Centre for Good Governance.

Ross, S.F., & Szymanski, S. (2008.) *Fans of the world unite*. Palo Alto: Stanford University Press.

Special Olympics. (2012). What we do: Special Olympics mission. www.specialolympics.org/mission.aspx.

Stapenhurst, R., & O'Brien, M. (2012). Accountability in governance. World Bank. http://siteresources.worldbank.org/PUBLICSECTORANDGOVERNANCE/Resources/AccountabilityGovernance.pdf.

United Nations. (2012). Global issues: Governance. www.un.org/en/globalissues/governance.

Washington Capitals. (2012). Ted Leonsis bio. http://capitals.nhl.com/club/page.htm?id=62951.

Chapter 6

Ammon, R., Nagel, M.S., & Southall, R. (2010). *Sport facility management* (2nd ed.). Morgantown, WV: FIT Publishing.

Bishop, G. (2011, November 11). Season tips off in location unlike any other. *New York Times*. www.nytimes.com/2011/11/12/sports/ncaabasketball/unc-and-michigan-state-tip-off-on-an-aircraft-carrier.html?pagewanted=all.

Cagan, J., & deMause, N. (1998). *Field of schemes*. Monroe, ME: Common Courage Press.

Cousens, L., & Bradish, C. (2012). Sport and sponsorship. In L. Trenberth & D. Hassan (Eds.), *Managing sport business*. (pp. 264–284). New York: Routledge.

Gaffney, C.T. (2008). *Temples of the earthbound gods*. Austin: University of Texas Press.

Gems, G.R., Borish, L.J., & Pfister, G. (2008). *Sports in American history: From colonization to globalization*. Champaign, IL: Human Kinetics.

Horrow, R., & Swatek, K. (2011). *Beyond the scoreboard*. Champaign, IL: Human Kinetics.

John, G., & Sheard, R. (2000). *Stadia*. Oxford, UK: Architectural Press.

Kitchin, P. (2012). Planning and managing the stadium experience. In L. Trenberth & D. Hassan (Eds.), *Managing sport business*. (pp. 350–366). New York: Routledge.

Lussier, R. N., & Kimball, D. C. (2009). *Applied sport management skills*. Champaign, IL: Human Kinetics.

Masteralexis, L.P., Barr, C.A., & Hums, M.A. (2012). *Principles and practice of sport management* (4th ed.). Sudbury, MA: Jones & Bartlett.

Mulrooney, A., & Styles, A. (2005). Managing the facility. In B.L. Parkhouse (Ed.), *The management of sport* (4th ed.). (pp. 137–163). New York: McGraw-Hill.

O'Connor, S. (2012). Sport event management. In L. Trenberth & D. Hassan (Eds.), *Managing sport business*. (pp. 389–411). New York: Routledge.

Paramio, J.L., Campos, C., & Buraimo, B. (2012). Promoting accessibility for fans with disabilities to European stadia and arenas. In L. Trenberth & D. Hassan (Eds.), *Managing sport business*. (pp. 367–388). New York: Routledge.

Pedersen, P.M., Parks, J.B., Quarterman, J., & Thibault, L. (Eds.). (2011). *Contemporary sport management* (4th ed.). Champaign, IL: Human Kinetics.

Puhalla, J.C., Krans, J.V., & Goatley, J.M., Jr. (2010). *Sports fields design, construction and maintenance* (2nd ed.). New York: Wiley.

Robinson, M.J. (Ed.). (2010). *Sport club management*. Champaign, IL: Human Kinetics.

Robinson, M.J., & Sgarzi, C.A. (2010). Club facilities. In M.J. Robinson (Ed.), *Sport club management* (pp. 159–183). Champaign, IL: Human Kinetics.

Shonk, D., & Bravo, G. (2010). Interorganizational support and commitment: A framework for sporting event networks. *Journal of Sport Management* 24(3), pp. 272–290.

Shultz, B., Caskey, P. H., & Esherick, C. (2011). *Media relations in sport*. Morgantown, WV: Fitness Information Technologies.

Ueberroth, P. (with Levin, R., & Quinn, A.). (1985). *Made in America*. New York: Morris.

U.S. Department of Justice. (2010, September 15). Americans with Disabilities Act, Title III Regulations: Part 36: Nondiscrimination on the basis of disability in public accommodations and commercial facilities. www.ada.gov/regs2010/titleIII_2010/titleIII_2010_regulations.htm.

Chapter 7

American Law Institute. (n.d.). About the American Law Institute. Retrieved from www.ali.org/doc/thisisALI.pdf.

Americans With Disabilities Act of 1990, 42 U.S.C.A. § 12101 *et seq.* (West 1993).

Associated Press. (2005, October 10). Former Alabama coach, Time Inc. settle defamation suit. www.usatoday.com/sports/college/football/2005-10-10-price-settlement_x.htm.

Byrne, J. (2005). Contracts Texts: *Restatement 2d contracts and US UCC Article 2* (2nd ed.). Montgomery Village, MD: Institute of International Banking Law & Practice.

Champion, W.T., Jr. (2004). *Fundamentals of sports law* (2nd ed.). St. Paul, MN: Thomson/West.

Education Amendments of 1972, Title IX, 20 U.S.C. § 1681 (1972).

Federal Arbitration Act of 1925, 9 U.S.C. § 1 (1925).

Federal Baseball Club v. National League, 259 U.S. 200 (1922).

Franklin v. Gwinnett County Public Schools, 503 U.S. 60 (1992).

Garner, B. (Ed.). (2009). *Black's law dictionary*. St. Paul, MN: West.

Hogshead-Makat, N., & Zimbalist, A. (2007). *Equal play*. Philadelphia: Temple University Press.

Kionka, E.J. (2005). *Torts in a nutshell* (4th ed.). St. Paul, MN: Thomson/West.

Lanham (Trademark) Act, 15 U.S.C. § 1051 (1946).

NCAA v. Board of Regents of the University of Oklahoma, 468 U.S. 85 (1984).

PGA Tour, Inc. v. Martin, 532 U.S. 661 (2001).

Reeb, M. (2006) The role and function of the court of arbitration for sport (CAS). I.S. Blackshaw, C.R. Seikmann & J. Soek (Eds) The court of arbitration for sport (1984-2004). West Nyack, NY: Cambridge University Press.

Roberts, G.R., & Weiler, P.C. (2004). *Sports and the law* (3rd ed.). St. Paul, MN: Thomson/West.

Rohwer, C.D., & Skrocki, A.M. (2010). *Contracts* (7th ed.). St. Paul, MN: West.

Sharp, L.A., Moorman, A.M., & Claussen, C.L. (2010). *Sport law* (2nd ed.). Scottsdale, AZ: Holcomb Hathaway.

Sports Broadcasting Act of 1961, 15 USC 1291.

Szalai, I. (2007). Modern arbitration values and the first world war. *American Journal of Legal History* *49*(4), 355–391.

Uniform Commercial Code. (2011). Philadelphia: American Law Institute.

Wong, G.M. (2010). *Essentials of sports law* (4th ed.). Santa Barbara: ABC-CLIO.

Chapter 8

American Marketing Association. (2012). Definition of marketing. www.marketingpower.com/AboutAMA/Pages/DefinitionofMarketing.aspx.

Boone, L.E., & Kurtz, D.L. (1992). *Contemporary marketing*. Fort Worth: Dryden Press.

Canada Newswire. (2012, April 2). Under Armour names Karl-Heinz ("Charlie") Maurath president of International. www.newswire.ca/en/story/948533/under-armour-names-karl-heinz-charlie-maurath-president-of-international.

Daniels, M., Baker, R.E., Backman, K., & Backman, S. (2007). What sponsors want. *International Journal of Sport Management, 8*(2), 131–146.

Dosh, K. (2012, February 3). NFL may be hitting stride with female fans. *ESPN.go*. http://espn.go.com/espnw/more-sports/7536295/nfl-finding-success-targeting-women-fans-merchandise-fashion.

Freedman, J. (2010, July 22). The 50 highest-earning American athletes. http://sportsillustrated.cnn.com/specials/fortunate50-2010/.

Gentilviso, C. (2010, September 28). NFL turns its marketing attention to female football fans. *Time*. http://newsfeed.time.com/2010/09/28/nfl-turns-its-marketing-attention-to-female-football-fans/.

Hoopedia. (2011a). NBA.com International. http://hoopedia.nba.com/index.php?title=NBA.com_International.

Hoopedia. (2011b). NBA in China. http://hoopedia.nba.com/index.php?title=NBA_in_China.

Lefton, T. (March 8, 2010). NFL licensing targets: 'Back to Football' and women's market. *Sports Business Daily*. www.sportsbusinessdaily.com/Journal/Issues/2010/03/20100308/Marketingsponsorship/NFL-Licensing-Targets-Back-To-Football-And-Womens-Market.aspx.

Lough, N. (2005). Sponsorship and sales in the sport industry. In A. Gillentine & R.B. Crow (Eds.), *Foundations of sport management* (pp. 99–109). Morgantown, WV: Fitness Information Technology.

Madkour, A. (Ed.). (2009). *Sports business resource guide and fact book 2010*. Charlotte: Street and Smith's Sports Group.

Mullin, B.J., Hardy, S., & Sutton, W. A. (2000). Sport marketing (2nd ed.). Champaign, IL: Human Kinetics.

National Basketball Association (NBA). (2012). 2011–2012 international broadcast information. www.nba.com/schedules/international_nba_tv_schedule.html.

Parks, J., Quarterman, J., & Thibault, L. (2007*). Contemporary sport management* (3rd ed.). Champaign, IL: Human Kinetics.

Pitts, B.G., & Stotlar, D.K. (2002). *Fundamentals of sport marketing* (2nd ed.). Morgantown, WV: Fitness Information Technology.

Plunkett, J.W. (2010). *Plunkett's sports industry almanac*. Houston: Plunkett Research.

Rovell, D. (January 25, 2011). Whose NFL jersey scores the most with women? CNBC. www.cnbc.com/id/41254306/Whose_NFL_Jersey_Scores_The_Most_With_Women.

Shank, M. (2005). *Sports marketing: A strategic perspective*. Upper Saddle River, NJ: Pearson.

Stotlar, D.K. (2001). *Developing successful sport marketing plans*. Morgantown, WV: Fitness Information Technology.

Under Armour. (2011). Under Armour business site. www.uabiz.com.

Vega, T. (August 25, 2010). Suiting up in jerseys suitable for women. *New York Times*. www.nytimes.com/2010/08/26/business/media/26adco.html.

Weprin, A. (September 27, 2010). NFL launches women-centric website. *Media Bistro*. www.mediabistro.com/tvnewser/nfl-launches-womens-website_b86275.

Chapter 9

Barber, R. (1970). *The broadcasters*. New York: Da Capo Press.

Bauder, D. (2010, February 8). Super Bowl 2010 ratings: 106 million watch, top-rated telecast EVER. www.huffingtonpost.com/2010/02/08/super-bowl-2010-ratings-m n 453503.html.

Bryant, J., & Holt, A.M. (2006). A historical overview of sports and media in the United States. In A.A. Raney & J. Bryant (Eds.), *Handbook of sports and media*. (pp. 21–43). Hillsdale, NJ: Erlbaum.

Cushnan, D. (2010, February 22). Europe's multimedia sports partner. SportsPro. www.sportspromedia.com/notes_and_insights/_a/europes_multimedia_sports_partner.

Davies, R.O. (2007). *Sports in American life*. Malden, MA: Blackwell.

Dempsey, J.M. (Ed.). (2006). *Sports talk radio in America*. New York: Haworth Press.

Gullifor, P.F. (2006). *WFAN and the birth of all-sports radio: Sporting a new format*. In J.M. Dempsey (Ed.), *Sports talk radio in America*. (pp. 53–64). New York: Haworth Press.

Harrison, M. (2011). Qualitative aspects of the talk radio audiences. Talkers.com. www.talkers.com/2011/10/20/qualitative-aspects-of-the-talk-radio-audiences.

Horrow, R., & Swatek, K. (2011). *Beyond the scoreboard.* Champaign, IL: Human Kinetics.

Kirsch, G.B. (1989). *The creation of American team sports.* Urbana: University of Illinois Press.

Laird, S. (2012, April 23). Kaka to be the world's first athlete with more than 10 million twitter followers. http://mashable.com/2012/04/23/kaka-to-be-worlds-first-athlete-with-10-million-twitter-followers.

Madkour, A. (Ed.). (2009). *Sports business resource guide and fact book 2010.* Charlotte: Street and Smith's Sports Group.

Mandell, R.D. (1976). *The first modern Olympics.* Berkeley: University of California Press.

Masteralexis, L.P., Barr, C.A., & Hums, M.A. (Eds.). (2012). *Principles and practice of sport management* (4th ed.). Sudbury, MA: Jones & Bartlett.

McArdle, M. (2009, July 1). Old media blues. The Atlantic online. www.theatlantic.com/business/archive/2009/07/old-media-blues/20490/.

McCarthy, M. (2011, June 7). NBC wins rights to Olympics through 2020; promises more live coverage. *USA Today.* http://content.usatoday.com/communities/gameon/post/2011/06/olympic-tv-decision-between-nbc-espn-and-fox-could-come-down-today/1#.T7gml9xrN_c.

National Basketball Association (NBA). (2012). www.nba.com.

Ourand, J. (2012, February 13). A strong signal. *Sports Business Daily.* www.sportsbusinessdaily.com/Journal/Issues/2012/02/13/In-Depth/Lead.aspx.

Pedersen, P.M., Parks, J.B., Quarterman, J., & Thibault, L. (Eds.). (2011). *Contemporary sport management* (4th ed.). Champaign, IL: Human Kinetics.

ProQuest. (2009). *Broadcasting cable yearbook.* New Providence, NJ: Author.

Schultz, B. (2005). *Sports media.* Burlington, MA: Focal Press.

Schultz, B., Caskey, P.H., & Esherick, C. (2010). *Media relations in sport* (3rd ed.). Morgantown, WV: Fitness Information Technology.

Stevens, J. (1987, Fall). The rise of the sports page. *Gannett Center Journal,* 1–11.

Swangard, P. (2008). Sport in the digital domain. In B.R. Humphreys & D.R. Howard (Eds.), *The business of sports, Volume I.* (pp. 253–271). New York: Praeger.

Williams, J. (2011). *Cricket and broadcasting.* Manchester, UK: Manchester University Press.

Chapter 10

Americans With Disabilities Act of 1990, 42 U.S.C.A. § 12101 *et seq.* (West 1993).

Antoniewicz, A. (2008). Perspectives on the sports industry in China. In B.R. Humphreys & D.R. Howard (Eds.), *The business of sports, Volume 1* (pp. 59–80). Westport, CT: Praeger.

Baade, R.A., & Matheson, V. (2011). An assessment of the economic impact of the American football championship, the Super Bowl, on host communities. In W. Andreff (Ed.), *Recent developments in the economics of sport, Volume I.* (pp. 207–229). Northampton, MA: Elgar.

Beech, J., & Chadwick, S. (2004). *The business of sport management.* Essex, England: Pearson Education.

Borland, J., & MacDonald, R. (2003). Demand for sport. *Oxford Review of Economic Policy, 19*(4), pp. 100–124.

Brown v. Board of Education, 347 U.S. 483 (1954).

DeSchriver, T.D., & Mahony, D.F. (2011). Finance and economics in the sport industry. In P.M. Pedersen, J.B. Parks, J. Quarterman, & L. Thibault (Eds.), *Contemporary sport management* (4th ed., pp. 290–311). Champaign, IL: Human Kinetics.

Education Amendments of 1972, Title IX, 20 U.S.C. § 1681 (1972).

Fantasy Sports Trade Association. (2012, June 12). CBSSports.com announces the fantasy football developer challenge. www.fsta.org/blog/fsta-press-release.

Fort, R.D. (2010). *Sports economics.* Englewood Cliffs, NJ: Prentice Hall.

Goff, B.L., & Tollison, R.D. (1990). Sportometrics. In R.E. McCormack & R.D. Tollison (Eds.), *Crime on the court.* (pp. 59–72). College Station: Texas A&M University Press.

Gollapudi, N. (2012, June 9). IPL corruption probe on sting allegations complete. *ESPN*. www.espncricinfo. com/india/content/story/567884.html.

Gupta, A. (2010). India: The epicenter of global cricket? In C. Rumford & S. Wagg (Eds.), *Cricket and globalization*. (pp. 41–58). Newcastle Upon Tyne, UK: Cambridge Scholars.

Leeds, M.A. (2005). Economics and sport. In B.L. Parkhouse (Ed.), *The management of sport*. (pp. 180–195). New York: McGraw-Hill.

Mahony, D.F., & DeSchriver, T.D. (2008). The big business of college sports in America. In B.R. Humphreys & D.R. Howard (Eds.), *The business of sports, Volume I*. (pp. 225–251). New York: Praeger.

Masteralexis, L.P., Barr, C.A., & Hums, M.A. (Eds.). (2012). *Principles and practice of sport management* (4th ed.). Sudbury, MA: Jones & Bartlett.

Matheson, V. (2008). Mega events: The effect of the world's biggest sporting events on local, regional, and national economies. In B.R. Humphreys & D.R. Howard (Eds.), *The business of sports, Volume I*. (pp. 81–99). New York: Praeger.

Niemann, A., Garcia, B., & Grant, W. (Eds.) (2011). *The transformation of European football*. New York: Manchester University Press.

Rascher, D. (1997). A model of a professional sport league. In W. Hendricks (Ed.), *Advances in the economics of sport, Volume 2* (pp. 27–76). London: Jai Press.

Sports Broadcasting Act of 1961. Public Law 87-331 (75 stat. 732).

Styles, A., Baker, R.E., & Hurley, T. (2004). *Factors contributing to the success of the 2003 World Special Olympics staged in Ireland: A case study*. Presented at the annual conference of the North American Society for Sport Management, Atlanta, GA.

Swangard, P. (2008). Sport in the digital domain. In B.R. Humphreys & D.R. Howard (Eds.), *The business of sports, Volume I*. (pp. 253–271). New York: Praeger.

Tan, T.C., & Bairner, A. (2011). Elite basketball policy in the People's Republic of China. *Journal of Sport Management, 25*, pp. 408–422.

Weiner, J. (2000). *Stadium games*. Minneapolis: University of Minnesota Press.

Chapter 11

Associated Press. (2006, January 10). Pickens sets record with $165 million Oklahoma State gift. http:// sports.espn.go.com/ncaa/news/story?id=2286820.

Berenson, H. (2011, June 17). Cal baseball officially reinstated as team preps for College World Series. UC Berkeley News Center. http://newscenter.berkeley.edu/2011/06/17/cal-baseball-officially-reinstated-as-team-preps-for-college-world-series.

Brown, G., & Morrison, M. (2008). *ESPN sports almanac*. New York: Ballantine Books.

Clark, K. (2009, September 29). At long last, the sports mortgage. *The Wall Street Journal*. http://online. wsj.com/article/SB10001424052748704471504574441213411789746.html.

Conrad, M. (2006). *The business of sports*. Hillsdale, NJ: Erlbaum.

Duderstadt, J.J. (2000). *Intercollegiate athletics and the American university*. Ann Arbor: University of Michigan Press.

Fried, G., Shapiro, S.J., & DeSchriver, T.D. (2008). *Sport finance* (2nd ed.). Champaign, IL: Human Kinetics.

Garcia, B., Olmeda, A.P., & Gonzalez, C.P. (2011). Spain: Parochialism or innovation. In A. Niemann, B. Garcia, & W. Grant (Eds.), *The transformation of European football*. (pp. 134–151). New York: Manchester University Press.

Garland, J., Malcolm, D., & Rowe, M. (Eds.). (2000). *The future of football: Challenges for the 21st century*. Portland, OR: Cass.

Grant, R.R., Leadley, J., & Zygmont, Z. (2008). *The economics of intercollegiate sports*. Hackensack, NJ: World Scientific.

Ham, L. (2005). Accounting and budgeting. In B. Parkhouse (Ed.), *The management of sport* (4th ed.). (pp. 196–214). New York: McGraw-Hill.

Horrow, R., & Swatek, K. (2011). *Beyond the scoreboard: An insiders guide to the business of sport.* Champaign, IL: Human Kinetics.

Humphrey, J.H. (2002). *Principles and practices in interscholastic athletics.* New York: NOVA Science.

Jensen, C.R., & Overman, S.J. (2003). *Administration and management of physical education and athletic programs* (4th ed.). Prospect Heights, IL: Waveland Press.

Keilman, J. (2011, October 28). High school football has high expenses, low revenue. *Chicago Tribune.* http://articles.chicagotribune.com/2011-10-28/news/ct-met-football-money-main-20111028_1_high-school-football-football-field-coaching.

Klayman, B. (2009, September 4). College sports license market tackled by recession. Reuters. www.reuters.com/article/sportsNews/idUSTRE5835UD20090904?pagenumber=2&virtualBrandChannnel=11604.

Krotee, M.L., & Bucher, C.A. (2007). *Management of physical education and sport* (13th ed.). Boston: McGraw-Hill.

Madkour, A. (Ed.). (2009). *Sports business resource guide & fact book 2010.* Charlotte: Street and Smith's Sports Group.

Masteralexis, L.P., Barr, C.A., & Hums, M.A. (Eds.). (2012). *Principles and practice of sport management* (4th ed.). Sudbury, MA: Jones & Bartlett.

Muret, D. (2011, November 16). Practice facilities heat up construction market. *Sporting News.* http://aol.sportingnews.com/ncaa-basketball/story/2011-11-16/practice-facilities-heat-up-construction-market#ixzz1yLIj9aRC.

National Collegiate Athletic Association (NCAA). (2008). NCAA Division I Men's Basketball Championship: Tournament history. www.ncaamarchmadness2008.com/mens/pdf/Tourney_History_41207.pdf.

National Collegiate Athletic Association. (NCAA) (2012, January 17). *Revenue.* www.ncaa.org/wps/wcm/connect/public/NCAA/Finances/Revenue.

O'Toole, T. (2010, April 22). NCAA reaches 14-year deal with CBS/Turner for men's basketball tournament, which expands to 68 teams for now. *USA Today.* http://content.usatoday.com/communities/campusrivalry/post/2010/04/ncaa-reaches-14-year-deal-with-cbsturner/1#.T9-vXhdrOkM.

Regan, T. H., & Bernthal, M. J. (2005). Sport Finance. In A. Gillentine & R. B. Crow (Eds), *Foundations of sport management* (pp. 67–82). Morgantown, WV: Fitness Information Technology.

Robinson, M.J. (2010). *Sport club management.* Champaign, IL: Human Kinetics.

Schultz, B., Caskey, P.H., & Esherick, C. (2010). *Media relations in sport.* Morgantown, WV: Fitness Information Technology.

Stotlar, D. (2005). Sponsorship. In B. Parkhouse (Ed.), *The management of sport* (4th ed.). (pp. 256–270). New York: McGraw-Hill.

Swangard, P. (2008). Sport in the digital domain. In B.R. Humphreys & D.R. Howard (Eds.), *The business of sports, Volume I.* (pp. 253–271).New York: Praeger.

Whisenant, W.A., & Forsyth, E.W. (2011). Interscholastic athletics. In P.M. Pedersen, J.B. Parks, J. Quarterman, & L. Thibault (Eds.), *Contemporary sport management* (4th ed.). (pp. 142–163). Champaign, IL: Human Kinetics.

Yost, M. (2009, December 19). Building teams, brick by brick. *The Wall Street Journal.* http://online.wsj.com/article/SB10001424052748704541004574600002554600262.html.

Chapter 12

Baker, R.E. (1999). Ensuring integrity in coaching. *Strategies: A Journal for Physical and Sport Educators, 13*(1), 21–24.

Feinstein, J. (2006, March 7). GMU's Larranaga taking Patriots down the right path. *The Washington Post,* p. E3.

Gilligan, C. (1982). *In a different voice.* Cambridge, MA: Harvard University Press.

Goff, S. (2006, March 13). Mason relieved to be included. *The Washington Post,* p. F7.

Haidt, J. (2001). The emotional dog and its rational tail: A social intuitionist approach to moral judgment. *Psychological Review, 108,* 814–834.

Held, R. (2011, August 5). Former UConn star Nykesha Sales makes her point at Basketball Hall of Fame's Legend of the Game series. MassLive.com. www.masslive.com/sports/index.ssf/2011/08/former_uconn_star_nykesha_sale.html.

Hursthouse, R. (1999). *On virtue ethics*. Oxford: Oxford University Press.

International Olympic Committee. (2009). *Ethics*. www.olympic.org/Documents/Reports/EN/Code-Ethique-2009-WebEN.pdf.

Kant, I. (1993). *Grounding for the metaphysics of morals* (J.W. Ellington, Trans.). Indianapolis: Hackett. (Original work published 1785)

Kohlberg, L. (1981). *Essays on moral development*. New York: Harper & Row.

Mahony, D.F. Geist, A.L., Jordan, J., Greenwell, T.C., & Pastore, D. (1999). Codes of ethics used by sport governing bodies: Problems in intercollegiate athletics. *Proceedings of the Congress of the European Association for Sport Management, 7*, 206–208.

Malloy, D.C., Ross, S., & Zakus, D.H. (2003). *Sport ethics* (2nd ed.). Toronto: Thompson Educational.

Mill, J.S. (1861) *Utilitarianism*. www.utilitarianism.com/jsmill.htm.

National Association of Basketball Coaches (NABC). (1987). Code of ethics. www.nabc.org/programs/ethics/index.

Niiler, E. (2011, July 1). Tour de France doping: Should it be legal? *Discovery News*. http://news.discovery.com/adventure/cycling-doping-drugs-sports-110701.html.

Ridinger, L., & Greenwell, T.C. (2005). Ethics in the sport industry. In J.A. Gillentine & R.B. Crow (Eds.), *Foundations of sport management* (pp. 155–168). Morgantown, WV: Fitness Information Technology.

Rokeach, M. (1973). *The Nature of Human Values*. New York: Free Press.

Starratt, R.J. (1991). Building an ethical school: A theory for practice in educational leadership. *Educational Administration Quarterly, 27*(2), 185–202.

Tucker, R., & Dugas, J. (2011, July 23). A doping-free Tour de France? *The New York Times*. www.nytimes.com/2011/07/24/opinion/sunday/24tour.html.

United States Anti-Doping Agency. (2010). *What Sport Means in America: A Survey of Sport's Role in Society.*

Epilogue

Black, A. (2012, March 8). Soccer—That American sport. Huffingtonpost.com. www.huffingtonpost.com/alan-black/soccer-popularity_b_1328136.html.

Danylchuk, K. (2012). The internationalization of sport management academia. In A. Gillentine, R.E. Baker, & J. Cuneen (Eds.), *Critical essays in sport management: Exploring and achieving a paradigm shift.* (pp. 149–162). Scottsdale, AZ: Holcomb Hathaway.

DeSensi, J. (2012). The power of one for the good of many. In A. Gillentine, R.E. Baker, & J. Cuneen (Eds.), *Critical essays in sport management: Exploring and achieving a paradigm shift.* (pp. 125–132). Scottsdale, AZ: Holcomb Hathaway.

Hums, M. (2010). The conscience and commerce of sport management: One teacher's perspective. *Journal of Sport Management 24*(1), 1–9.

Mahony, D.F. (2008). NASSM Ziegler Lecture. *Journal of Sport Management 22*(1), pp. 1–10.

Schorn, D. (2009). Mixed martial arts: A new kind of fight. CBS News. www.cbsnews.com/2100-18560_162-2241525.html.

Schultz, B., Caskey, P.H., & Esherick, C. (2010). *Media relations in sport.* Morgantown, WV: Fitness Information Technology.

Wertheim, J. (2007). The new main event. *Sports Illustrated*. http://sportsillustrated.cnn.com/2007/more/05/22/ultimate0528/index.html.

Wollman, D. (2011, April 15). E-book sales triple year-over-year, paper books decline in every category. www.engadget.com/2011/04/15/e-book-sales-triple-year-over-year-paper-books-decline-in-every/.

Index

Note: The italicized *f* and *t* following page numbers refer to figures and tables, respectively.

About the Authors

Robert E. Baker, EdD, is an associate professor, the coordinator of sport management, and the founding director of the Center for Sport Management at George Mason University in Fairfax, Virginia. Baker has decades of experience working in the sport industry and more than 13 years in higher education. Baker, along with coauthor Craig Esherick and Dr. Pamela Hudson Baker, works in conjunction with the U.S. Department of State on the implementation of projects using sport for development, peace, and diplomatic purposes.

In 2011 Baker received the Outstanding Achievement in Sport Management Award from the National Association for Sport and Physical Education (NASPE). In 2010 he was the recipient of the North American Society for Sport Management (NASSM) Distinguished Sport Management Educator Award. Baker served on the inaugural board of the Commission on Sport Management Accreditation (COSMA) and on several editorial boards. He has also served as president of NASSM.

Baker is a sports enthusiast who also enjoys travel and classic cars. He and his wife, Pamela, reside in Haymarket, Virginia.

Craig Esherick, JD, is an assistant professor of sport management and associate director of the Center for Sport Management at George Mason University in Fairfax, Virginia. Esherick has a varied background in the sport industry, having spent 25 years coaching basketball at various levels, including serving as a high school assistant coach, an assistant coach for the 1988 Olympic team, and the head coach at Georgetown University. He also has worked as a television sports commentator and has taught in the field of sport management since 2005.

Fundamentals of Sport Management is Esherick's second book. He is a member of the North American Society for Sport Management (NASSM), the National Association of Basketball Coaches, and the American Federation of Television and Radio Artists. Esherick earned a bachelor's degree in finance in 1978 and a degree in law in 1982 from Georgetown University.

He lives with his wife, Theo Stamos, and two sons, Nicko and Zachary, in Arlington, Virginia. In his free time he enjoys playing golf, gardening, and reading.